Bullying

M000031420

Bullying: Experiences and discourses of sexuality and gender provides a valuable insight into the experiences of young people and how bullying can impact upon them in the school environment. The book offers an introduction to the key issues associated with bullying on the grounds of sex and sexual orientation, and points to key policies and guidance on these difficult issues.

With cutting-edge research and applied studies from leading academics and practitioners in the field, *Bullying* combines theory with suggestions for practical intervention for practitioners in education and social work. Chapter by chapter, the book strengthens the reader's knowledge base, and demonstrates how best to develop both academic and advocacy arguments to confront bullying, formulate intervention through examples of research findings, and recommend advice and guidance in professional contexts. *Bullying* offers multiple perspectives to challenge bullying related to gender, sexuality and transgender status.

The book includes the latest work on:

- sexual bullying and the implications for policy and practice
- sexual dimensions of cyberbullying
- homophobia
- sex differences in bullying
- lesbian, gay, bisexual and transgender issues in educational contexts
- planning and delivering interventions in schools.

Bullying: Experiences and discourses of sexuality and gender will appeal to education professionals, as well as researchers and postgraduate students in the social sciences, social work, and educational and clinical child psychology.

Ian Rivers is Professor of Human Development in the School of Sport and Education at Brunel University, UK.

Neil Duncan is Reader in Education for Social Justice at the University of Wolverhampton, UK.

Foundations and Futures of Education

Peter Aggleton School of Education and Social Work,
University of Sussex, UK
Sally Power Cardiff University, UK
Michael Reiss Institute of Education, University of London, UK

Foundations and Futures of Education focuses on key emerging issues in education as well as continuing debates within the field. The series is interdisciplinary, and includes historical, philosophical, sociological, psychological and comparative perspectives on three major themes: the purposes and nature of education; increasing interdisciplinarity within the subject; and the theory–practice divide.

Being a University
Ron Barnett

Education: An 'Impossible Profession'?
Tamara Bibby

Radical Education and the Common School
Michael Fielding and Peter Moss

Re-Designing Learning Contexts: Technology-rich, learner-centred ecologies
Rosemary Luckin

Schools and Schooling in the Digital Age: A critical analysis
Neil Selwyn

The Irregular School
Roger Slee

Gender, Schooling and Global Social Justice
Elaine Unterhalter

Language, Learning, Context: Talking the talk
Wolff-Michael Roth

School Trouble
Deborah Youdell

The Right to Higher Education: Beyond widening participation
Penny Jane Burke

Postfeminist Education? Girls and the sexual politics of schooling
Jessica Ringrose

Bullying: Experiences and discourses of sexuality and gender
Ian Rivers and Neil Duncan

Education and Masculinities: Social, cultural and global transformations
Chris Haywood and Mairtin Mac an Ghaill

Bullying

Experiences and discourses of sexuality
and gender

Edited by Ian Rivers and Neil Duncan

LONDON AND NEW YORK

First published 2013
by Routledge
2 Park Square, Milton Park, Abingdon, Oxon OX14 4RN

Simultaneously published in the USA and Canada
by Routledge
711 Third Avenue, New York, NY 10017

Routledge is an imprint of the Taylor & Francis Group, an informa business

British Library Cataloguing in Publication Data
A catalogue record for this book is available from the British Library

Library of Congress Cataloging-in-Publication Data
Bullying : experiences and discourses of sexuality and gender /
edited by Ian Rivers and Neil Duncan.
pages cm
ISBN 978-0-415-50502-4 (hardback) – ISBN 978-0-415-50503-1
(paperback) – ISBN 978-0-203-07677-4 (ebook) (print)
1. Harassment in schools. 2. Sexual harassment in education.
3. Bullying in schools. 4. Bullying in schools–Psychological aspects.
I. Rivers, Ian. II. Duncan, Neil, 1956-
LC212.82.B85 2012
371.5'8–dc23
2012027702

ISBN: 978-0-415-50502-4 (hbk)
ISBN: 978-0-415-50503-1 (pbk)
ISBN: 978-0-203-07677-4 (ebk)

Typeset in Garamond
by Saxon Graphics Ltd, Derby

MIX
Paper from
responsible sources
FSC
www.fsc.org   **FSC® C004839**

Printed and bound in Great Britain by
TJ International Ltd, Padstow, Cornwall

To Chris and Barbara (IR)

To Carol and Alex (ND)

Contents

Contributors

Eric Anderson, University of Bath, UK

Helen Cowie, University of Surrey, UK

Craig D. DiGiovanni, Boston College, USA

Neil Duncan, University of Wolverhampton, UK

Dorothy L. Espelage, University of Illinois, USA

Dawn Jennifer, Open University, UK

Kate Klein, Wilfrid Laurier University, Canada

Mark McCormack, Durham University, UK

Ethan H. Mereish, Boston College, USA

Lauren Munro, Wilfrid Laurier University, Canada

Debbie Ollis, Deakin University, Australia

V. Paul Poteat, Boston College, USA

Ian Rivers, Brunel University, UK

Jillian R. Scheer, Boston College, USA

Margaret Schneider, University of Toronto Ontario Institute for Studies in Education, Canada

Alex St. John, Wilfrid Laurier University, Canada

Robb Travers, Wilfrid Laurier University, Canada

Siân Williams, London Borough of Lewisham, UK

Figures and tables

Figures

Tables

Acknowledgements

The editors would like to thank those colleagues who have supported us in the development of this book. We are indebted to Peter Aggleton, Sally Power and Michael Reiss for offering us an opportunity to contribute to their series Foundations and Futures of Education. We are grateful to our excellent cast of authors who have provided us with a series of chapters that challenge our thinking about sexuality and gender in educational contexts. We are also indebted to Archie Panjabi for supporting this book with her foreword, and to Clare Ashworth for keeping a check on our progress.

Ian Rivers
Brunel University

Neil Duncan
University of Wolverhampton

July, 2012

Foreword

Archie Panjabi

In April 2012 I was invited to attend the inaugural lecture of Professor Ian Rivers at Brunel University where I had once been a student. The focus of this lecture was Ian's twenty-year career researching bullying behaviour, particularly his work on gender-based and homophobic bullying. This book, co-edited with Neil Duncan, brings together the work of a group of researchers who have dedicated their careers to combating bullying in schools, thereby ensuring that issues of sexuality and gender are no longer barriers to education.

Bullying is always damaging and destructive. It is unacceptable that one person feels he or she has the right to torment another because he or she does not like what the other stands for. Being a woman, being lesbian, gay, bisexual, transgender or questioning, being mentally or physically disabled, being in any vulnerable state, being a member of a minority or of different faith, ethnicity, body type or being a combination of any of these does not make a person less worthy of our care and protection. It does not mean that they are less entitled to be educated in a safe and supportive environment, free from fear of intimidation and harassment. Finally and most importantly of all, it does not mean that their lives are of less value.

As a child I was encouraged to learn about and to respect people who were different from me. In retrospect I think that is partly what drew me to acting and has enabled me to play a wide range of characters that have challenged cultural, social and gender stereotypes. These women have often been forced to choose between family or cultural expectations and be true to themselves. In CBS's *The Good Wife*, my character Kalinda Sharma is an independent, bisexual, working-class woman of colour who continually challenges cultural norms regarding how, who, and what women 'should' be. She refuses to be defined or confined by preconceived norms, and from the letters of support that come from fans, many of them identify with Kalinda and feel that she gives a 'voice' to them.

Regrettably, we live in a world where some people believe that they have greater worth and that their preferences are right, so that they therefore are entitled to threaten or impose their preferences over others who are different. This form of discrimination is 'bullying', and ironically this behaviour often begins at a time of greatest vulnerability: in childhood. It makes sense that to address 'bullying in society', we should train our educators, childcare workers and parents to identify manifestations of this behaviour at its onset.

This book explains that historically, bullying is linked to other forms of violence including sexual violence; how those who are bullied and also those who bully suffer from mental health difficulties, and again, how identifying bullying early on and acknowledging diversity promotes well-being.

This book serves as a brilliant tool for educators and parents who wish to see positive change so that all children are free to thrive in our school systems and thereafter as adults in society. Ultimately, the lesson from *Bullying: Experiences and discourses of sexuality and gender* is that where there is a failure to recognise and address the differences that exist among us, bullying will continue to thrive.

1 Introduction

Neil Duncan and Ian Rivers

About bullying

The study of bullying is now a worldwide phenomenon, but it surprises many to hear that this is a fairly recent area for scientific and academic investigation. In 1978, Ludwig Lowenstein published his academic paper 'Who is the bully?', perhaps the first text written in English (rather than translations) with that keyword, and it then took more than a decade for the first books on bullying written in English to appear. Valerie Besag (1989), Delwyn Tattum, David Lane (Tattum and Lane, 1989), Yvette Ahmad and Peter Smith (Ahmad and Smith, 1994) were among the earliest wave of British researchers, developing and extending the pioneering work of Dan Olweus (1973), Anatol Pikas (1975), Kaj Björkqvist (Björkqvist *et al.*, 1982), Erling Roland (1989) and the other Scandinavians. The original work on bullying was focused on overt pupil behaviour in schools as researchers struggled to define it, measure it and, ultimately, reduce it in all its forms in order to improve the quality of life for the countless children it affected. The exponential production of research material really took off in the 1990s, and continues to this day with contributions from around the globe where studies of *bat nat* in Vietnam, *ijime* in Japan and *mobbning* in Scandinavia offer insight into the cultural distinctiveness of a world-wide school problem.

Today, the motive for research into bullying in schools is the same; a desire to make school life more civilised and enjoyable for everyone and to cultivate pro-social values in the next generation of adults. However the foci are more varied than they once were, and investigations now seek knowledge on the many sub-types of bullying that were once subsumed in the generic studies. The taxonomy of these sub-types is ever-expanding, but to date it includes racist, disablist, sexist and relational forms of aggression. In addition to these forms of bullying are added the modes through which it is carried out; cyberbullying, for example, is now a fixture in most anti-bullying policies.

Despite the enormous amount of research into bullying in schools, and the prodigious efforts to develop interventions, it appears that we are still not close to finding the means to effectively prevent it. This statement does not require protracted argument and supporting statistics, just a simple reminder of some cultural indicators that ought to speak for themselves. In the United

Kingdom in 2011, Kate Middleton, the fiancée of Prince William and the object of feverish media scrutiny, declined the offer of gifts for her wedding, preferring that well-wishers donate to the anti-bullying charity *Beatbullying,* as she herself had been badly bullied during her time at a prestigious private school. In the same year, that charity was a leading agent in the UK's national anti-bullying week in which television, radio, live music and sporting events highlighted the problem of school bullying and the national commitment to beat it. The blue wristband of anti-bullying week has been worn by hundreds of celebrities and thousands of others to demonstrate their solidarity with the campaign. The prevalence of the issue is further reflected in the plethora of publications on bullying: 'how-to-deal-with-it' books, 'how-to-avoid-it' books, story books for infants, 'mis-lit' books that wallow in the painful memory of experience, triumphal 'how-I-overcame-it' testaments and many more. A search of the online bookstore *Amazon* using the word 'bully' returns more than two thousand titles, while even greater numbers of academic texts populate university libraries.

What all this means, unfortunately, is that bullying is still with us and is foregrounded in the national consciousness. The profile of bullying could hardly be any higher in the UK. The word and the deed is pervasive and extends throughout all echelons of British society, as it does in many other countries, and continues to resist our attempts to reduce it, let alone eradicate it. So what is it about the phenomenon, a fairly clear set of aggressive behaviours, which enables it to prevail today in virtually every school? The answer, as one might expect, is not straightforward.

By its nature, bullying is not a socially accepted activity and though tolerated amongst some groups and in some contexts, it remains largely covert and secretive. One of bullying's least-noted (at least among the academic community) but common features is its intimacy. Unlike overt physical or verbal attacks, bullying can be insidious and get 'under a person's skin'. It can hurt deeply even though the act itself, such as a look or a stare, may seem mild to others. Indeed, it might even be invisible to onlookers, for example, a group pointedly ignoring their victim. Intimacy in bullying works on a level of psychological entrapment, ensnaring the victim in a social relationship or situation where they are disempowered and placed at the mercy of the aggressor. One such example of this 'quality' in bullying that differentiates it from other forms of peer aggression is the 'where I live test'. Each year Neil sets undergraduate students this problem, and we offer it to you now:

> You are on your way back to your house. On the street near your front door entrance is a gang of youths that looks threatening. Their demeanour and behaviour, dress and language, all intimidate you. As you pass by on the way into the house one of them nudges you; another calls you a humiliating name while a third demands money. You ignore them and go inside, glad to be away from their harassment.

The question is posed: which would be the worse situation; that this happened outside your permanent home, or outside a holiday flat in a foreign country? Some students state the latter, arguing that they would feel worse if they were on holiday because they are outside their comfort zone – away from friends, family and a familiar police service. Before they have finished answering, however, they usually readjust and agree with those students who state the former would be worse, as the situation is linked to their home. They ask: What if these youths are there all the time? They know where you live. You are vulnerable to an aspect of their intimate knowledge of you. Even if they are not there every day, until you know for sure, just coming round the corner of your street will fill you with dread. An important part of your everyday happiness is now under the control of a malignant other.

Naturally, different students have different takes on this vignette, and some students respond to the situation in a predictably robust manner! But the point here is that bullying, unlike other variants of interpersonal aggression, has an elusive affective dimension that is associated with being trapped in some form of relationship with the aggressor, be it the workplace, neighbourhood or school. Whatever the underlying reason for the aggression, its perpetuation is often based upon the convenience of the aggressor who then realises that the target has few opportunities to extricate himself or herself from the situation. In schools, this is often exacerbated by a child-culture or code of 'not-telling' and further reinforced by the high risk of retaliation if the code is broken.

Of all the aspects of bullying that have been researched, we know least about why bullying happens. What is apparent is that power and opportunity play a major part, and that aggression is usually targeted at those who are presumed or are perceived to be different. Knowing this does not adequately prevent or reduce the bullying but it does give leverage for further investigation, and in this regard there are two major schools of thought, though these often do not recognise their own existence in that sense.

The first school of thought – and the one most powerfully supported and most actively pursued – is what might be termed the individual model. In this model, the object of study is the individual person whose personal characteristics or background are considered to be the defining reasons why one person rather than another participates in bullying. This approach studies the actors' home backgrounds, relationships with parents and families, biological differences (such as levels of testosterone) and psychological differences (such as levels of empathy or coldness, aggression and compassion). The individual model views the exceptional individual actor, whether victim, bully or bystander, as the necessary unit of change, and this conceptualisation of bullying is usually associated with typical strategies such as counselling, anger management, assertiveness training and whole-school policies on behaviour. The deployment of whole-school policies in this case does not challenge the individualised responsibility for bullying, as the policy expects the exceptional children to conform rather than for the system to change.

The second school of thought might be called the collective model. It is differentiated from the individual model by its preoccupation with systems, cultures and institutions, rather than personalities. The object of scrutiny is the school or workplace, and the responsibility for change is on institutional ethos rather than individual children, some of whom, it is argued, will always be exceptionally more aggressive or passive than their peers. The underpinning belief here is that unless the system changes to reduce opportunity or benefit for bullying, when you get rid of one bully, another takes their place. In effect, the problem is the unwanted and unintended production of bullying relationships within organisations due to, for example, power hierarchies, authoritarianism or aggressive competitiveness. The collective model has fewer adherents – perhaps due to its more diffuse interests – but there is a growing appreciation for more systemic approaches across the research community, and an increasing overlap of work between the two models. Each of these approaches is well represented in this book.

About this book

This is an exceptional book because it takes us beyond the generic constructions of bullying. By including the dimension of sexuality as an organising principle we aim to consider current and recent work on bullying in a new light. The variety of contributors, and the perspectives held by them, offer a uniquely wide lens through which the reader can explore the interrelationship of bullying and sexuality in school-based contexts. Although these two phenomena are widely written and spoken about, it is rare to find them conjoined in academic research, and certainly not as thoroughly explored as they are here.

Following the development of feminist scholarship in the 1960s and onwards, the link between sex and bullying in schools was framed by the term 'sexual harassment', and the key writers in the UK scene of the 1970s and 1980s included Debbie Epstein (1999), Valerie Walkerdine (1987), AnnMarie Wolpe (1988) and many others. Their take on sexual harassment was predominantly (and understandably) one-way: men (both young and old) preyed upon women (both young and old) in a school system that was dominated by patriarchal values. Their work was the foundation for emergent masculinities studies in which Connell (1989) and Mac an Ghaill (1994) led the way, deconstructing the monolithic schoolboy and finding complexities and varieties that shed light upon male behaviours not only towards girls, but towards boys too.

These research trends overlapped and interpenetrated with one another, and throughout the period described, the work of Michel Foucault, Judith Butler and postmodernist thinkers nourished the thinking of writers in the field of schoolbased sexual aggression. However, these ideas appeared to sit apart from the prodigious output of mainstream work on bullying, and only recently have the two big ideas in this volume been brought together. *Bullying: Experiences and Discourses of Sexuality and Gender* delivers its readers a diverse range of writers drawing on a multitude of discourses and experiences from the standpoints of practitioners and theoreticians. The collection of personal and ideological writings offers a unique insight into bullying in schools that informs and stimulates, and hopefully drives forward its collective agenda for social change and social justice.

Overview of chapters

In Chapter 2, we begin our exploration of bullying by focusing upon the reasons why this form of aggressive behaviour must be addressed. Helen Cowie examines ways in which young people are affected by their experiences of bullying, and reports on recent large-scale longitudinal research that indicates the potential damage that being bullied can cause particularly to young people's sense of self, their sense of others, their capacity for trust and their ability to establish and enjoy relationships with peers. Attention is paid to those young people who bully others, examining their risk of emotional or mental health difficulties and how this is influenced by the type of bully that they are: aggressive, anxious, reinforcers or bully-victims. It is argued that although bullies may appear confident and, in some cases, popular with the peer group, they also tend to display a lack of empathy and an unrealistic or narcissistic justification for their anti-social behaviour. Such deficits disrupt the development long-term of pro-social skills and values and reduce the repertoire of responses available to these young people in interacting with their peers.

Next, in Chapter 3, Ian Rivers focuses on the phenomenon that has become known as 'cyberbullying'. Here he discusses the complexities of defining this form of interaction and the dissonance that exists between the 'online presence' and the 'offline person'. He argues that many of the facets of cyberbullying and cyberaggression are grounded in issues associated with sex, and particularly the exploitation of sexual desire of others online. He argues that for many young people, online lives differ in many ways from offline lives, and where they intersect or collide, so young people are rendered sexually and emotionally vulnerable. Ian also discusses the role anonymity plays in the online sexualisation of youth and how perpetrators are not always as they seem. Finally the chapter discusses some of the recommendations arising from the UK's Byron Review in 2008, and their implementation to date. There is still a long way to go in understanding and combating this form of aggressive behaviour.

In Chpater 4 Dorothy Espelage reviews research on the potential role of traditional masculinity, dominance, and peer influence on the association between bullying, homophobic teasing and sexual harassment. She provides definitions to contextualise the constructs that she examines across the wide range of studies of adolescent behaviour. Subsequently, she discusses prevalence rates of bullying, homophobic teasing and sexual harassment directed at straight-identified and lesbian, gay, bisexual and transgender (LGBT) youth. She then explores the research on the relationships between bullying, homophobic teasing and also sexual harassment perpetration and demonstrates how these three types of behaviour are inter-linked. Dorothy goes on to discuss traditional masculinity and dominance at the individual and peer-group level, which she describes in terms of explanatory variables to better understand the association between bullying, homophobic teasing and sexual harassment. Finally, she discusses the implications of this research for prevention programmes in schools.

The gendered aspect of pre-adolescent bullying is explored in Chapter 5 by Dawn Jennifer who focuses on young girls' use of indirect aggression as a means to bullying others. Here, Dawn discusses the nature of such behaviours, specifically the spreading of false rumours, peer exclusion and the manipulation of peer relationships. The aim of the chapter is to provide a succinct and accessible overview of the phenomenon's distinct manifestations among pre-adolescent girls. Using key research findings and perspectives from participants themselves, the chapter explores the complex nature of girls' bullying in terms of their friendships, their emerging sexual identities and the social power structures prevalent within schools. Findings demonstrate that, despite their pre-adolescence, girls' friendships are subject to a sexualised and gendered discourse of social aggression. The chapter provides examples of best practice and explores a range of effective interventions that can be used to address girls' bullying both within the school context and in other youth settings.

Linked to the chapters of both Dorothy and Dawn, Siân Williams describes in Chapter 6 one local authority's initiative in investigating sexual bullying within young persons' peer relationships. Uniquely, Siân's original research design spanned primary school, high school and post-compulsory college settings, giving a cross-section of student life in a single London borough. Her study collected data by both Q-methodology and interviews with young people. From this empirical base she describes key aspects of the sexual bullying young people report having experienced. The findings include some possible changes in behaviour trends, and links between young people's aggressive sexual behaviour and its relationship with new technology and the mass media. As the study is contextualised within a single local authority, the work develops some pedagogical ideas and recommendations for further strategic intervention at local governmental level. This chapter serves as an example of the quality of work possible within a progressive authority.

The focus of this book then turns more explicitly to issues of sexuality, and three chapters are offered that provide a context in which to better understand the roles of sexual orientation and, more widely, issues of sexual climate at school. In Chapter 7 Paul Poteat and his colleagues explore the issue of homophobic bullying and provide a conceptualisation of this phenomenon and how this is similar to, but also distinct from, general non bias-motivated bullying behaviour. This chapter offers a review of research that has documented the prevalence of homophobic bullying over the past decade, as well as demographic information on individuals who more typically engage in this behaviour and those who are targets of it. It elaborates on the individual factors that contribute to and predict engagement in homophobic bullying, for example dominance, gender-norm ideology and sexual prejudice. In addition, Paul discusses homophobic bullying from a broader ecological framework by examining how peers and the peer group social climate contribute to and influence this behaviour. He examines how certain school characteristics account for differences in this behaviour and discusses mental health, academic and behavioural outcomes related to homophobic bullying and victimisation. The chapter concludes with a discussion of the implications for prevention and intervention that arise from our understanding of homophobic bullying, and he points to options for future research in this area.

Taking a different standpoint, in Chapter 8 Mark McCormack challenges the predominant discourse of homophobia language and explores not only the literature associated with homophobic discourse but also the development of alternative interpretations of the language used by young people today. Mark suggests that homophobia conveyed through language was perhaps most prevalent in the 1980s and 1990s and that words such as 'gay' and 'fag' no longer have the meaning or significance they once had in the lives of young people. Through his research and through a critical review of fag discourse he arrives at a new model of 'homosexually-themed language' where context and intent require interrogation as much as the words spoken. 'That's so gay!' may not have the same meaning it once had when uttered by young people in classes today.

In Chapter 9 Neil Duncan explores the intersection of sexuality, disability and bullying. There is an existing body of research that confirms that disabled students and those with special needs are disproportionately the victims of bullying at school. In this chapter, Neil seeks to interrogate the links between schooling, disability and sexuality to examine how, and perhaps why, differences between students play out in forms of peer aggression. This theory-rich chapter draws upon a tradition of critical socio-cultural writing, and is intended to challenge conceptions of disability as it develops ideas on adolescent competition for an esteemed sexual reputation.

In the last part of the book, three authors describe both their personal experiences and their professional research that combats bullying on the grounds of sexuality and gender. In Chapter 10, Eric Anderson opens with an intensely personal viewpoint on homophobic bullying cultures in sport and education. This area of life, a central feature for many young men, has become renowned for its hypermasculine ethos and aggressive competitiveness. Male athletes, especially in team sports, are often regarded as the epitome of heteronormativity. Eric's experiences as a coach, and later as a researcher, are explored across a range of situations and he provides us with an insight into the worlds of competitive team sports, coaching and education. This chapter contributes a distinctive voice on homophobia, its practices, its impact and its capacity for change, as Eric supports the view that recent developments show a reduction in homophobia in this area and there is now a genuine potential for the inclusion of sexual minorities.

In Chapter 11 Margaret Schneider and her colleagues provide a very much needed review of the value of Gay–Straight Alliances (GSAs) in schools, primarily basing their observations on research conducted in Canada. Here, qualitative data is introduced from interviews with teachers and from students that shows the benefits and limitations on GSAs. A clear impact is made not only in terms of awareness but also on young people's connectedness to school and their comfort with being themselves. However, this research also shows that while overt homophobia may be challenged, ingrained heterosexism remains, and is perhaps only buried a little deeper than it was before. While there is evidence that GSAs can work to make schools safer for young people who are lesbian, gay, bisexual, transgender or questioning, Marg and her colleagues remind us that GSAs have yet to be systematically investigated, and we do not as yet know if they have met their full potential.

In Chapter 12, Debbie Ollis aims to assist those working with young people to translate research and understandings of the issues addressing gender, sexuality and bullying presented in this book into practice. Drawing on current research relating to effective sexuality education, teacher practice, building respectful relationships and challenging gender-based violence, the chapter offers suggestions for the planning and delivery of successful interventions for young people in schools. Debbie focuses on a number of potentially challenging, complex and interrelated gender and sexuality issues commonly encountered by educators as they attempt to provide safe and supportive learning environments for all young people. Additionally Debbie focuses on the role of professional learning/continuous professional development in supporting gender and sexual diversity in schools. Her data suggests that without a commitment to inclusion and the provision of professional learning, tackling bullying on the grounds of sexuality and gender will remain an uphill battle.

In the final chapter, Chapter 13, we consider what we have learned from this collection of essays and consider what the next steps are in our development of resources that will promote the safety of young people in school and online.

Summary

A key feature of this book is the provision of both theoretical and applied perspectives on the experiences of bullying, and its impact within the school environment. Chapter by chapter, we hope that *Bullying: Experiences and Discourses of Sexuality and Gender* develops readers' understanding and knowledge to reflect upon how best to formulate both an academic and advocacy argument to challenge bullying, defend the implementation of intervention through examples of research findings or provide advice and guidance in professional contexts. In addition to offering an authoritative conceptual underpinning, this book provides evidence, drawn from rigorous research, of what can be achieved at school level, local authority level and state level where there is a commitment to ensuring that young people are educated in safe learning environments.

References

Ahmad, Y. and Smith, P. K. (1994) 'Bullying in schools and the issue of sex difference', in J. Archer (ed.), *Male Violence*, London: Routledge.

Besag, V. E. (1989) *Bullies and Victims in Schools*, Milton Keynes: Open University Press.

Björkqvist, K., Ekman, K. and Lagerspetz, K. M. J. (1982) 'Bullies and victims: their ego picture, ideal ego picture, and normative ego picture', *Scandinavian Journal of Psychology*, 23: 281–290.

Connell, R. W. (1989) 'Cool guys, swots and wimps: the interplay of masculinity and education', *Oxford Review of Education*, 3: 291–303.

Epstein, D. (1999) (ed.) *Challenging Lesbian and Gay Inequalities in Education*, London: Routledge.

Lowenstein, L. F. (1978) 'Who is the bully?', *Bulletin of the British Psychological Society*, 31: 147–149.

Mac an Ghaill, M. (1994) *The Making of Men: Masculinities, Sexualities and Schooling*, Buckingham: Open University Press.

Olweus, D. (1973) *Hackkycklingar och Oversittare: Forskning om Skolmobbning*, Stockholm: Almqvist och Wicksell.

Pikas, A. (1975) *Så Bekämpar vi Mobbning*, Stockholm: Prisma.

Roland, E. (1989) 'Bullying: the Scandinavian tradition', in D. P. Tattum and D. A. Lane (eds), *Bullying in Schools*, Stoke-On-Trent: Trentham.

Tattum, D. P. and Lane, D. A, (1989) (eds) *Bullying in Schools*, Stoke-on-Trent: Trentham.

Walkerdine, V. (1987) 'Sex, power and pedagogy', in M. Arnot and G. Weiner (eds), *Gender and the Politics of Schooling*, London: Hutchinson.

Wolpe, A. M. (1988) *Within School Walls: The Role of Discipline, Sexuality and the Curriculum*, London: Routledge.

2   The immediate and long-term effects of bullying

Helen Cowie

Introduction

Most educators and healthcare professionals are aware of the serious consequences that school bullying can have for victims. What is less well understood is the complexity of bullying behaviour as a social phenomenon embedded in the peer group as a whole in a particular cultural context (Jones *et al.*, 2011). According to Salmivalli *et al.* (1996), bullying involves more than perpetrators and targets since it is experienced within a group, where those involved, whether as active agents, targets or as bystanders, take on a range of participant roles. 'Bullies' are often supported by assistants and are reinforced by others who encourage the aggressive behaviour by jeering at the victim or keeping a look-out for adults (teachers or other member of staff at school). Bullying is further supported by those bystanders who observe what is happening but who frequently take no action to prevent it. Only a minority of students will act as defenders of the victim and this proportion decreases as children grow older (Rigby and Slee, 1991). As a result, bullying is likely to have an impact on individuals, on the class group and on the school as a whole. This chapter examines key ways in which children and young people who are directly or indirectly involved in school bullying are affected by the behaviours they experience, perpetrate and/or observe. It considers the immediate and long-term effects that bullying behaviour can have on individual children as well as on the emotional climate of the whole school.

Outcomes for children who are bullied

Olweus (1993) has distinguished between *passive/submissive* victims, who typically signal to others that they are vulnerable, insecure individuals who will not retaliate if attacked and *provocative* victims, who typically exhibit anxious and aggressive reactive behaviours and annoy their peers, so provoking attack from bullies. Becoming a target of bullying appears to be influenced by such risk factors as temperament, previous experiences of loss or rejection, the history of intimate relationships and friendships and the presence or absence of personal resilience. The quality of friendship is a particularly important factor in preventing a child from being bullied.

Children whose friends are low in protective qualities have an increased chance of being bullied and also of developing internalising problems such as depression.

A substantive body of research confirms that there are damaging outcomes for victims, especially when the bullying is long-term. The experience undermines children's capacity to trust others and frequently results in social isolation (Boulton *et al.*, 1999; LaGreca and Harrison 2005; Marini *et al.*, 2006; Nangle *et al.* 2003). It affects the victims' physical, psychological and social health and well-being (Espelage *et al.*, 2000; Gini and Pozzoli, 2009; Ttofi *et al.*, 2011) by heightening their feelings of loneliness and by undermining their sense of self (Glover *et al.*, 2000). Hawker and Boulton (2000), in a meta-analysis of cross-sectional studies of bullying carried out between 1978 and 1997, found that the experience of being bullied was positively associated with depression; victims of bullying were consistently more depressed than non-victims. Similarly, they found that loneliness was also positively associated with the experience of being bullied. Both social and generalised anxiety was significantly related to bullying, though the effects were not as strong as those for depression. Bullied children were also found to have significantly lower self-esteem than non-victims.

Cyberbullying is the most recent form of bullying and usually targets those who are already being bullied in traditional, face-to-face ways (Dooley *et al.*, 2009; Gradinger *et al.*, 2009; Perren *et al.*, 2010; Riebel *et al.*, 2009; Sourander *et al.*, 2010). As in the case of traditional bullying, cyberbullying often occurs as a result of such relationship difficulties as the break-up of a friendship or romance, envy of a peer's success, intolerance of particular groups on the grounds of gender, ethnicity, sexual orientation or disability, and ganging up on one individual (Hoff and Mitchell, 2009). Being a victim of cyberbullying emerges as an additional risk factor for the development of depressive symptoms in adolescents involved in bullying (Perren *et al.* 2010; Gradinger *et al.*, 2009; Juvonen and Gross, 2008) and of psychosomatic symptoms like headaches, abdominal pain and sleeplessness (Sourander *et al.*, 2010). Moreover, some adolescent victims of cyber-bullying also engage in other types of problematic behaviour, such as increased alcohol consumption, a tendency to smoke and poor school grades (Mitchell *et al.*, 2007).

Bosacki *et al.* (2007) took account of earlier research in their large-scale survey of the multiple dimensions of adolescent peer relationships, including quality of friendships, perceived loneliness and peer victimisation. This study is important for our understanding of the effects of bullying on young people's emotional well-being since the researchers were able to investigate the impact of self-esteem on the outcomes of being bullied. In their sample of 7,290 young people aged between 13 and 18 years, the researchers investigated the ways in which these dimensions were linked to depression and social anxiety. They were especially interested to find out the extent to which self-esteem acted as a mediator between being bullied and the resultant social isolation, on the one hand, and the 'internalising problems' of both depression and social anxiety, on the other. As predicted, they found that social isolation, friendship alienation and lack of trust in others were significantly related to low self-esteem, depression and social anxiety. At the same time, low self-esteem was significantly related to depression and social anxiety, independent of peer relationship difficulties. Of particular importance was the finding that the direct association between peer relational difficulties and depression, and, to a lesser extent, social anxiety was significantly reduced once self-esteem was entered into the equation. Victims who retained high self-esteem despite their suffering were better able to cope with its negative effects. Conversely, those with low self-esteem found it much more difficult. In other words, the individual experience of an apparently similar event is likely to vary depending on that young person's emotional makeup, their history of friendship and intimate attachments or their own resilience in the face of adversity.

Longitudinal studies confirm the evidence that children who are already emotionally vulnerable are at greater risk of being bullied. This process can begin in the early years at school. For example, Arseneault *et al.* (2006), as part of a longitudinal study of 2,232 twins, identified those who had experienced bullying between the ages of 5 and 7 years, either as 'pure' victims (that is, children who are bullied but who do not retaliate) or as bully-victims (that is, those who both bully and are bullied). A significant number of the children identified in this study as victims of bullying had come to school with pre-existing problems and were already less happy than non-bullied peers during their first year at school. The authors suggest the possibility that bullied children may exhibit some behaviours or characteristics that elicit aggression from peers; as a consequence, the bullies may identify them as vulnerable and so target them from the start. Both pure victims and bully-victims showed more adjustment difficulties and unhappiness at school than controls. In comparison with non-bullied peers, the pure victims showed a higher incidence of internalising problems and unhappiness at school. Girls (but not boys) who were pure victims also showed more externalising problems than controls. However, the bully-victims had the highest levels of difficulty since they showed more internalising problems than either pure victims or controls. Similarly, Hay and Meldrum (2010), in a longitudinal study of 426 young people aged between 10 and 21 years, studied the effect of parenting styles and self-control on buffering the negative impact of traditional bullying and cyberbullying. They found an association between being bullied and reports of self-harm and suicidal ideation. However, the presence of authoritative (as opposed to authoritarian) parenting practices and a strong sense of self-control on the part of the targeted young person moderated the negative effects of being bullied. Hay and Meldrum (2010) recommend cognitive behavioural therapy (CBT) in helping vulnerable young people to change their own responses to peer aggression and to strengthen their resilience and belief in self.

Outcomes for perpetrators of bullying

Children who bully others are also at risk of emotional or mental health difficulties though this is influenced by the type of bully that they are. Aggressive bullies play a leadership role, anxious bullies assist the aggressor to compensate for their own feelings of insecurity, reinforcers of the bully provide a willing audience and, as we saw earlier, bully-victims are both aggressors and targets. Although bullies may appear confident and, in some cases, are popular with the peer group, they also tend to display a lack of empathy for the suffering of others (Sutton *et al.*, 1999), joy and pride about the suffering of others (Wilton *et al.*, 2000) and an unrealistic or narcissistic justification for their anti-social behaviour (Baumeister *et al.*, 1996; Terranova *et al.*, 2008). Bullying behaviour is also affected by attitudes and values of the peer group in the context of the school and wider community (Österman, 2000). Children who bully are less likely to feel connected to their school and are more likely to gravitate towards aggressive, anti-social groups which reinforce their behaviour.

Low fear reactivity is also a risk factor for aggressive behaviour and this prevents the development of a sense of conscience about harming others. Terranova *et al.* (2008), in a sample of 124 middle-school children (average age 10.3 years), investigated whether the children's fear reactivity and their 'effortful control' (that is, their ability to inhibit dominant responses) would influence whether they engaged in bullying. They found that children who carry out direct physical bullying (as opposed to psychological or indirect bullying) lack the qualities of self-regulation and also do not fear the consequences of their aggression. They noted that deficits in effortful control disrupt the development of pro-social skills and values so reducing the repertoire of responses available to bullies when they interact with their peers. The callousness with which some young people engage in bullying behaviour is shown in qualitative interview data gathered from girl bullies by Owens, Shute and Slee (2000). Some reported that by socially excluding selected peers, they affirmed their own inclusion in the in-group. Others reported that they bullied through boredom, attention-seeking, revenge and the need for power. Bullies frequently justify their aggressive behaviour and minimise the outcomes for victims. For example, bullies will often state that the victim provoked them in some way and so deserved the treatment that they had received.

The immediate outcomes for bullies are often experienced by them as rewarding in terms of the power and status that they gain (Andreou and Metallidou, 2004; Caravita *et al.*, 2010). Longer term, however, the emotional and social outcomes for bullies are serious. Children who regularly bully have learned to use their power and aggression to control others, a mode that is not conducive to healthy relationships either in the present or in their future lives. Such deficits disrupt the development long term of pro-social skills and values and reduce the repertoire of responses available to these children in interacting with their peers.

There is evidence that they are more likely to be morally disengaged from school (Almeida *et al.*, 2010). Aggressors are at increased risk for school problems, conduct disorders, and substance use (Hinduja and Patchin, 2008; Sourander *et al*., 2010). Being a bully is linked to later violence, use of weapons and gang membership (Holmes and Brandenburg-Ayres, 1998) as well as to domestic violence and crime (Farrington, 1995; 2002).

Furthermore, children who bully are more likely to have mental health problems that persist into adult life. Kumpulainen and Räsänen (2000) found that children involved in bullying had more psychiatric symptoms at the age of 15 years than did children who were not bullies. The probability of being deviant at the age of 15 years was higher among children involved in bullying at the age of 8 or 12 years than among non-involved children. When concurrent psychiatric deviance was taken into account, involvement in bullying increased the probability of teacher-defined deviance at the age of 15 years. Similarly, Kaltiala-Heino *et al*. (2000), in a large-scale survey of 14- to 16-year-old Finnish adolescents taking part in the School Health Promotion Study (8,787 in 1995 and 7,643 in 1997), found that anxiety, depression and psychosomatic symptoms were most frequent among bully-victims and equally common among bullies and victims. Frequent excessive drinking and substance misuse were most common among bullies and additionally among bully-victims. Among girls, eating disorders were associated with involvement in bullying in any role, among boys with being bully-victims. These authors conclude that bullying should be seen as an indicator of risk of various mental disorders in adolescence.

These examples of the bully's personal characteristics also appear to confirm what some researchers have identified as a narcissistic preoccupation with the self and over-sensitivity to any form of actual or perceived criticism. Those high in narcissism appear to be self-confident with high levels of self-esteem but they are often considered by others to be egotistical and conceited individuals who have a grandiose conception of themselves. Narcissistic individuals also tend to be self-focused, highly competitive, exhibitionistic and aggressive people who lack empathy and who tend to be manipulative and self-seeking in their interpersonal relationships (Raskin and Novacek, 1989). Baumeister *et al*. (1996) further propose that aggression is related to high self-esteem through what they define as defensive egotism – a tendency to hold favourable self-appraisals that may be not grounded in reality or may be exaggerated, combined with difficulty in accepting any criticism. Threats to such self-appraisals are met with aggression. This type of self-focussed person tends to be highly competitive, manipulative, lacking in empathy and self-seeking in their relationships with others; they also score highly on measures of narcissism. Baumeister *et al*. argue that it is at the point where such a person's self-appraisal is perceived to be under threat that they become aggressive.

The effects upon peers

Much research has focused on the individual aspects of bullying behaviour by exploring the characteristics of perpetrators and targets, so overlooking the powerful influence of the social contexts where the bullying is enacted. Jones *et al.* (2011) indicate the crucial part played by peer group membership, peer group norms and in-group identification in shaping the outcomes of bullying episodes. In particular, these researchers examine the emotional reactions of the peer group in the context of their group affiliation, taking account of the strong impact of the social group to which individuals belong in directing their emotional responses to the actions of the group with which they most strongly identify. Jones *et al.* (2011) propose that group-based emotions are important here since this perspective can cast light on the fact that children and young people do not always respond with empathy to the victim of bullying and can also experience pride in the aggressive actions of the bully.

As indicated earlier, bullies seek dominance within the group and use aggression and psychological manipulation to maintain their power. They take advantage of the social structures in their peer groups and their skill at manipulating others to gain power and status, and to deflect perceived threats to their own self-esteem. However, the group has the potential to challenge the aggressors, as Besag (2006), in a longitudinal observational study of girls' relationships, observed. Skill at manipulating others (often covertly) may be an effective means of retaining dominance over others in the short term, but it can backfire if the group collectively decides that the behaviour is unacceptable. For example, Besag described one girl's unsuccessful bids for leadership that failed since her repertoire of tactics included a bullying, autocratic manner and the tendency to act in such a way that vulnerable members were disadvantaged. She was large and powerfully built so could be very intimidating but in the end the others usually managed to reject her attempts to dominate, so indicating the potential of the group to challenge the power of the bully, if it chooses.

Concluding remarks

The research evidence offers useful insights into a chain of events that may arise from the experience of being bullied, and indicates the crucial part that peer relationships play in the emotional health and well-being of young people. The findings suggest that students who are already emotionally vulnerable in some way need support to build up their resilience in the face of rejection or intimidation at the hands of bullies or indifference on the part of bystanders. Adults need to be aware of the risk factors for bullying in order to anticipate difficulties before they become entrenched. They need to be sensitive to the fact that some young people will be trapped in a vicious cycle in which they are unable to protect themselves, so they become even more vulnerable and experience further bullying as a consequence. Low self-esteem and interpersonal difficulties may interact with one another over time. Children with low self-esteem may be more vulnerable to attack in the first place; the bullying undermines their self-esteem even further; in turn, this leads to further victimisation and so the cycle continues if nothing is done to intervene. A further outcome is likely to be that they learn to expect bad treatment from peers and so experience events more negatively than would emotionally resilient peers (Escobar *et al.*, 2011; Verkuyten and Thijs, 2001).

A major outcome for the peer group as a whole is that the school climate suffers if bullying and bystander apathy go unchallenged. A range of approaches is available to create emotionally literate school communities that value the right of everyone to feel safe at school and to be valued. The presence of bullying behaviour challenges educators and young people to reflect on the injustice of actions that hurt and socially exclude children and young people. Schools have a substantial role to play in facilitating positive harmonious relationships as part of a whole-school approach to counteracting bullying. The outcomes then are safer schools where students and educators can embark collectively on active participation and social inclusion.

References

Almeida, A., Correia, I. and Marinho, S. (2010) 'Moral disengagement, normative beliefs of peer group, and attitudes regarding roles in bullying', *Journal of School Violence*, 9: 23–36.

Andreou, E. and Metallidou, P. (2004) 'The relationship of academic and social cognition to behaviour in bullying situations among Greek primary school children', *Educational Psychology: An International Journal of Experimental Educational Psychology*, 24: 27–41.

Arseneault, L., Walsh, E., Trzesniewski, K., Newcombe, R., Caspi, A. and Moffitt, T. (2006) 'Bullying victimization uniquely contributes to adjustment problems in young children: a nationally representative cohort study', *Pediatrics*, 118: 130–138.

Baumeister, R. F., Smart, L. and Boden, J. M. (1996) 'Relation of threatened egotism to violence and aggression: the dark side of high self-esteem', *Psychological Review*,103: 5–33.

Besag, V. (2006) *Understanding Girls' Friendships, Fights and Feuds: A Practical Approach to Girls' Bullying*, Maidenhead: Open University Press.

Bosacki, S. L., Dane, A. V., Marini, Z. A. and YLC-CURA (2007) 'Peer relationships and internalizing problems in adolescents: mediating role of self-esteem', *Emotional and Behavioural Difficulties*, 121: 261–282.

Boulton, M. J., Trueman, M., Chau, C., Whitehand, C. and Amatya, K. (1999) 'Concurrent and longitudinal links between friendship and peer victimization: Implications for befriending interventions', *Journal of Adolescence*, 22: 461–466.

Caravita, S., Di Blasio, P. and Salmivalli, C. (2010) 'Early adolescents' participation in bullying: is ToM involved?,' *Journal of Early Adolescence*, 30: 138–170.

Dooley, J., Pyzalski, J. and Cross, D. (2009) 'Cyberbullying versus face-to-face bullying. a theoretical and conceptual review', *Zeitschrift für Psychologie/Journal of Psychology*, 217: 182–188.

Espelage, D., Bosworth, K. and Simon, T. (2000) 'Examining the social context of bullying behaviours in early adolescence', *Journal of Counseling and Development*, 78: 326 333.

Escobar, M., Fernandez-Baen, F. J., Miranda, J., Trianes, M. V. and Cowie, H. (2011) 'Low peer acceptace and emotional/behavioural maladjustment in schoolchildren: effects of daily stress, soping and sex', *Anales de Psicologia*, 27: 4122–4217.

Farrington, D. P. (1995) 'The development of offending and anti-social behaviour from childhood: key findings from the Cambridge Study in Delinquent Development', *Journal of Child Psychology and Psychiatry*, 36; 929–964.

Farrington, D. P. (2002) 'Risk factors for youth violence', in E. Debarbieux and C. Blaya (eds), *Violence in Schools and Public Policies*, Oxford: Elsevier Science.

Gini, G. and Pozzoli, T. (2009) 'Association between bullying and psychosomatic problems: a meta-analysis', *Pediatrics*, 123: 1059–1065.

Glover, D., Gough, G. and Johnson, M. (2000) 'Bullying in 25 secondary schools: incidence, impact and intervention', *Educational Research*, 42: 141–156.

Gradinger, P., Strohmeier, D. and Spiel, C. (2009) 'Traditional bullying and cyberbullying: identification of risk groups for adjustment problems', *Zeitschrift fur Psychologie/Journal of Psychology*, 217: 205–213.

Hawker, D. S. J. and Boulton, M. J. (2000) 'Twenty years' research on peer victimization and psychosocial maladjustment: a meta-analytic review of cross-sectional studies', *Journal of Child Psychology and Psychiatry*, 41: 441–455.

Hay, C. and Meldrum, R. (2010) 'Bullying victimization and adolescent self-harm: testing hypotheses from General Strain Theory', *Journal of Youth and Adolescence*, 39: 446–459.

Hinduja, S. and Patchin, J.W. (2008) 'Cyberbullying: an exploratory analysis of factors related to offending and victimization', *Deviant Behavior*, 29: 129–156.

Hoff, D. L. and Mitchell, S. N. (2009) 'Cyberbullying: causes, effects, and remedies', *SO – Journal of Educational Administration*, 47: 652–665.

Holmes, S. R. and Brandenburg-Ayres, S. J. (1998) 'Bullying behaviour in school: a predictor of later gang involvement', *Journal of Gang Research*, 5: 1–6.

Jones, S. E., Manstead, A. S. R. and Livingstone, A. G. (2011) 'Ganging up or sticking together? Group processes and children's responses to text-message bullying', *British Journal of Psychology*, 102: 71–96.

Juvonen, J. and Gross, E. F. (2008) 'Extending the school grounds? Bullying experiences in cyberspace', *The Journal of School Health*, 78: 496–505.

Kaltiala-Heino, R., Rimpela, M., Rantanen, P. and Rimpela, A. (2000) 'Bullying at school – an indicator of adolescents at risk for mental disorders', *Journal of Adolescence*, 23: 661–674.

Kumpulainen, K. and Räsänen, E. (2000) 'Children involved in bullying at elementary school age: their psychiatric symptoms and deviance in adolescence: an epidemiological sample', *Child Abuse and Neglect*, 24: 1567–1577.

LaGreca, A. and Harrison, H. (2005) 'Adolescent peer relations, friendships and romantic relationships: do they predict social anxiety and depression', *Journal of Clinical Child and Adolescent Psychology*, 34: 49–61.

Marini, Z. A., Dane, A., Bosacki, S. and YLC-CURA (2006) 'Direct and indirect bully-victims: differential psychosocial risk factors associated with adolescents involved in bullying and victimization', *Aggressive Behavior*, 32: 551–569.

Mitchell, K. J., Ybarra, M. and Finkelhor, D. (2007) 'The relative importance of online victimization in understanding depression, delinquency, and substance use', *Child Maltreatment*, 12: 314.

Nangle, D., Erdley, C., Newman, J., Mason, C. and Carpenter, E. (2003) 'Popularity, friendship quantity, and friendship quality: interactive influences on children's loneliness and depression', *Journal of Clinical Child and Adolescent Psychology*, 32: 546–555.

Olweus, D. (1993) *Bullying: What We Know and What We Can Do*, Oxford: Basil Blackwell.

Owens, L., Shute, R. and Slee, P. (2000) '"Guess what I just heard!": Indirect aggression among teenage girls in Australia', *Aggressive Behavior*, 26: 67–83.

Österman, K. F. (2000) 'Students' need for belonging in the school community', *Review of Educational Research*, 70: 323–367.

Perren, S., Dooley, J., Shaw, T. and Cross, D. (2010) 'Bullying in school and cybersace: associations with depressive symptoms in Swiss and Australian adolescents', *Child and Adolescent Psychiatry and Mental Health*, 4: 28.

Raskin, R. and Novacek, J. (1989) 'An MMPI description of the narcissistic personality', *Journal of Personality Assessment*, 53: 66–80.

Riebel, J., Jaeger, R. S. and Fischer, U. C. (2009) 'Cyberbullying in Germany – an exploration of prevalence, overlapping with real life bullying and coping strategies', *Psychology Science Quarterly*, 51: 298–314.

Rigby, K. and Slee, P. (1991) 'Bullying among Australian school children: reported behaviour and attitudes towards victims', *Journal of Social Psychology*, 131: 615–627.

Salmivalli, C., Lagerspetz, K., Björkqvist, K., Österman, K. and Kaukiainen, A. (1996) 'Bullying as a group process: participant roles and their relations to social status within the group', *Aggressive Behavior,* 22: 1–15.

Sourander, A., Brunstein Klomek, A. B., Ikomen, M., Lindroos, J., Luntamo, T., Koskelainen, M., Ristkari, T. and Helenius, H. (2010) 'Psychosocial risk factors associated with cyberbullying among adolescents', *Archives of General Psychiatry*, 67: 720–728.

Sutton, J., Smith, P. K. and Swettenham, J. (1999) 'Bullying and theory of mind: a critique of the "social skills deficit" view of anti-social behaviour', *Social Development*, 8: 117–127.

Terranova, A. M., Sheffield Morris, A. and Boxer, P. (2008) 'Fear reactivity and effortful control in overt and relational bullying: a six-month longitudinal study', *Aggressive Behavior*, 34: 104–115.

Ttofi, M. M., Farrington, D. P. and Lösel, F. (2011) 'Editorial: health consequences of school bullying', *Journal of Aggression, Conflict and Peace Research*, 3: 60–62.

Verkuyten, M. and Thijs, J. (2001) 'Peer victimization and self-esteem of ethnic minority group children', *Journal of Community and Applied Social Psychology*, 11: 227–234.

Wilton, M. M. M., Craig, W. M. and Pepler, D. J. (2000) 'Emotional regulation and display in classroom victims of bullying: characteristic expression of affect, coping styles and relevant contextual factors', *Social Development*, 9: 226–245.

3 Cyberbullying and cyberaggression

Sexualised and gendered experiences explored

Ian Rivers

Introduction

Today children and young people have the potential to interact with others in ways that only a decade ago we could not envisage. The evolution of internet-ready mobile/cell phones, greater access to the internet through games consoles and our increasing reliance upon electronic forms of communication mean that electronic information about individuals is globally accessible and therefore also readily available to those who seek to discriminate, intimidate or exploit vulnerable others. In this chapter, the focus turns to the sexualised and gendered nature of hostile electronic and online interactions between young people (principally adolescents) and other 'users', both peers and adults. While there is ever-increasing evidence that young people represent a particularly vulnerable group of users of technology, they are, more than any other generation, also experts or 'digital natives' in the manipulation of this technology for their own ends. From a relatively early age they have learnt, more so than many adults, how to navigate around net-nannies, hide illicit conversations, delete tracking histories and explore worlds once considered 'adult', without a parent or guardian ever knowing. Yet, for all this expertise, . rarely do the skills they show online incorporate an understanding of risk avoidance or risk management (Byron, 2008), and perhaps more pertinently research has shown that these digital 'natives'not only fail to maintain control of their online identities but their investment in online relationships is such that they fail to see the threats associated with increased disclosure of personal information. Ultimately, online disclosure can result in offline vulnerability to many different forms of exploitation.

Definitions of cyberbullying and cyberaggression

Cyberbullying is a form of aggressive behaviour that occurs through electronic devices such as mobile/cell phones (calls and SMS/text messages), e-mail and the internet (blogs, chatrooms, newsgroups, social networks and web-pages). Like other forms of bullying, cyberbullying is usually defined in terms of intentional and repeated interactions on the part of the perpetrator who is perceived to be more powerful than the victim: the perpetrator's ability to act anonymously is indicative of a form of power he or she holds over the victim (Wolak *et al.*, 2007). The perpetrator then seeks to harm, exploit or denigrate the status of that individual.

By way of contrast, cyberaggression can be defined as any form of communication mediated through an electronic device where the purpose is to harm or otherwise exploit an individual physically, sexually and/or emotionally (Grigg, 2010). Cyberaggression can include single incidents as well as those that are repeated. It can include behaviours such as 'trolling' (sending or posting messages mean to shock, threaten or intimidate viewers), 'flaming' (escalating or intensifying an interaction through aggressive messaging), 'flooding' (dominating chat) and 'kicking' (excluding people from chat or a game by reporting them to a moderator or service provider; Rivers *et al.*, 2011: 212). Cyberaggression can also include sexual solicitation, especially when the online interactions make demands of the victim, or where he or she feels obliged to engage in behaviours that increase his or her vulnerability (disclosing personal information or posting/emailing compromising or intimate images).

The transformative nature of online 'presence'

Orgad (2005: 141) has argued that online communication has a 'transformative potential' in the lives of individuals, particularly those who, in times of difficulty, wish to seek out and be supported by others who understand or share those difficulties. Here, the internet becomes a positive resource, a befriending service and facilitator of support groups. It allows those in need of advice or guidance to interact in meaningful ways with similar others and also with those who have succesfully navigated their way through a particular hardship or challenging experience. Orgad goes further to say that, in her study which focused on online communication among breast cancer patients, the internet provides a special level of anonymity and security which she describes as follows:

> The situation of being behind a screen when one is not physically visible and present, and where one can remain anonymous, constitutes a supportive context for one to step back from one's personal experience
> (Orgad, 2005: 152)

Orgad's description of the internet experience of cancer patients provides two useful insights into the ways in which many individuals (including children) interact with others online. Firstly, in the minds of internet users there exists a mythical status known as 'anonymity' where each user can create and retain control of her or his identity. Secondly, and perhaps much more importantly, the user is a disembodied 'presence' and thus the physical or offline form (the body) and the online form (the 'presence') can be separated, or are perceived to be unrelated (at least in the minds of users).

Users, regardless of their motivation to be online, are thus transformed by their desire to interact with others in cyberspace. Attempts to ensure anonymity and a belief that the two worlds are in some way separate, particularly when conversing with strangers, mean that the identity portrayed online is different to that portrayed in offline interactions with others. Boundaries may be crossed, assumptions may be made and limits may be transgressed by an online 'presence' that would not (and probably could not) be transgressed by the same person offline (Suler, 2004). Thus, behaviours such as the sexual solicitiation of minors, trolling and flaming are perpetrated by women and men who, in the offline world, may not only be well-educated, but also understand and enforce the limits society places upon social interactions with vulnerable others, especially children (Kyrik, 2005).

When the offline and online worlds collide

Sexually aggressive solicitations

For those supporting or caring for children and young people there are justifiably concerns about safe-guarding. For over 10 years, David Finkelhor and his colleagues at the University of New Hampshire in the USA have been monitoring young people's use of the internet – the Youth Internet Safety Surveys – YISS. While the data they have gathered suggests that there is a downward trend in young people's exposure to sexually aggressive or distressing sexual solicititations online (see Table 3.1), it remains the case that girls are far more likely to receive such solicitations, whereas boys are more likely to be exposed to unwanted pornographic images (see Table 3.2). It is important to note the sexual content of the material young people are receiving, and the fact that their lives online are, in part, constructed around others' desire to provide these young people with opportunities for sexual exploration and knowledge, perhaps leading to a physical sexual interaction. The sexually exploitative nature of online interactions, while often discussed in the media, is not understood fully within the educational context, nor is there a full appreciation of how online interactions can impact upon young people's understandings of sex and sexuality. Yet, educationally, parents, teachers, administrators, politicians and community leaders are hesitant to provide young people with the skills and resources to understand the complexity of sex and sexuality and, more importantly, manage the risk of exposure to sexually explicit or aggressive material online. Furthermore, as the offline and online worlds merge with face-to-face interactions blending with online communication, exposure to sexual material via the internet is not matched by a concomitant exposure to sex education and sexual-risk management skills which ultimately leave young people unprepared to deal

Tables 3.1 and 3.2 Trends in online sexual solicitation: percentages

Unwanted experiences on internet	Youth Internet Safety Survey		
	2000 *(n = 1,500)* %	*2005* *(n = 1,500)* %	*2010* *(n=1,560)* %
Any sexual solicitation			
10–12 years of age	10	5	2
13–15 years of age	21	17	8
16–17 years of age	23	17	14
Distressing sexual solicitation			
10–12 years of age	5	3	1
13–15 years of age	4	5	3
16–17 years of age	3	6	3
Aggressive sexual solicitation			
10–12 years of age	1	1	1
13–15 years of age	3	5	3
16–17 years of age	4	5	4
Unwanted exposure to pornography			
10–12 years of age	9	19	15
13–15 years of age	28	35	23
16–17 years of age	33	44	28
Distressing exposure to pornography			
10–12 years of age	2	10	6
13–15 years of age	8	9	5
16–17 years of age	7	9	5

Unwanted experiences on internet	Youth Internet Safety Survey		
	2000 *(n = 1,500)* %	*2005* *(n = 1,500)* %	*2010* *(n=1,560)* %
Any sexual solicitation			
Girls	27	18	13
Boys	12	8	4
Distressing sexual solicitation			
Girls	8	7	4
Boys	2	2	1
Aggressive sexual solicitation			
Girls	4	7	5
Boys	2	2	1
Unwanted exposure to pornography			
Girls	23	31	22
Boys	27	37	24
Distressing exposure to pornography			
Girls	6	10	5
Boys	6	8	5

Sources: Tables reprinted from the *Journal of Adolescent Health*, Vol. 50, Jones, L. M., Mitchell, K. J. and Finkelhor, D., 'Trends in youth internet victimization: Findings from three youth internet safety surveys 2000–2010', p. 183 and p. 184, Copyright (2012), with permission from Elsevier.

with the advances they receive online. For example, in the second of three studies, Mitchell, Finkelhor and Wolak (2007) noted that levels of disclosure of personal information were greatest when young people received sexually aggressive solicitations (see Table 3.3). In other words, as a contact became more demanding or more threatening online, so the young people in Mitchell *et al*.'s study were more likely to acquiesce to those demands, post increasingly personal information about themselves which eventually placed them at even greater emotional and physical risk. Indeed, Mitchell *et al.* noted that in 60 per cent of cases where the young people in their study had received sexually aggressive solicitations online, they were also experiencing offline victimisation. In every sense, therefore, the threat to young people from electronic media is a real one.

Table 3.3 Youth Online Behaviour and Perpetrator Response: YISS 2 (2005)

Youth Online Behaviour	*No sexual solicitation (n=1,300)* %	*Aggressive sexual solicitation (n=63)* %	*Limited sexual solicitation (n=137)* %
Posted personal information	53	81	72
Sent personal information to someone	21	75	47
Talked about sex	3	29	16
Person on buddy list never met in person	31	78	58
Other office interpersonal victimisation	37	60	45

Source: Reprinted from *American Journal of Preventative Medicine*, Vol. 32, Mitchell, K.J., Finkelhor, D. and Wolak, J., 'Youth internet users at risk for the most serious online sexual solicitations', p. 535, Copyright (2007), with permission from Elsevier.

In a related study to that cited above, Wolak, Mitchell and Finkelhor (2007) reported that in 43 per cent of cases young people definitely know the offline identities of those who are aggressive towards them online. While this suggests that in the majority of online interactions young people are unlikely to come into physical contact with their aggressor, this does not mean that those young people cannot be sexually exploited in other ways (e.g. through the posting of intimate photographs that they have shared with their online 'friends', see Finkelhor and Ormrod, 2004 for more on this). Online 'grooming' is both subtle and strategic. It can begin with friendly banter in a chatroom, followed by a request to chat 'in private'. As a young person becomes more confident in the trust she or he can place in their online friend, pictures and personal details may be exchanged, secrets shared. Gradually, there is an escalation in requests (and this can happen over days, weeks or even months) where pictures and webcam interactions are recorded and saved by the perpetrator. Where requests to meet are made they can be accompanied by threats to shame or expose the young person's images to others; fear and shame may compel some young people to meet their online 'friends' (Childnet International, 2012).

Gendered misunderstandings

Numerous assumptions are made about the intentions of perpetrators in online interactions based upon the sex and age of the victim. However, for over a decade we have known that all is not as it seems. A study conducted by the American Association of University Women – AAUW (1999) suggested that many young women find the online environment liberating in terms of releasing them from traditional expectations allowing them to explore other aspects of themselves (see Berson, 2003). By way of contrast, Berson *et al.* (2002) argued that many online interactions initiated or entered into by young people involve a degree of deception where the primary communication devices are verbal harassment or sexually suggestive chat. Berson *et al.* noted that, particularly in email or chat-rooms, insults, sexual innuendoes and challenges to the opinions of others were everyday occurrences. Additionally, for some young women the age of those with whom they flirted was immaterial. For some, being online was a fictional space where they could be whomever they chose to be, with elective gender, age and personality.

The evolution of social networking sites such as *Myspace, Facebook* and *Twitter* has also afforded individuals of all ages the opportunity to talk with one another, often in real-time regardless of their location. Just as the opportunities for global communication emerge with advances in technology, so too do opportunities for global bullying and the posting of statements and comments that are meant to shock or cause emotional distress without having any 'come-back' for the perpetrator hiding behind her or his veil of anonymity or pseudo-identity. Yet, as before, there is often a 'gendered' assumption at play here because most of the victims of internet grooming or harassment are female and most of the online identities they interact with are male. However, even seemingly innocent interactions supervised by parents are not always what they seem, and can conceal identities and purposes that are almost unthinkable.

The case of Megan Meier provides an early example where assumptions made by this young person and her parents about the honesty of an online interaction were shattered by the intentional behaviours of two adults who sought to hurt her. Megan was 13 years of age in the summer of 2006 when she struck up an online relationship with a 16-year-old boy named 'Josh Evans' on *Myspace*. Megan was only allowed to use the computer when she was supervised by a parent, and to those who knew about Josh this online relationship was to all intents and purposes innocent. Megan had a history of depression and had recently fallen out with a friend after she had moved schools. Thus, this online relationship had lifted Megan's spirits.

The relationship was described as 'flirtatious' in the trial memorandum and Josh had described Megan as 'sexi'. This relationship continued unabated until 16 October when Josh posted a message that included a statement which read 'the world would be a better place without you'. Others who were linked to Josh Evans' *Myspace* account also began to post hurtful messages. A short time after Megan was found dead: she had hanged herself. 'Josh Evans' vanished from *Myspace* soon after Megan's death was made public. His account was deleted and his offline identity remained unknown, at least for a time. Who was Josh Evans, and why did he post that hurtful statement? Josh was in fact a 49-year-old woman named Lori Drew who was also the mother of the friend with whom Megan had fallen out. Drew, together with her daughter and an employee, deliberately sought to humiliate their victim by making public some of the things Megan and Josh had talked about online. Lori Drew was indicted on four counts associated with unauthorised use of a computer and breaching *Myspace*'s terms and conditions of use. Drew was eventually found guilty of these misdemeanours, but she was never charged with the death of Megan Meier, and even her conviction was overturned on appeal. Although Drew retained her freedom, the outrage caused by her actions resulted in a change in legislation, and led to laws on using the internet to harass another person.

The significance of this case not only lies in the fact that it caused outrage, but also in the fact that it demonstrated how girls' offline relationships can be manipulated online when they go sour. We do not know what information Lori Drew used to create Josh, but in all likelihood this online 'presence' was created by exploiting the knowledge gained by Drew's daughter when she was friendly with Megan. Was Josh this adolescent girl's ideal, drawn from the secrets she shared with Lori Drew's daughter?

Cyberbullying: how different is it from other forms of bullying?

As noted above, sexual content, and particularly aggressive sexual content of online interactions, is often presumed to be by members of the opposite sex (if heterosexual youth) and same-sex (if lesbian, gay, bisexual or transgender youth) and interactions that can be characterised as internet bullying or cyberbullying often assume an existing offline relationship between perpetrator and victim. To date, however, no quantitative studies have demonstrated this link other than commenting on possibility that there has been an offline interaction between the two (see Smith *et al.*, 2008; Williams and Guerra, 2007).

In the current literature associated with bullying, it is always assumed that a relationship has been established between the perpetrator and the victim or, at the very least, each has a working knowledge of the other. Most definitions describe bullying in terms of a series of deliberate acts whereby the perpetrator's intention is to inflict physical or emotional pain upon the victim repeatedly. However, the majority of studies conducted so far have tended to apply one generic definition that encompasses both the behaviours of perpetrators and the responses of victims without necessarily considering if victims can discern deliberate acts, and can understand their significance in terms of their day-to-day relationship with those perpetators. In the offline world there are instances where this intentionality to inflict suffering by the perpetrator is apparent as a result of the way in which the victim is attacked, but is this necessarily the case in the online world where interactions can be easily misinterpreted or sent without premeditation (an emotional response to a hastily or poorly-phrased e-mail is one such example)? For any interaction to be considered bullying or, indeed, cyberbullying, it is necessary to interrogate the relationship between the parties involved, and not assume, as so many anonymous school surveys do, that 'X' number of perpetrators in a school are responsible for the bullying of 'Y' number of victims. More pertinently, it becomes even more problematic if an assumption is made that 'Y' number of victims of cyberaggression, sexual solicitation or cyberbullying are the targets of 'X' number of known perpetrators who engage in similar behaviour offline.

Asking young people about the content on the hurtful posts, messages or websites they see or receive is one way of establishing whether cyberaggression or cyberbullying is likely to be a local phenomenon perpetrated by young people against young people, and one that can be tackled within the school setting. As part of a five-year study of text and email bullying, students aged between 11 and 14 years were asked to provide the researchers with examples of the hurtful messages they had received (Rivers and Noret, 2010). Text messages were provided by 38 boys and 109 girls and email messages were submitted by 17 boys and 75 girls. Overall, ten categories of content were identified in the texts and e-mails. These categories included: threats of physical violence, abusive or hate-related statements, name-calling (including homophobia), death threats, the ending of platonic relationships, sexual acts, demands/instructions, threats to damage existing relationships, threats to home/family life and menacing chain messages.

Overall the results indicated that boys received more hate-related messages than girls, while girls were subjected to name-calling more often than boys. In terms of content of the hurtful messages that students received, the majority indicated either an offline relationship or some knowledge of the recipient by the perpetrator – 'I'm going to kick your head in when you least expect it', 'I'm going to tell him that you said…', 'I will get you and your family too', 'you're going to be knocked out after school', 'I know where you live, I'm going to kill you', 'I'm going to make your mates turn against you'. Additionally, in terms of the relationships between online and offline bullying, it was observed that boys were more likely to receive hurtful text and email messages if they were being bullied because of their weight, size or body shape, general appearance, ethnicity, perceived sexual orientation or because of the brand of clothes they were wearing to school. Girls were more likely to receive hurtful text and email messages if they were also being bullied because they were good at school work, or because they were either very good or not so good at sports. Although the data suggested that the online and offline worlds were interconnected for the young people in this study, as noted earlier, it is not always the case that we can make assumptions about the nature of the relationships that lead to incidents of cyberaggression and cyberbullying.

Addressing cyberaggression and cyberbullying

To effectively challenge cyberaggression and cyberbullying, it is important for parents and teachers to better understand the prejudices, beliefs and dislikes young people hold, and how they have arrived at those prejudices or beliefs. Some undoubtedly will come from the offline world where conversations with family and friends are logged and either rejected or assimilated, but others will come from the so-called 'information super-highway' which is largely unregulated and where extreme beliefs are posited as politically legitimate and rational standpoints (Resnick *et al.*, 1994). Any interventions that are designed to challenge the prejudices that are expressed online, or limit young people's exposure to potentially exploitative interactions with unknown users, necessarily require the imposition of a degree of monitoring or censorship that may, in some circumstances infringe civil liberties and the expression of free speech. This is, in essence, where government policy in the UK is directed. However, rather than be a framework for ensuring the welfare of individuals online, it is primarily a mechanism to counter terrorism and ensure national security.

Both monitoring online interactions and censorship are likely to have little effect in the case of cyberbullying if those undertaking that monitoring do not understand the context in which such online behaviour takes place or seek to understand its meaning and resonance with the victim. As noted by Rivers and Noret (2010: 665):

> To effectively challenge the negative perceptions or beliefs that inform a perpetrator's decision to harass or otherwise abuse a peer online, it is important that we understand the significance of the messages that victims receive, not simply record their frequency, and interrogate the context and interpersonal dynamics that underpin the relationship between the perpetrator and the victim.

This is, however, contingent upon us being able to identify perpetrators or, at the very least, identify their sex – which we can do in less than 50 per cent of incidents (Wolak *et al.*, 2007).

In an independent review sponsored by the then British Prime Minister, Gordon Brown, media psychologist Tanya Byron looked at the risks of young people being exposed to harmful or inappropriate material on the internet and in video games (Byron, 2008). In her report, Byron argued that there is a need to look at ways of empowering young people to manage risk effectively on the internet and to recognise that there is a need for age-related restrictions or classifications for video games to ensure that children and young people are not exposed to violent media early in their development. Although Byron also recommended a more stringent regulation of the internet, she only briefly mentioned issues associated with cyberbullying, recommending that this should be the responsibility of teacher training institutions (i.e. universities) that were charged with assessing knowledge of e-safety against professional standards of competence.

In a follow-up report published in 2010, progress against the recommendations made by Tanya Byron was submitted to the Secretary of State for Education (Byron, 2010). While there were clear attempts to improve the safety of children and young people on the internet, the recommendations remained focused on censure and reporting rather than on risk management skills in young people. Furthermore, changes in the way in which teaching training is delivered in the UK mean that universities are no longer the sole providers of intial teacher education (ITE). There are now teaching schools that deliver in partnership with a university ITE, and 'Free Schools' that do not require any formal qualifications in teaching whatsoever. In effect, the diversification of ITE in the UK and the lack of requirement for teachers to be appropriately qualified if they teach in 'Free Schools' (similar to Charter Schools in the USA) means that the requirement for teachers to demonstrate professional standards of competence in promoting e-safety among children and young people may be compromised without further legislative intervention.

Notwithstanding the development of the United Kingdon Council for Child Internet Safety (UKCCIS) – recommended by Byron (2008) – has produced a very simple guide to online safety which can be understood by children and young people of all ages: 'Zip It, Block It, Flag It' (Byron, 2010: 13):

> Zip It – Keep your personal stuff private and think about what you say online.
>
> Block It – Block people who send nasty messages and don't open unknown links and attachments.
>
> Flag It – Flag up with someone you trust if anything upsets you or if someone asks to meet you offline.

The success of such an initiative has yet to be evaluated fully, but it is a useful starting point for the development of a training programme from children and young people in schools, although, as noted earlier, the training of teachers and parents has yet to be fully addressed.

Conclusion

Cyberaggression and cyberbullying are commonplace phenomena. Since 2000, there have been numerous reports of young people taking their own lives because they have been the victims of taunts not only at school but also online. Many of the online taunts and slurs experienced by these young people have focused on issues of sexuality and sexual orientation which seem to have been an index of an escalation in offline bullying. Sexuality, sexual orientation, gender typicality and atypicality are aspects of young people's lives that constantly appear in developmental literature. The internet provides an environment in which it is possible for young people to explore these most personal aspects of lives often anonymously. However, the internet also provides forums where others can express their likes and dislikes, their prejudices and their suspicions about others without having the social cues and restrictions that regulate face-to-face interactions. Add to this the presence of other users searching for vulnerable young people to exploit and we are left with a world where there are few immediate sanctions for extremes of behaviour and, perhaps, even fewer opportunities to hide once an online identity is known. While Jones *et al.*'s (2012) data indicates that there was been a general downturn in young people's exposure to sexual solicitation and pornography on the internet, cyberbullying remains a significant issue and the exploitation and denigration of another's sexuality remains a key weapon for perpetrators.

References

American Association of University Women – AAUW (1999) *Voices of a Generation: Teenage Girls on Sex, School and Self*, Washington, DC: Author.

Berson, I. R. (2003) 'Grooming cybervictims: the psychosocial effects of online exploitation for youth', *Journal of School Psychology*, 2: 5–18.

Berson, I. R., Berson, M. J. and Ferron, J. M. (2002) 'Emerging risk of violence in the digitial age: lessons for educators from an online study of adolescent girls in the United States', *Journal of School Violence*, 1: 51–71.

Byron, T. (2008) *Safer Children in a Digital World: The Report of the Byron Review*. Avaliable at: http://www.education.gov.uk/ukccis/about/a0076277/the-byron-reviews (accessed 1 April 2012).

Byron, T. (2010) *Do We Have Safer Children in a Digital World? A Review of Progress Since the 2008 Byron Review*. Available at: http://www.education.gov.uk/ukccis/about/a0076277/the-byron-reviews (accessed 1 April 2012).

Childnet International (2012) Online Grooming and UK Law. Available at: http:www.childnet-int.org/downloads/online-grooming.pdf (accessed 11 April 2012).

Finkelhor, D. and Ormrod, R. (2004) *Child Pornography: Patterns from NIBRS*. Available at: http://www.ncjrs.gov/pdffiles1/ojjdp/204911.pdf (accessed 1 April 2012).

Grigg, D. W. (2010) 'Cyber-aggression: definition and concept of cyberbullying', *Australian Journal of Guidance and Counselling*, 20: 143–156.

Jones, L. M., Mitchell, K. J. and Finkelhor, D. (2012) 'Trends in youth internet victimization: findings from three Youth Internet Safety Surveys 2000–2010', *Journal of Adolescent Health*, 50: 179–186.

Kyrik, K. (2005) 'Trolling for predators: more and more law enforcement officers are actively working the internet to track, apprehend and prosecute pedophiles', *Police: The Law Enforcement Magazine*, 29: 32–34, 36, 38–40.

Mitchell, K. J., Finkelhor, D. and Wolak, J. (2007) 'Youth internet users at risk for the most serious online sexual solicitations', *American Journal of Preventive Medicine*, 32: 532–537.

Orgad, S. (2005) 'The transformative potential of online communication', *Feminist Media Studies*, 5: 141–161.

Resnick, P., Zeckhauser, R. and Avery, C. (1994) *Roles for Electronic Brokers*. Available at: http://ccs.mit.edu/papers/CCSWP179.html (accessed 1 April 2012).

Rivers, I. and Noret, N. (2010) '"I h 8 u": findings from a five-year study of text and email bullying', *British Educational Research Journal*, 36: 643–671.

Rivers, I., Chesney, T. and Coyne I. (2011) 'Cyberbullying', in C. P. Monks and I. Coyne (eds), *Bullying in Different Contexts*, Cambridge: Cambridge University Press.

Smith, P. K., Mahdavi, J., Carvalho, M., Fisher, S., Russell, S. and Tippett, N. (2008) 'Cyberbullying: its nature and impact in secondary school pupils', *Journal of Child Psychology and Psychiatry*, 49: 378–385.

Suler, J. (2004) 'The online disinhibition effect', *CyberPsychology and Behavior*, 7: 321–326.

Williams, K. R. and Guerra, N. G. (2007) 'Prevalence and predictors of internet bullying', *Journal of Adolescent Health,* 41 (Supplement): 14–21.

Wolak, J., Mitchell, K. J. and Finkelhor, D. (2007) 'Does online harassment constitute bullying? An exploration of online harassment by known peers and online-only contacts', *Journal of Adolescent Health*, 41 (Supplement): 51–58.

4 Bullying and sexual violence

Definition, prevalence, outcomes and moderators

Dorothy L. Espelage

Introduction

Youth bullying experiences and sexual violence perpetration are major public health problems. The US Centers for Disease Control and Prevention (CDC; Basile and Saltzman, 2002) define sexual harassment as a component of sexual violence and bullying that is homophobic in nature and in some cases can be viewed as sexual harassment. While existing literature suggests that bullying and sexual violence may share some correlates, only a handful of studies have attempted to establish an empirical link in the literature between bullying and co-occurring or subsequent sexual violence perpetration during the middle school years (Basile *et al.*, 2009). Despite a dearth of literature on the link between bullying and sexual violence, prevention educators who are charged to prevent sexual violence and rape in schools have increasingly focused on implementing bullying prevention programmes in schools because it is easier to gain access to schools with bullying prevention over sexual violence prevention initiatives. Thus, it is imperative that research be conducted to identify the association between bullying and sexual violence during early adolescence, but it is also important to identify mediators and moderators of this association that are malleable to school-based intervention.

This chapter is framed by the *Bully-Sexual Violence Pathway*, an emerging theory in which bullying perpetration and homophobic teasing perpetration/victimisation are suggested to be predictive of sexual violence perpetration in later years (Espelage *et al.*, 2012). This theory is supported by a longitudinal study of middle school students, where it was found that both bullying and the perpetration of homophobic teasing were associated with sexual harassment over time (Espelage *et al.*, 2012; Espelage *et al.*, under review). Within the context of the *Bully-Sexual Violence Pathway* theory, we not only find that as perpetrators of traditional bullying mature, they increase their use of homophobic teasing, we also find that students who are targets of nonsexualised bullying are also at-risk for being the target of homophobic bullying over time. Additionally, among young men, there is a concern that some of those victims may engage in the sexual harassment of other students to demonstrate their heterosexuality. Thus, the *Bully-Sexual Violence Pathway* needs to be probed further to identify mediators and moderators of such behaviour.

In this chapter, I will review the research on the potential role of traditional masculinity, dominance and peer influence on the association between bullying, homophobic teasing and sexual harassment. First, some definitions will be provided to elucidate the constructs that are being examined across the wide range of studies of adolescents. Second, prevalence rates of bullying, homophobic teasing and sexual harassment directed at straight-identified and lesbian, gay, bisexual and transgender (LGBT) youth will be presented. Third, research on the relations between bullying, homophobic teasing and sexual harassment perpetration will be reviewed. Fourth, traditional masculinity and dominance at the individual and peer-group level will be considered as explanatory variables of the association between the three major constructs. Finally, implications of this research for prevention programming in schools will be identified.

Definitons, prevalence rates

Bullying

According to Olweus (2001) 'A student is being bullied or victimised when he or she is exposed, repeatedly and over time, to negative actions on the part of one or more students'. Bullying is recognisably a major problem in US schools today, estimates suggest that nearly 30 per cent of US students are involved in bullying in some capacity (Nansel *et al.*, 2001). Findings from this nationally representative sample of 6th to 10th graders indicate that 13 per cent had bullied others, 11 per cent had been bullied and 6 per cent had both bullied and been bullied.

Homophobic teasing

Homophobia includes negative beliefs, attitudes, stereotypes and behaviours toward gays and lesbians or those perceived to be gay and lesbian (Wright *et al.*, 1999). Heterosexual students might also be victims of homophobia, not because of their sexual orientation, but because of their perceived differences and departure from traditional masculine/feminine gender role expectations (Kimmel and Mahler, 2003). Homophobic teasing can be considered a potential subtype of both bullying and sexual harassment. For instance, a large percentage of bullying among students involves the use of homophobic teasing and slurs, particularly among adolescents (Poteat and Espelage, 2005; Poteat and Rivers, 2010). Espelage *et al.* (2012) found 34 per cent of boys and 20 per cent of girls in a large middle school sample directed homophobic language toward students. Rivers (2001) reported that name-calling, being hit or kicked and teasing were frequent forms of bullying experienced by gay and lesbian students (82 per cent, 60 per cent and 58 per cent, respectively). Rumour spreading (59 per cent) and social isolation (27 per cent), which could be considered relational forms of aggression, were also reported, as well as sexual assault by a peer or teacher (11 per cent).

Bullying and homophobic victimisation occur more frequently among LGBT youth in US schools than among students who identify as heterosexual (Birkett *et al.*, 2009; Kosciw *et al.*, 2009). A recent nationwide survey of LGBT youth reports that 84.6 per cent of LGBT students reported being verbally harassed, 40.1 per cent reported being physically assaulted at school in the past year because of their sexual orientation (Kosciw *et al.*, 2010). A population-based study of over 200,000 California students found that 7.5 per cent reported being bullied in the last year because they were 'gay or lesbian or someone thought they were' (O'Shaughnessy *et al.*, 2004: 3). Of note, among sexual minority youth, transgender youth remain an especially understudied and underserved population who are often victimised because of their gender expression (Kosciw *et al.*, 2009).

Even without being a direct target of homophobic bullying, a student may feel isolated from friends and teachers because of the anti-gay attitudes and behaviours present in schools; 91.4 per cent of a LGBT middle/high school sample reported that they sometimes or frequently heard homophobic remarks in school, such as 'faggot', 'dyke' or 'queer'. Of these students, 99.4 per cent said they heard remarks from students and 63 per cent heard remarks from faculty or school staff (Kosciw and Diaz, 2006; Kosciw *et al.*, 2008). The pervasiveness of anti-gay language in schools suggests that most school environments are hostile for LGBT students and create negative environments for their heterosexual peers as well (Poteat and Espelage, 2007).

Sexual violence and sexual harassment

Sexual violence encompasses a continuum of acts from unwanted non-contact exposures of a sexual nature (e.g. verbal harassment) to forcible penetration (Basile and Saltzman, 2002). Examining completed penetration only, the 2007 Youth Risk Behaviour Survey, a national survey of students in grades 9–12, found a lifetime reported prevalence of unwanted physically forced sexual intercourse of 10.5 per cent for females and 4.5 per cent, for males (Centers for Disease Control, 2010). Further, Banyard and colleagues (2006) found that of a sample of 980 adolescents in grades 7–12, 10 per cent of boys and 2.5 per cent of girls reported perpetrating sexual coercion (e.g. unwanted kissing, touching or intercourse). Within the US national data for current rates of sexual teen dating violence perpetration and victimisation also are underreported. Moreover, existing estimates at the local level vary widely. Prevalence rates for various types of forced sexual activity or sexual coercion within dating relationships range from 15 per cent (Foshee, 1996; Jezl *et al.*, 1996) to 59 per cent (Jackson *et al.*, 2000). However, these data suggest that more research needs to examine the prevalence and predictors of sexual violence within teenage dating relationships and the extent to which this predicts engagement in intimate partner violence into adulthood.

In the USA, sexual harassment is a form of sex discrimination under federal law Title IX (1972), and is defined as unwelcome sexual advances, requests for sexual favors and other verbal or physical contact of a sexual nature when the conduct is sufficiently severe, persistent or pervasive to limit a student's ability to participate in or benefit from the education programme, or to create a hostile or abusive educational environment. Further, the CDC (Basile and Saltzman, 2002) recently defined sexual harassment as a component of sexual violence. Sexual harassment perpetration is common among school-aged adolescents, with one national study reporting peer harassment rates of 66 per cent and 52 per cent, for boys and girls, respectively (American Association of University Women, 1993). Also, a study of 1,300 middle school students found that 32 per cent of boys and 22 per cent of girls reported often making sexual comments to other students (Espelage *et al.*, 2012).

Linking paths between bullying homophobic teasing and sexual harassment

Bullying and homophobic teasing

Evidence indicates that there exists a strong association between aggression and homophobic behaviour among early adolescents, particularly the use of homophobic language. Students who report higher levels of aggression, including bullying, fighting and relational aggression, also report more frequent use of homophobic epithets (Phillips, 2007; Phoenix *et al.*, 2003; Plummer, 2001; Poteat and Espelage, 2005). Poteat and Rivers (2010) found among a sample of 253 high school students that the use of homophobic epithets was significantly associated with the primary bully role and the supportive roles of reinforcing and assisting the bully for boys and girls. Remaining uninvolved was associated with less use of homophobic language only for girls. Furthermore, engaging in multiple bullying roles predicted more frequent use of homophobic epithets among boys. However, a more complex relation existed for girls. The reinforcer role significantly predicted more frequent use of homophobic epithets for girls, but to a greater extent for those who also engaged in the primary bully role.

Recent studies indicate that homophobic language often reflects the content expressed during many aggressive episodes regardless of the actual or perceived sexual orientation of the victim (Kimmel and Mahler, 2003; Phoenix *et al.*, 2003; Plummer, 2001; Poteat and Espelage, 2005). These broader school-wide studies, in combination with those specifically among LGBT youth samples, underscore the connection between aggression and the use of homophobic language. Also, the associations between forms of aggression and use of homophobic epithets apply for boys and for girls (Poteat and Espelage, 2005). Being the target of homophobic epithets is associated with psychological and social concerns for both LGBT and heterosexual youth (D'Augelli *et al.*, 2002; Poteat and Espelage, 2007; Rivers, 2001; Williams *et al.*, 2003). Among LGBT youth, psychosocial concerns have been connected to experiences of victimisation (D'Augelli *et al.*, 2002; Rivers, 2001), and Williams *et al.* (2003) found that victimisation mediated differences between LGBT and heterosexual students on mental health concerns. Within the general student population, being the target of homophobic epithets predicted higher levels of psychosocial concerns among middle school students (Poteat and Espelage, 2007).

Bullying, homophobic teasing and sexual harassment

In many ways, the behaviours that constitute homophobic teasing overlap conceptually with 'bullying' or 'sexual violence', as it may include, for example, relational aggression or sexual harassment or assault. Homophobic teasing may play an important role in the link between bullying and sexual violence perpetration. What conceptually distinguishes homophobic teasing from bullying and sexual violence appears to be the direct intention of homophobic teasing to express and promote masculinity for all students, not just LGBT youth.

While there are few studies that have examined associations between bullying and sexual harassment, such studies have consistently found these behaviours to be related. Pepler and colleagues (2002) found that sexual harassment perpetration in 5th to 8th grade students was associated with increased bullying rates. DeSouza and Ribeiro (2005) examined a sample of Brazilian high school students and found that for both males and females, peers who self-reported bullying perpetration were more likely to sexually harass the same peers. Pepler and colleagues (2006) also found a positive association between sexual harassment perpetration and bullying perpetration among students. In this cross-sectional study of nearly 2,000 adolescents, sexual harassment perpetration was more prevalent among students who bullied others than those who did not report bullying others. Finally, research suggests that whereas some students experience bullying victimisation in isolation of other victimisation forms, targets of sexual harassment typically incur victimisation in additional realms, including bullying (Holt and Espelage, 2005).

With respect to associations among homophobic teasing, bullying and sexual harassment, we found a strong connection among these behaviours in our own work (Espelage *et al.*, 2011; Poteat and Espelage, 2005). Specifically, we have found that bullying perpetration is an antecedent of homophobic teasing and the two are causally linked in middle school. Further, bullying and homophobic teasing predicted longitudinal sexual harassment among middle school students (Espelage *et al.*, 2012) and homophobic teasing moderated the bully-sexual harassment relation (Espelage *et al.*, under review). These findings suggest that homophobic teasing is well-established by middle school, and are likely precursors to more extreme forms of homophobic behaviours and sexual violence.

Teen dating violence/intimate partner violence

Although theoretical overlaps exist in the bullying and SV literature, much more work needs to be conducted on unpacking the *Bully-Sexual Violence Pathway* during early adolescence (Espelage *et al.*, 2012). According to this theory, we posit that bullying might be a precursor to SV perpetration. Further, the research is beginning to support the contention that the need for control and dominance that underlies bullying is transferred to increasingly escalating forms of aggression and into relationships characteristic of the developing adolescent, including dating relationships. Following from this literature, it is likely that involvement in bullying, homophobic bantering and/or violence might be precursors to teen dating violence or intimate partner violence-victimisation and/or perpetration. Indeed, early antisocial behaviour and aggression have been shown to predict later use of violence against dating partners in three longitudinal studies (Capaldi and Clark, 1998; Lavoie *et al.*, 2002; Simons *et al.*, 1998) and a study by Brendgen and colleagues (2001) showed aggression perpetrated by young adolescent boys was associated with dating violence perpetration at the age of 16 and 17 years. Efforts to address teen dating violence or intimate partner violence could be informed by the potential overlap among dating violence, bullying perpetration and sexual harassment. Pepler and colleagues (2002) found that sexual harassment perpetration among students in Grades 5 to 8 (10–14 years of age) was associated with increased rates of bullying. Similarly, students who reported bullying their peers also reported more violence in their dating relationships (both physical and social) than non-bullies (Connolly *et al.*, 2000). In a recent study of 1,279 9th graders (14–15 years of age) in Canada (50 per cent boys), Ellis and colleagues found that girls who were perpetrators of psychological teen dating violence were more likely to report increases in delinquent behaviour (Ellis *et al.*, 2009).

Indeed, it seems that Arriaga and Foshee's 2004 experimental study is the only longitudinal study on the role of peer attitudes and teen dating violence involvement. In their study 526 8th and 9th graders (13–15 years of age) completed self-report measures over two time periods six months apart. Youth were asked to report about their dating violence experiences as well as their friends' involvement in their dating violence. Cross-lag analyses indicated that those with friends who were involved in teen dating violence were significantly more likely to report subsequent dating violence involvement themselves.

Applying a traditional masculinity framework to bullying, homophobia and sexual harassment

Theoretical explanations of adult sexual harassment have emphasised the role of gender and power, viewing sexual harassment as 'the product of a gender system maintained by a dominant, normative form of masculinity' (Uggen and Blackstone, 2004: 66). Feminist sociocultural theories posit that the socialisation of men into traditional masculine gender roles that encompass a need for power and dominance in relationships and hostility toward women promotes violence against women (Russell, 1975; Sanday, 1990). Traditional masculinity ideology is characterised by anti-femininity, homophobia, emotional restrictiveness, competitiveness, toughness and aggressiveness (Pleck, 1995), and this form of heterosexual masculinity continues to be privileged over all forms of femininity and alternative masculinities in the US gender system. It has been argued that sexual harassment is a form of sexism that serves to uphold patriarchy by enforcing a primarily masculine worldview and keeping women in less powerful positions (O'Neil and Egan, 1993).

As boys reach adolescence, conforming to traditional male norms becomes even more important. There is pressure within groups of boys to prove their masculinity to one another, to project an image of traditional masculinity. As stated by Kimmel (2008), male peer groups can act as 'gender police' and are quick to point out any time another boy crosses the gender boundary and behaves as less than masculine. This causes boys to constantly monitor themselves and hide any form of sensitivity that they may be experiencing. And it is because of this necessary confirmation of masculinity that we see bravado come to the forefront in adolescence as well as misogynistic attitudes toward girls. One of the strongest predictors of homophobic attitudes has been traditional masculinity, or masculinity that values dominance, assertiveness and a lack of emotion (Epstein, 2001; Mandel and Shakeshaft, 2000 Phoenix *et al.*, 2003). In Whitley's 2001 meta-analysis of gender-role variables and their prediction of homophobia, traditional gender-role beliefs, modern sexism and hypermasculinity predicted increased homophobic attitudes. Thus, these findings suggest that bullying and homophobic bullying is associated with adopting traditional masculinity ideologies which then could contribute to the development of sexual harassment.

Peer group influences and norms

A few studies have examined homophobic behaviour from a broader social perspective (Korobov, 2004; Poteat, 2007, 2008; Rivers, 2001; Rivers *et al.*, 2007). As has been documented for general forms of aggression, including bullying and fighting (Espelage *et al.*, 2003), the frequency of reported homophobic behaviour varies significantly across peer groups (Poteat, 2007). Also, the social climate of peer groups predicts the extent to which students engage in homophobic banter (Poteat, 2008). Rivers *et al.* (2007) reported that, in terms of homophobic bullying directed towards students perceived to be LGBT, in the majority of cases the perpetrators were groups of peers (both boys and girls) rather than single individuals. Among male peers, in addition to its connection with aggression, homophobic discourse can be used to assert heterosexuality and to enforce gender normative behaviour (Korobov, 2004; Meyer, 2009).

In addition, thus far it appears that perhaps the strongest link between bullying and sexual harassment perpetration is the influence of peer group norms and peer support. Both forms of violence are reinforced and maintained by peer group norms that support bullying (Espelage *et al.*, 2003; Ojala and Nesdale, 2004; Pellegrini, 2002) and sexual violence (Ageton, 1983; DeKeserdy and Schwartz, 1998; DeKeserdy and Kelly, 1993).

More recently, Birkett and Espelage (in press) examined peer group contextual and socialisation effects on masculinity attitudes, homophobic and non-homophobic bullying perpetration in a young early adolescent sample. Participants included 493 5th–8th grade students from two middle schools (10–14 years of age). Social network analysis and multilevel modeling results indicated that peer groups play an important role in the formation of homophobic name-calling. Additionally, students who were victims of homophobic name-calling over time increased their own perpetration of homophobic name-calling. Non-homophobic bullying was also related to homophobic name-calling, but only for male peer groups. And finally, the role of masculinity attitudes was shown to be complex, as peer group masculinity attitudes were significantly predictive of an individual's homophobic perpetration; however this effect did not remain significant over time. Results suggest that homophobic name-calling during early adolescence is strongly influenced by peers.

Implications

Significant evidence is accumulating to support substantial and meaningful associations among bullying, homophobic teasing and sexual harassment across the course of adolescence. Furthermore, the *Bully-Sexual Violence Pathway* appears to be explained by the potential mediating and moderating role of homophobic teasing and adoption of a traditional masculinity ideology. However, much more scholarship needs to conducted to expand on this research to understand how these behaviours are influenced by other factors, including school, family, community, neighborhood and society in general.

What is clear is that homophobic teasing during early adolescence is predicted by bully involvement and predicts development of later sexual violence and dating violence/intimate partner violence. The issue of homophobic teasing is particularly salient given evidence suggesting it often is associated with acts of severe school violence. For instance, Kimmel and Mahler (2003) retrospectively examined the association among bullying, victimisation and homophobia as experienced by school shooters in the past two decades. They found that almost all school shooters had been bullied, and more specifically, had been repeatedly teased as being gay (although no evidence suggested the shooters were gay). Despite this, a study of 23 comprehensive anti-bullying programmes found that none of them covered issues of sexual orientation, homophobia, sexual harassment and sexual violence sufficiently enough to warrant any efficacy (Birkett *et al.*, 2008).

Given the high occurrence of homophobic teasing in US schools, and the lack of prevention programmes that address these behaviours, it is no surprise that school-based bully prevention programmes yielded null findings. Two meta-analyses found that effects were non-existent or too small to be practically helpful (Merrell *et al.*, 2008; Ttofi *et al.*, 2008). A third found that programmes reduced bullying in non-US countries by 23 per cent but effects for US studies were significantly lower. The efficacy of the *Olweus Bullying Prevention Program*, considered the gold-standard of bully prevention, which is found in thousands of US school districts is questionable. Efficacy is based on one peer-review article that included a randomised controlled trial of 10 schools and reductions of bullying were reported only for white students (Bauer *et al.*, 2007). Thus, three things need to happen in bully prevention. First, there must be recognition that gender-based bullying is highly prevalent in schools in the USA and outside of the USA. Second, prevention efforts targeted need to include materials related to traditional masculinity, gender nonconformity and sexual harassment. Third, because both bullying, homophobic teasing, sexual violence and dating violence perpetration appear to be (in part) the result of peer group socialisation, more basic research needs to be conducted on whether and how the socialisation of these forms of aggression can be modified. Clarifying complexities of bullying and sexual harassment at the individual and peer levels should assist educators and other professionals in developing more effective prevention and intervention strategies.

Conclusion

It is very clear that equating bullying with sexual harassment is problematic and should not continue. Conceptualising adolescent sexual harassment from a bullying framework has recently been criticised for ignoring the role of gender and removing sexual harassment 'from the discourse of rights by placing it into a more psychological, pathologising realm' (Brown *et al.*, 2007: 1257). Brown *et al.* argue that, "bullying" has become the stand-in for other behaviours that school and public health officials, scholars, legislators, and researchers do not want to name, such as racism, homophobia, sexism, or hate crimes' (2007: 1260). Therefore, Brown *et al.* argue that 'effective bully-prevention programs in the US must start with research on diverse groups of children and take into account social location (such as gender, race, class and sexual identity), and they must distinguish peer-to-peer bullying from more egregious forms of sexual and racial harassment' (2007: 1267).

In 2010 the US Department of Education Office of Civil Rights released a document to school administrators across the country to clarify concepts of bullying and sexual harassment in order to guide schools in their prevention efforts. In this 'Dear Colleague' letter, bullying is defined as a form of harassment, which can include verbal, written or cyber name-calling, can be physically threatening or humiliating, and 'does not necessarily have to include an intent to harm, be directed at a specific target, or involve repeated incidents' (p. 2). In contrast to bullying, sexual harassment is a form of sex discrimination – 'unwelcomed behaviour of a sexual nature' that interferes with the right to receive an equal educational opportunity – and is part of federal law Title IX of the Education Amendments of 1972 (Title IX of the Education Amendments of 1972). Under Title IX, a school is required to distribute a formal policy addressing sexual harassment to students, parents and employees, to respond promptly with a thorough investigation when a complaint has been filed and to prevent retaliation (Stein, 2003). Thus, it behooves schools to take seriously homophobic teasing and sexual harassment in their schools to prevent violating the civil rights of their students and families. Only then can we start to create safe schools for all.

References

Ageton, S. S. (1983) *Sexual Assault among Adolescents*, Lexington, MA: Lexington Books.

American Association of University Women (1993) *Hostile Hallways: The AAUW Survey on Sexual Harassment in America's Schools*, Washington, DC: Harris/Scholastic Research.

Arriaga, X. B. and Foshee, V. A. (2004) 'Adolescent dating violence: do adolescents follow in their friends' or their parents' footsteps?', *Journal of Interpersonal Violence*, 19: 162–184.

Banyard, V., Cross C. and Modecki, K. (2006) 'Interpersonal violence in adolescence: ecological correlates of self-reported perpetration', *Journal of Interpersonal Violence*, 21: 1314–1332.

Basile, K. C. and Saltzman, L. E. (2002) *Sexual Violence Surveillance: Uniform Definitions and Recommended Data Elements (Version 1.0)*, Atlanta, GA: Centers for Disease Control and Prevention.

Basile, K. C., Espelage, D. L., Rivers, I., McMahon, P. M. and Simon, T. R. (2009) 'The theoretical and empirical links between bullying behavior and sexual violence perpetration', *Aggression and Violent Behavior*, 14: 336–347.

Bauer, N. S., Lozano, P. and Rivara, F. P. (2007) 'The effectiveness of the Olweus Bullying Prevention Program in public middle schools: a controlled trial', *Journal of Adolescent Health*, 40: 266–274.

Birkett, M. and Espelage, D.L. (in press) 'Homophobic name-calling, peer-groups, and masculinity: the socialization of homophobic behavior in adolescents', *Social Development*.

Birkett, M., Espelage, D. L. and Koenig, B. (2009) 'LGB and questioning students in schools: the moderating effects of homophobic bullying and school climate on negative outcomes', *Journal of Youth and Adolescence*, 38: 989–1000.

Birkett, M.A., Espelage, D.L. and Stein, N. (2008, August) *Have School Anti-Bullying Programs Overlooked Homophobic Bullying?* Poster presented at the American Psychological Association Annual Convention, Boston, MA.

Brendgen, M., Vitaro, F., Tremblay, R. E. and Lavoie, F. (2001) 'Reactive and proactive aggression: predictions to physical violence in different contexts and moderating effects of parental monitoring and caregiving behavior', *Journal of Abnormal Child Psychology*, 29: 293–304.

Brown, L. M., Chesney-Lind, M. and Stein, N. (2007) 'Patriarchy matters: toward a gendered theory of teen violence and victimization', *Violence Against Women*, 13: 1249–1273.

Capaldi, D. M. and Clark, S. (1998) 'Prospective family predictors of aggression toward female partners for at-risk young men', *Developmental Psychology*, 34: 1175–1188.

Centers for Disease Control and Prevention (2010) *Youth Risk Behavior Surveillance – United States, 2009*, Atlanta, GA: Centers for Disease Control and Prevention.

Connolly, J., Pepler, D. J., Craig, W. M. and Taradash, A. (2000) 'Dating experiences of bullies in early adolescence', *Child Maltreatment: Journal of the American Professional Society on the Abuse of Children*, 5: 299–310.

D'Augelli, A. R., Pilkington, N. W. and Hershberger, S. L. (2002) 'Incidence and mental health impact of sexual orientation victimization of lesbian, gay, and bisexual youths in high school', *School Psychology Quarterly*, 17: 148–167.

DeKeseredy, W. and Kelly, K. (1993) 'The incidence and prevalence of woman abuse in Canadian university and college dating relationships', *Canadian Journal of Sociology*, 18: 137–159.

DeKeseredy, W. S. and Schwartz, M. D. (1998) 'Male peer support and woman abuse in postsecondary school courtship: suggestions for new directions in sociological research', in R. Bergen (ed.), *Issues in Interpersonal Violence*, Thousand Oaks, CA: Sage.

DeSouza, E. R. and Ribeiro, J. (2005) 'Bullying and sexual harassment among Brazilian high school students', *Journal of Interpersonal Violence*, 20: 1018–1038.

Ellis, W. E., Crooks, C. V. and Wolfe, D. A. (2009) 'Relational aggression in peer and dating relationships: links to psychological and behavioral adjustment', *Social Development*, 18: 253–269.

Epstein, D. (2001) 'Boyz' own stories: masculinities and sexualities in schools', in W. Martino and B. Meyenn (eds), *What About the Boys? Issues of Masculinity in Schools*, Maidenhead: Open University Press.

Espelage, D.L., Basile, K.C. and Hamburger, M.E. (2012) 'Bullying experiences and co-occurring sexual violence perpetration among middle school students: shared and unique risk factors', *Journal of Adolescent Health*, 50: 60–65.

Espelage, D. L., Basile, K. C., Hamburger, M. E. and De La Rue, L. (under review) 'Longitudinal associations among bully, homophobic teasing and sexual violence perpetration among middle school students', *Journal of Interpersonal Violence*.

Espelage, D. L., Holt, M. K. and Henkel, R. R. (2003) 'Examination of peer-group contextual effects on aggression during early adolescence', *Child Development*, 74: 205–220.

Espelage, D. L., Rao, M., Little, T. and Rose, C. A. (2011, August) *Linking Bullying Perpetration to Homophobic Name-Calling During Early Adolescence*, Poster presented at the annual meeting of the American Psychological Association, Washington, DC.

Foshee, V. A. (1996) 'Gender differences in adolescent dating abuse prevalence, types and injuries', *Health Education Research*, 11: 275–286.

Holt, M. and Espelage, D. (2005) 'Multiple victimization of adolescents', in K. Kendall-Tackett and S. Giacomoni (eds), *Victimization of Children and Youth: Patterns of Abuse, Response Strategies*, Kingston, NJ: Civic Research Institute.

Jackson, S. M., Cram, F. and Seymour, F. W. (2000) 'Violence and sexual coercion in high school students' dating relationships', *Journal of Family Violence*, 15: 23–36.

Jezl, D. R., Molidor, C. E. and Wright, T. L. (1996) 'Physical, sexual and psychological abuse in high school dating relationships: prevalence rates and self-esteem issues', *Child and Adolescent Social Work Journal*, 13: 69–87.

Kimmel. M. (2008) *Guyland: The Perilous World Where Boys Become Men*, New York: Harper.

Kimmel, M. S. and Mahler, M. (2003) 'Adolescent masculinity, homophobia, and violence: random school shootings, 1982–2001', *American Behavioral Scientist,* 46: 1439–1458.

Korobov, N. (2004) 'Inoculating against prejudice: a discursive approach to homophobia and sexism in adolescent male talk', *Psychology of Men and Masculinity*, 5: 178–189.

Kosciw, J. G. and Diaz, E. M. (2006) *The 2005 National School Climate Survey: The Experiences of Lesbian, Gay, Bisexual and Transgender Youth in Our Nation's Schools*, New York: GLSEN.

Kosciw, J. G., Diaz, E. M. and Greytak, E. A. (2008) *The 2007 National School Climate Survey: The Experiences of Lesbian, Gay, Bisexual and Transgender Youth in Our Nation's Schools*, New York: GSLEN.

Kosciw, J. G., Greytak, E. A. and Diaz, E. M. (2009) 'Who, what, when, where, and why: demographic and ecological factors contributing to hostile school climate for lesbian, gay, bisexual, and transgender youth', *Journal of Youth and Adolescence*, 38: 976–988.

Kosciw, J. G., Greytak, E. A., Diaz, E. M. and Bartkiewicz, M. J. (2010) *The 2009 National School Climate Survey: The Experiences of Lesbian, Gay, Bisexual and Transgender Youth in Our Nation's Schools*, New York: GLSEN.

Lavoie, F., Hebert, M., Tremblay, R., Vitaro, F., Vezina, L. and McDuff, P. (2002) 'History of family dysfunction and perpetration of dating violence by adolescent boys: a longitudinal study', *Journal of Adolescent Health*, 30: 375–383.

Mandel, L. and Shakeshaft, C. (2000) 'Heterosexism in middle schools', in N. Lesko (ed.), *Masculinities at School*, Thousand Oaks, CA: Sage.

Merrell, K. W., Gueldner, B. A., Ross, S. W. and Isava, D. M. (2008) 'How effective are school bullying intervention program? A meta-analysis of intervention research', *School Psychology Quarterly*, 23: 26–42.

Meyer, E. (2009) *Gender, Bullying and Harassment: Strategies to End Sexism and Homophobia in Schools.* New York: Teacher's College Press.

Nansel, T. R., Overpeck, M., Pilla, R. S., Ruan, W. J., Simons-Morton, B. G. and Scheidt, P. (2001) 'Bullying behaviors among US youth: prevalence and association with psychosocial adjustment', *Journal of the American Medical Association*, 285: 2094–2100.

Ojala, K. and Nesdale, D. (2004) 'Bullying and social identity: the effects of group norms and distinctiveness threat on attitudes towards bullying', *British Journal of Developmenta Psychology*, 22: 19–35.

Olweus, D. (2001) 'Peer harassment: a critical analysis and some important issues', in J. Juvonen and S. Graham (eds), *Peer Harassment in Schools: The Plight of the Vulnerable and the Victimized*, New York: Guilford.

O'Neil, J. M. and Egan, J. (1993) 'Abuses of power against women: sexism, gender role conflict, and psychological violence', in E. P. Cook (ed.), *Women, Relationships, and Power: Implications for Counseling*, Alexandria, VA: American Counseling Association.

O'Shaughnessy, M., Russell, S. T., Heck, K., Calhoun, C. and Laub, C. (2004) *Safe Place to Learn: Consequences of Harassment Based on Actual or Perceived Sexual Orientation and Gender Non-Conformity and Steps for Making Schools Safer*, San Francisco, CA: California Safe Schools Coalition.

Pellegrini, A. D. (2002) 'Bullying, victimization, and sexual harassment during the transition to middle school', *Educational Psychologist*, 37: 151–163.

Pepler, D. J., Craig, W. M., Connolly, J. and Henderson, K. (2002) 'Bullying, sexual harassment, dating violence, and substance use among adolescents', in C. Wekerle and A.-M. Wall (eds), *The Violence and Addiction Equation: Theoretical and Clinical Issues in Substance Abuse and Relationship Violence*, New York: Brunner-Routledge.

Pepler, D. J., Craig, W. M., Connolly, J. A., Yuile, A., McMaster, L. and Depeng, J. (2006) 'A developmental perspective on bullying', *Aggressive Behavior*, 32: 376–384.

Phillips, D. A. (2007) 'Punking and bullying: strategies in middle school, high school, and beyond', *Journal of Interpersonal Violence*, 22: 158–178.

Phoenix, A., Frosh, S. and Pattman, R. (2003) 'Producing contradictory masculine subject positions: narratives of threat, homophobia, and bullying in 11–14 year old boys', *Journal of Social Issues*, 59: 179–195.

Pleck, J. H. (1995) 'The gender role strain paradigm: an update', in R. F. Levant and W. S. Pollack (eds), *A New Psychology of Men*, New York: Basic Books.

Plummer, D. C. (2001) 'The quest for modern manhood: masculine stereotypes, peer culture and the social significance of homophobia', *Journal of Adolescence*, 24: 15–23.

Poteat, V. P. (2007) 'Peer group socialization of homophobic attitudes and behavior during adolescence', *Child Development,* 78: 1830–1842.

Poteat, V. P. (2008) 'Contextual and moderating effects of the peer group climate on use of homophobic epithets', *School Psychology* Review, 37, 188–201.

Poteat, V. P. and Espelage, D. L. (2005) 'Exploring the relation between bullying and homophobic verbal content: the Homophobic Content Agent Target (HCAT) Scale', Violence and Victims, 20: 513–528.

Poteat, V. P. and Espelage, D. L. (2007) 'Predicting psychosocial consequences of homophobic victimization in middle school students', *Journal of Early Adolescence*, 27: 175–191.

Poteat, V. P. and Rivers, I. (2010) 'The use of homophobic language across bullying roles during adolescence', *Journal of Applied Developmental Psychology*, 31: 166–172.

Rivers, I. (2001) 'The bullying of sexual minorities at school: its nature and long-term correlates', *Educational and Child Psychology*, 18: 33–46.

Rivers, I., Duncan, N. and Besag, V. E. (2007) *Bullying: A Handbook for Educators* and Parents, Westport, CT: Praeger Publishers.

Russell, D. (1975) *The Politics of Rape*, New York: Stein and Day.

Sanday, P. (1990) *Fraternity Gang Rape*, New York: New York University Press.

Simons, R. L., Lin, K. and Gordon., L. C. (1998) 'Socialization in the family of origin and male dating violence: a protective study', *Journal of Marriage and Family*, 60: 467–478.

Stein, N. (2003) 'Bullying or sexual harassment: the missing discourse of rights in an era of zero tolerance', *University Arizona Law Review*, 45: 783–799.

Title IX of the Education Amendments of 1972, 20 U.S. C. §1681, §1687.

Ttofi, M. M., Farrington, D. P. and Baldry, A. C. (2008) *Effectiveness of Programmes to Reduce School Bullying*, Stockholm: Swedish Council for Crime Prevention, Information, and Publications.

Uggen, C. and Blackstone, A. (2004) 'Sexual harassment as a gendered expression of power', *American Sociological Review*, 69: 64–92.

US Department of Education Office for Civil Rights (2010), *Dear Colleague Letter*. Available at: http: www2.ed.gov/about/offices/list/ocr/letters/colleague-201010. pdf (accessed 12 December 2011).

Whitley, B. E., Jr. (2001) 'Gender-role variables and attitudes toward homosexuality. *Sex Roles*, 45: 691–721.

Williams, T., Connolly, J., Pepler, D. and Craig, W. (2003) 'Questioning and sexual minority adolescents: high school experiences of bullying, sexual harassment and physical abuse', *Canadian Journal of Community Mental Health*, 22: 47–58.

Wright, L. W., Adams, H. E. and Bernat, J. (1999) 'Development and validation of the homophobia scale', *Journal of Psychopathology and Behavioral Assessment*, 21: 337–347.

5 Girls and indirect aggression

Dawn Jennifer

Introduction

This chapter focuses on girls' use of indirect aggression to bully other girls and manipulate peer relationships, such as spreading false rumours about others and excluding peers from the group. Drawing on recent qualitative research with pre-adolescent girls, this chapter provides a succinct and accessible overview of the phenomenon of bullying among girls. Using key research findings and perspectives from girls themselves, this chapter explores the complex nature of girls' bullying in terms of their friendships, their emerging sexual identities and the social power structures prevalent within schools. The chapter demonstrates that, despite their pre-adolescence, girls' friendships are subject to a sexualised and gendered discourse of indirect aggression, and it provides examples of best practice to explore a range of effective interventions that can be used to address girls' bullying both within the school context and within other youth settings.

Definitions of indirect aggression

While much cross-national research since the 1970s has been conducted into the issue of indirect aggression, there has been minimal focus on the influence of sexuality and gender on such behaviour (Duncan, 1999). What limited research does exist has tended to focus on secondary school-aged students (e.g., Duncan, 1999; Shute *et al.*, 2008; Timmerman, 2005; Witkowska and Menckel, 2005). One of the reasons for this omission may be due to dominant discourses of childhood innocence (Meyer, 2007) and school practices such as 'protecting' young children that maintain the primary school as an asexual environment (Wallis and Van Every, 2000). That younger primary school-aged students have largely been overlooked is to the detriment of young girls, since research with this age group demonstrates that the impact of indirect aggression results in negative emotional health and well-being, such as loss of self-esteem and confidence (Besag, 2006a), social-psychological adjustment difficulties such as loneliness, depression and isolation (Crick and Grotpeter, 1996) and internalising problems such as anxiety, withdrawal and somatic complaints (Murray-Close *et al.*, 2007). Hence, the aim of this chapter is to provide an overview of indirect aggression among young girls with particular reference to the sexualised and gendered aspects of such behaviour.

Traditionally, early research into peer-to-peer bullying focused on aggressive physical behaviour in boys, partly because physical aggression was more easily observable (Underwood *et al.*, 2001). Subsequently, researchers have focused their attention on other forms of bullying including verbal and psychological (e.g., Farrington, 1993). Björkqvist *et al.*, (1992a) distinguished between three types of aggression: direct physical, direct verbal and indirect aggression. Direct physical aggression includes behaviours such as pushing, hitting, punching or kicking. Direct verbal aggression may take the form of yelling abuse at another, name-calling, using insulting expressions or making verbal threats. As the term implies, indirect aggression uses less direct forms of aggressive behaviour such as spreading malicious rumours about another, excluding a person from the group or disclosing another's secrets to a third person (Björkqvist *et al.*, 1992b). In contrast to direct aggression, which involves harm delivered face-to-face, indirect aggression is delivered covertly. Thus, Björkqvist *et al.* (1992b: 52) define indirect aggression as 'a kind of social manipulation: the aggressor manipulates others to attack the victim, or, by other means, makes use of the social structure in order to harm the target person without being personally involved in the attack'. It should be noted that indirect aggression has sometimes been referred to as relational aggression (Crick and Grotpeter, 1995) or social aggression (Cairns *et al.*, 1989). Relational aggression has been defined as 'behaviours that are intended to significantly damage another child's friendships or feelings of inclusion by the peer group' (Crick and Grotpeter, 1995: 711) and social aggression has been defined as 'hurting another person by doing harm to her self-concept or social standing' (Galen and Underwood, 1997: 589). Archer and Coyne's (2003) review of the three terms – indirect, relational and social – suggests that there are very few differences among them, for example they are all dependent on good verbal skills and the manipulation of social networks, and each ultimately harms the social status of the victim. For the purposes of this chapter, indirect aggression will be used since this term was established at the outset of research in this field (Björkqvist, 2001), although relational aggression and social aggression will be used when discussing research that has employed these specific terms.

To complicate matters even further, indirect aggression has been divided into subtypes: reactive (e.g. an angry or defensive response to provocation) and proactive aggression (e.g. to obtain a desired goal) (Crick and Dodge, 1996; Salmivalli and Nieminen, 2002). While most research has focused on reactive aggression, whereby aggressive behaviours under investigation are a response to provocation employed to express anger and cause harm, Underwood *et al.* (2001) suggest that indirect aggression might be employed for more proactive reasons, for example, to gain or preserve social status, or even to provide entertainment value through manipulating others' social relationships or self-esteem. Research in Australia, which supports this possibility, has found that adolescent girls mention alleviating boredom, creating excitement and managing peer relationships as major motivations for using indirect aggressive behaviours (Owens *et al.*, 2000). Thus the social structure of girl's friendship groups and the manipulation of peer relationships appear to be important factors that may provide opportunities for, and even facilitate, indirect aggression.

Girls' friendship groups, friendships and social power structures

In her essay about social groupings in childhood, Maccoby (1986) drew attention to the gender-differentiated styles of children's behaviour in naturally occurring gender-segregated peer groups, suggesting that these might contribute to anti-social behaviour in different ways for boys and girls. She demonstrates that outside of environments that are regulated by adults (e.g. family, school) natural segregation by gender occurs among children from as young as 3 to 5 years of age. Observational research in the US suggests that such spontaneous gender segregation decreases as children reach the age of 12 years (Pellegrini, 2001).

Early research in this field has also highlighted a number of key characteristics of children's friendship groups, pertinent to the issue of young girls' use of indirect aggression. For example, in her study of friendships in children aged 10 and 11, Lever (1976, 1978) found that girls were more inclined than boys were to play indoors in private spaces, with play occurring mostly in small groups. Girls reported that they were most comfortable in pairs and least comfortable in groups of four or more. In addition, girls were more likely to have one 'best friend' and these friendships had a tendency to be exclusive, with self-disclosure playing a key role in both maintaining the friendship bond and in facilitating the break up, for example when secrets were divulged to third parties.

This fragility of friendship bonds is clearly demonstrated by the findings from Besag's (2006b) ethnographic study of a sample of young girls aged between 10 and 12 years old. Her research revealed instabilities in girls' close friendships, with membership fluctuating and changing over a 16-month period; only one 'best friend' dyad identified at the start of the research was maintained over the duration of the study. Girls' identified a number of key threats to the stability of their close relationships, including jealousy of other girls' dyadic relationships, 'anxiety … about another girl "sneaking" her friend away' (Besag, 2006b: 541) and 'girls "waiting in the wings" to be the next best friend' (546). In other words, some girls were jealous of the close friendships of others and some felt in danger of losing a close friend to another. Not only does this kind of social structure make relationships among young girls emotionally important to group members, it increases the opportunities for indirect aggression (Lagerspetz *et al.*, 1988; Murray-Close *et al.*, 2007).

Besag (2006b) suggests that changeability and instability in the social structure of young girls' friendships appears to be at the core of the low-level bickering, quarrels and conflicts that occur on a daily basis among young females. Indeed, not only might a girl be excluded from the group, or ignored by another girl who was previously her friend, she might also experience having false rumours spread about her and being given dirty looks (Shaughnessy and Jennifer, 2007).

A dominant feature of children's friendship groups is the 'popular clique-structure' that serves to regulate peers' social relationships (Adler and Adler, 1995: 145). Based on their longitudinal participant observation and interview study of children in elementary school, Adler and Adler (1995: 149) found that popular groups 'embodied systems of dominance whereby individuals with more status and power exerted control over others' lives' and leaders used their power and authority to influence group membership and intra-group stratification. They also identified peer group processes such as inclusion (e.g. membership screening) and exclusion (e.g. rejection, expulsion) techniques used to influence group membership and social stratification among the group (Adler and Adler, 1995).

The notion of a clique structure supports the findings from a novel study that explored 10- and 11-year-olds' ($N = 64$) understanding of the role of the social group context in which school bullying takes place by revealing what children themselves think about how and why their peers become involved in bullying others. Using pictorial vignettes that depicted a hypothetical story of peer bullying (adapted from the Scripted-Cartoon Narrative of Bullying, Almeida *et al.*, 2001), combined with semi-structured interviews and focus group discussions, the findings revealed a rich and illuminating wealth of detail regarding children's understanding of the social group hierarchy (Jennifer, 2007).

Analysis showed that participants drew attention to the hierarchical structure of the bully group, identifying three key roles: leader, assistant and follower, with each role ascribed a distinct function. Participants described the role of the leader bully in terms of his or her pro-active, leader-like behaviour, and primarily focused on the bully's sense of power and authority in terms of his or her dominating and oppressive behaviours, such as taking control, giving orders and initiating bullying episodes. Female accounts drew attention to the bullies' manipulation of interpersonal relationships within the peer group, for example, deciding who was or was not a member of the 'popular' group and deciding who followers could or could not befriend. The assistant character was perceived as playing an active role in bullying others by supporting the leader in terms of offering assistance, encouragement and providing support by 'tagging along' (Jennifer, 2007: 373). While the follower character was perceived as minimally involved in bullying others, they were, nevertheless, perceived to be reinforcing the bullying episodes by providing support and encouragement to the bullies.

Furthermore, Jennifer's (2007) analysis drew attention to the nature of the attachments and interpersonal relationships among members of the bully group and characters' motivation for participation in bullying. Generally, participants perceived that connection with the group offered protection of some kind for each of the bully characters. Female participants perceived that the leader's attachment with other members of the bully group was offered protection from the consequences of engaging in bullying behaviour, for example, by telling or forcing other group members what to do. In terms of the assistant character, female participants cited protection from being bullied by the leader as a motive for attachment to the bully group, whereas they cited fear of isolation as a motive for the follower's attachment (Jennifer, 2007). In sum, this research revealed children's understanding of the hierarchical structure of the bully group, which embodied a system of dominance whereby the high-status leader exerted control over other members and their behaviour. Not only do these behaviours enable leaders to manipulate social relationships by making use of the social structure, thereby remaining unidentified (Lagerspetz *et al.*, 1988), they also serve to maintain the leaders' dominance, status and social standing (Adler and Adler, 1995; Pepler *et al.*, 1999).

Young girls and indirect aggression

In the last twenty years or so, several pioneering studies have investigated the phenomenon of indirect aggression among pre-adolescent girls (e.g., Besag, 2006b; Crick *et al.*, 1996; Lagerspetz *et al.*, 1988; Tapper and Boulton, 2004). It is evident from the early research literature that young girls are more likely to engage in indirect aggression than their male counterparts (although not exclusively so). For example, using peer-rating techniques with a Finnish sample of 10- and 11-year-olds, Lagerspetz *et al.* (1988) demonstrated that while boys employed direct means of aggression, physical as well as verbal, girls more typically used indirect means such as gossiping about another girl behind their back and manipulating the social structure of the peer group. In the USA, Cairns *et al.* (1989) tracked children from fourth- to ninth-grade (N = 220) to identify peers in school who bothered them and to establish descriptions of recent conflicts with peers, one same-gender and one opposite-gender conflict. Thematic coding of the conflict descriptions revealed that while girls reported themes of indirect aggression in same-gender conflicts, including behaviours such as excluding individuals from the group, slander and defamation of reputation by gossip, and alienation of affections, such themes were rarely reported by boys. In addition, analysis revealed a developmental increase in girls' reporting of indirect aggression. In fourth-grade, 10 per cent of girl-to-girl conflicts involved manipulation of peer group acceptance through alienation, ostracism or character defamation with this figure rising to over one-third of girls in the seventh grade (Cairns *et al.*, 1989).

Recent research on indirect aggression and girls has produced similar findings. For example, in a short-term longitudinal study of fourth graders (N = 385) to assess the trajectory of relational aggression in middle childhood, Murray-Close *et al.* (2007) found a statistically significant gender difference at the first assessment, with girls exhibiting greater relational aggression than their male peers. In addition, the results demonstrated that relational aggression for girls increased in a linear fashion over the course of the year, suggesting that indirect aggression becomes an increasingly common occurrence for females during the latter years of primary school. Furthermore, results indicated that, for girls only, increases in intimate self-disclosure by a close friend were associated with increases in relational aggression. This finding is consistent with the notion that increasing knowledge of close friends may provide opportunities for relationally aggressive behaviour (Murray-Close *et al.*, 2007).

That a gender difference is apparent in the use of indirect aggression may provide evidence that within the social world of females, bullying has a different meaning and purpose compared with that of males (Salmivalli *et al.*, 1998). For boys, who typically engage in direct aggression, it might be a question of power, domination and showing off, whereas for girls who engage in more indirect aggression, it might pertain to social relationships and social situations (Salmivalli *et al.*, 1998). Indeed, researchers have suggested a number of reasons for pre-adolescent girls' use of indirect aggression: for example, to regulate sex-gender identities (Kehily *et al.*, 2001); to regulate group membership (Currie *et al.*, 2007); as a means of acquiring social status and popularity within the peer group (Smith *et al.*, 2003); and as a means of competing for access to boys (Pellegrini and Long, 2002).

Sexualised and gendered discourse in indirect aggression

As we have seen above, indirect aggression among girls is collective in nature and based on interpersonal relationships within the peer group (Lagerspetz *et al.*, 1982), with certain dimensions of the social power structure, for example, desire for peer group acceptance and attempts to achieve social dominance, underlying the indirect aggression that takes place (Besag, 2006a, 2006b; Lagerspetz *et al.*, 1988). Research demonstrates that, despite their pre-adolescence, young girls' use of indirect aggression is subject to a sexualised and gendered discourse. For example, in a survey of middle and high school girls (N = 568), Gruber and Fineran (2007) measured the frequency of bullying and sexual harassment by perpetrator. They found that middle school girls (N = 369) were the main perpetrators of several types of sexual bullying behaviours against other young girls. These behaviours included public sexual bullying such as spreading sexual rumours, telling sexual jokes and gay/lesbian harassment, and ridiculing other girls, which included teasing, making fun of other girls and name-calling. Besag's (2006a) study of girls' close friendships supports the above, and revealed a number of indirectly aggressive behaviours that were subject to a sexualised and gendered discourse. These behaviours included spreading gossip about another girl's sexual reputation (e.g., about losing one's virginity, about having sexual relations with a boy) and ridiculing another's physical appearance behind their back (e.g. discussing another's breast development).

Studies by Besag (2006a) and Owens *et al.* (2000) showed that girls' emerging interest in boys, evidenced by investment in appearance and clothing, physical attractiveness, behaviour and sexual reputation, provided a rich source of material for indirect aggression. Furthermore, during observations of conflicts among girls in an unsupervised context, Besag (2006a: 119) noted that girls would adopt offensive terms of abuse commonly used by older children and adults in their local communities that were intended to shock (e.g. 'slapper', 'slag', 'tart', 'tramp').

Renold's (2002) study of sexual harassment in primary school children aged 10- to 11-years-old, also revealed that much of the bullying among girls was gendered in nature. In addition, she observed that girls directed their bullying behaviour against girls who they positioned as 'outsiders' and 'others' (p. 426), that is, those girls who did not develop their feminine identity within dominant heterosexual and feminine discourses. Bullying behaviour took the form of girls regulating both their own and other girls' bodies, appearances, behaviours and romantic interest in boys through, for example, indirect aggression, including social exclusion as well as the use of direct verbal aggression such as sexualised verbal abuse and teasing (Renold, 2002; 2006). Renold (2006) suggests that the deployment of gendered and sexualised discourses is the predominant means by which children can create and consolidate gender and sexual norms, identities and hierarchies.

Notwithstanding the discussion above, it should be noted that while young girls' friendships are subject to a sexualised and gendered discourse, this is not a phenomenon that is exclusive to girls. For example, using Q method combined with group discussions to explore children and young people's (N = 57) experiences of sexual bullying in education settings, Jennifer and Williams (2010) found that both same-sex and cross-sex relationships in primary school were subject to such discourses. As Spears *et al.* (2011) suggest, girls in co-educational settings are potentially experiencing a 'double whammy', that is, experiencing sexualised and gendered forms of indirect aggression from boys as well from girls.

Understanding girls' use of indirect aggression

Even though psychologists have developed theories about aggression in general, few researchers have concentrated on explanations of bullying per se (Boulton, 1993). In previous research, there has been a tendency to focus on explanations of aggressive behaviour that are located in the individual, for example, as a response to frustration (Dollard et al., 1939), through the social learning principles of modelling and reinforcement (Bandura, 1977) and in terms of 'faulty' social information processing (Dodge and Coie, 1987). More recent theories, relating to youth violence, offer effective perspectives that take into account the wider context within which aggressive behaviour takes place, for example, the risk and protective factors framework (e.g., Farrington, 1995, 2002; Rutter, 2000) and the ecological model (World Health Organisation, 1999: 2002). A third perspective, the socio-cultural perspective, offers an alternative explanation for understanding aggression and conflict, which takes into account the gender differences in the use of indirect aggression outlined above and, in particular, bullying among young girls (Rogoff, 2003).

A socio-cultural perspective offers an account of how gender differences arise in the use of indirect aggression, an explanation which is consistent with the adult roles expected of men and women in many cultural communities around the world. Derived from neo-Vygotskian theory, a socio-cultural perspective suggests that gender differences in children's social relationships are consistent with the roles that adult males and females model within their cultures and communities (Rogoff, 2003). Such gender roles not only reflect the biological and reproductive roles of adult males and females, they also embody social learning of gender roles.

Rogoff (2003) suggests that the differences observed between men and women in social relations that involve bullying and aggression reflect the traditions and practices associated with the gender roles expected of adults in many cultural communities, roles for which children from their earliest years are participating in and preparing to assume. Thus, in terms of aggression, cultural observations systematically find boys being more physically aggressive than girls are, and girls show greater indirect aggression, such as malicious use of social exclusion, gossip and manipulation of relationships (Rogoff, 2003). From a socio-cultural perspective, boys' engagement in direct aggression reflects the expectation that men are aggressive and tough (Askew, 1989), whereas girls' use of indirectly aggressive tactics, such as malicious use of exclusion, gossip and relationship manipulation reflects the socio-cultural stereotypes which consign women to a passive and submissive role (Rogoff, 2003). Accordingly, if direct aggression is discouraged by society for women more than for men, it is possible that women (of all ages) will make greater use of indirect forms of aggression instead (Lagerspetz *et al.*, 1988).

Research into young children's friendship groups, as discussed earlier, is consistent with socio-cultural theory. As a rule, boys' friendships are characterised by physical play, centring on group games or activities, with boys congregating in larger groups compared with girls (Adler *et al.*, 1992; Lever, 1978; Maccoby, 1986). Conversely, girls' friendship groups are more likely to consist of pair or triad relationships, with a focus on intimacy and emotional expression (Adler *et al.*, 1992; Gilligan, 1993; Lever, 1978; Maccoby, 1986). Based on their study of indirect aggression among 11- and 12-year-olds Lagerspetz *et al.* (1988) suggested that not only do these tight friendship groups make relationships among girls emotionally important to group members they also increase the opportunities for indirect aggression by making it easier for girls to exploit and manipulate relationships in order to harm others. On the other hand, Lagerspetz *et al.* (1988) suggested that the social structure of girls' peer groups might encourage indirect forms of aggression.

That pre-adolescent girls' friendships are subject to a sexualised and gendered discourse of indirect aggression not only coincides with the onset of puberty (Rivers *et al.*, 2007), which on average occurs between nine and thirteen, but also reflects the 'media sexualisation of young girls, [whereby] girls are bombarded with images and messages about sex and sexuality' on a daily basis from a very young age (Durham, 2009: 12). Western culture is currently characterised by the hyper-sexualisation and objectification of females through, for example, sexualised media content and merchandise, and the mainstreaming of pornography (e.g. glamour modelling, lap-dancing) (Papadopoulos, 2010). Not only does such sexualisation devalue young girls, it encourages them to live up to unrealistic ideals. Thus, it could be argued that indirect aggression among girls is an adaptive response to a socio-cultural context that serves to devalue and sexualise females, and which emerges as a reaction to the increased feelings of competition towards other girls, particularly for the attention of boys (Sippola *et al.*, 2007). In their attempts to achieve social dominance and popularity, sexualised and gendered discourses of indirect aggression may provide a competitive edge for some young girls in terms of enabling them to maintain or advance their social status by, for example, denigrating another's sexual reputation or positioning other girls in such a way that makes them look unattractive to boys (Duncan, 1999, 2004) or defines them as 'other' (Renold, 2002, 2006).

Rogoff (2003) argues that such adversarial relations demonstrate a lack of respect for individual autonomy and self-determination and reflect a system of traditional leadership and organisation in which one person attempts to control what others do. Thus, in schools, young girls learn not only the formal academic curriculum, they also learn about ways of relating with each other and co-ordinating their activities that reflect the hierarchical, organisational and management structure of the institution (Rogoff, 2003). Moreover, in relation to their emerging gender and sexual identities, girls also learn about ways of relating with each other that reflect the school's values, expectations and codes of behaviour (Rivers *et al.*, 2007). With this in mind, this chapter will now discuss best practice opportunities that can be used to address girls' indirect aggression.

Implications for school-based interventions

This overview of young girls' use of indirect aggression, and the role of the social context in which school bullying takes place, emphasises the need for school intervention programmes that focus on fostering emotionally healthy interpersonal relationships that are directed towards the whole peer group in a conscious effort to utilise children as facilitators of change.

There are a number of strategies that might be employed to address the issue of indirect aggression that focus on developing social skills, understanding emotional issues and building empathy, including emotional literacy, restorative practices and peer support (Cowie and Jennifer, 2008). Emotional literacy takes an approach that develops emotional and social competency skills, such as the ability to understand, express and manage one's own emotional states, the ability to understand and respond to the emotional states of others in a socially competent fashion, and the ability to understand social situations and form interpersonal relationships (Weare, 2004). For example, the *Second Step* programme (Committee for Children, 2010), uses a class-based approach that includes lesson plans, DVDs, handouts, student activity cards, Home Link activities, posters and an online teaching guide that cover the teaching of empathy, impulse control, problem solving and anger management skills. Besides reducing bullying and aggressive behaviour in schools, emotional literacy approaches enhance learning and well-being in the school community, foster open communication among all members of the organisation, enable children and staff to find their own solutions to problems, and encourage staff and students to reflect on their relationships with each other (Cowie and Jennifer, 2008).

The aim of a restorative justice approach to interpersonal conflict, such as indirect aggression, is to transform the power imbalances that affect social relationships (Morrison, 2006). This is achieved by strengthening systems of support and accountability within the school community, promoting healthy shame management procedures and empowering those affected by harmful behaviour to take responsibility and address the harm they have experienced. Often using peer mediation or peer conferencing strategies, restorative practice draws upon a collaborative approach that involves all affected parties in the process to establish what happened, to facilitate the reparation of any harm done, to encourage the restoration of relationships and to support the reintegration of individuals back into the school community (Cowie and Jennifer, 2008). Not only does research suggest that restorative practice is an effective intervention against aggression and other harmful behaviour, this approach has the capacity to empower individuals and communities through building healthy and supportive relationships, and fostering democratic organisations (Morrison, 2006).

Peer support initiatives build on the resources that friends spontaneously offer one another, helping school communities to foster a safe and caring learning environment (Cowie and Wallace, 2000). This approach facilitates the use of basic listening skills, the development of empathy for the other's point of view, a problem solving style of dealing with interpersonal difficulties and a willingness to take a supportive role in dealing with peer relationship issues, such as providing support for victims of bullying. Peer support initiatives provide children with the opportunity to discuss matters of personal concern, including friendship problems and bullying, to develop a sense of belongingness and to promote experiences that enhance a positive and respectful ethos within the school. In addition to benefiting the users, a peer support service also benefits the peer supporters and the school community as a whole (Cowie and Wallace, 2000).

In the first instance, however, an important practical implication for addressing indirect aggression among young girls is that whole-school interventions may benefit from preliminary work directed towards general awareness raising, self-reflection and rehearsal at the classroom group level (Salmivalli, 1999). Raising awareness might involve facilitating young girls' understanding of indirect aggression and its consequences, and of the social group processes involved, while self-reflection could involve engaging children in discussions that encourage them to reflect on their behaviour using, for example, a narrative stimulus such as *My Secret Bully* (Ludwig, 2005) to facilitate reflection upon their attitudes, feelings and behaviours with regard to indirect aggression. Rehearsal activities would provide young girls with opportunities to practise new and different behaviours through activities such as drama exercises and role play. Such approaches have been found to have a positive impact on knowledge and understanding of peer-to-peer bullying and coping strategies (Jennifer *et al.*, 2006).

The over-arching challenge for school staff is to work in a variety of ways in partnership with each other, with children and with parents and carers, to shift what is becoming an accepted norm of sexualised and gendered discourse, thus enabling young girls to develop mutually respectful relationships of all kinds as they move into adolescence and transition to secondary school. However, while research suggests that staff understand and manage sexual bullying as a child protection issue, evidence also demonstrates a need to improve the response to young girls' use of indirect aggression that is subject to a sexualised and gendered discourse (Seager, 2009), for example, by raising awareness about the issues relating to indirect aggression with young girls, by incorporating opportunities for young girls to discuss their gender and sexual identities, and pro-social relationships into the curriculum and by providing training for all members of school staff (Seager, 2009).

Conclusion

This chapter has focused on young girls' use of indirect aggression to manipulate peer relationships through, for example, spreading rumours and social exclusion. Following a brief discussion of definitional issues, the topic of girls' friendship groups, friendships and social power structures were highlighted. Particular attention was paid to the hierarchical nature of girls' friendship groups and the notion of a dominant girl manipulating social relationships within the peer group. Young girls' use of indirect aggression was discussed, with a particular focus on an emerging sexualised and gendered discourse, which serves to denigrate others as a means of achieving social dominance. That young girls' friendships are subject to a sexualised and gendered discourse of indirect aggression suggests a number of interventions that focus on supporting the development of emotionally healthy peer relationships, which also provide opportunities for young girls to address issues of gender and sexual identity.

References

Adler, P. A. and Adler, P. (1995) 'Dynamics of inclusion and exclusion in preadolescent cliques', *Social Psychology Quarterly*, 58: 145–162.

Adler, P. A., Kless, S. and Adler, P (1992) 'Socialization to gender roles: popularity among elementary school boys and girls', *Sociology of Education*, 65: 169–187.

Almeida, A., del Barrio, C., Marques, M., Gutiérrez, H. and van der Meulen, K. (2001) 'A script-cartoon narrative of bullying in children and adolescents: a research tool to assess cognitions, emotions and coping strategies in bullying situations', in M. Martinez (ed.), *Prevention and Control of Aggression and the Impact on its Victims*, New York: Kluwer Academic/Plenum Publishers.

Archer, J. and Coyne, S. M. (2003) 'An integrated review of indirect, relational and social aggression', *Personality and Social Psychology Review*, 9: 212–230.

Askew, S. (1989) 'Aggressive behaviour in boys: to what extent is it institutionalized?' in D. P. Tattum and D. A. Lane (eds), *Bullying in Schools*, Stoke-on-Trent: Trentham Books.

Bandura, A. (1977) *Social Learning Theory*, Englewood Cliffs, NJ: Prentice Hall.

Besag, V. (2006a) *Understanding Girls' Friendships, Fights and Feuds: A Practical Approach to Girls' Bullying*, Maidenhead: Open University Press.

Besag, V. (2006b) 'Bullying among girls: friends or foes?' *School Psychology International*, 27: 535–551.

Björkqvist, K. (2001) 'Different names, same issue', *Social Development*, 10: 272–274.

Björkqvist, K., Lagerspetz, K. M. J. and Kaukiainen, A. (1992a) 'Do girls manipulate and boys fight? Developmental trends in regard to direct and indirect aggression', *Aggressive Behavior*, 18: 117–127.

Björkqvist, K., Lagerspetz, K. M. J. and Österman, K. (1992b) *Direct and Indirect Aggression Scales (DIAS)*, Vasa: Åbo Akademi University.

Boulton, M. J. (1993) 'Aggressive fighting in British middle school children', *Educational Studies*, 19: 19–39.

Cairns, R. B., Cairns, B. D., Neckerman, H. J., Ferguson, L. L. and Gariépy, J.-L. (1989) 'Growth and aggression: 1. Childhood to early adolescence', *Developmental Psychology*, 25: 320–330.

Committee for Children. (2010), *Second Step*. Available at: http://www.cfchildren.org/programs/ssp/overview/ (accessed 19 March, 2012).

Cowie, H. and Jennifer, D. (2008) *New Perspectives on Bullying*, Maidenhead: The Open University Press.

Cowie, H. and Wallace, P. (2000) *Peer Support in Action: From Bystanding to Standing By*, London: Sage Publications.

Crick, N. R., and Dodge, K. A. (1996) 'Social information-processing mechanisms in reactive and proactive aggression', *Child Development*, 67: 993–1002.

Crick, N. R. and Grotpeter, J. K. (1995) 'Relational aggression, gender, and social-psychological adjustment', *Child Development*, 66: 710–722.

Crick, N. R. and Grotpeter, J. K. (1996) 'Children's treatment by peers: victims of relational and overt aggression', *Development and Psychopathology*, 8: 367–380.

Crick, N. R., Bigbee, M. A. and Howes, C. (1996) 'Gender differences in children's normative beliefs about aggression: how do I hurt the? Let me count the ways', *Child Development*, 67: 1003–1014.

Currie, D. H., Kelly, D. M. and Pomerantz, S. (2007), '"The power to squash people": understanding girls' relational aggression', *British Journal of Sociology of Education*, 28: 23–37.

Dodge, K. A. and Coie, J. D. (1987) 'Social-information factors in reactive and proactive aggression in children's peer groups', *Journal of Personality and Social Psychology*, 53: 1146–1158.

Dollard, J., Doob, L. W., Miller, N. E., Mowrer, O. H. and Sears, R. R. (1939) *Frustration and Aggression*, New Haven, CT: Yale University Press.

Duncan, N. (1999) *Sexual Bullying: Gender Conflict and Student Culture in Secondary Schools*, London: Routledge.

Duncan, N. (2004) 'It's important to be nice, but it's nicer to be important: girls, popularity and sexual competition', *Sex Education*, 4: 137–152.

Durham, M. G. (2009) *The Lolita Effect*, London: Duckworth Overlook.

Farrington, D. P. (1993) 'Understanding and preventing bullying', *Crime and Justice*, 17: 381–458.

Farrington, D. P. (1995) 'The development of offending and antisocial behaviour from childhood: key findings from the Cambridge Study in Delinquent Development', *Journal of Child Psychology and Psychiatry*, 36: 929–964.

Farrington, D. P. (2002) 'Risk factors for youth violence', in E. Debarbieux and C. Blaya (eds.), *Violence in Schools and Public Policies*, London: Elsevier.

Galen, B. R. and Underwood, M. K. (1997) 'A developmental investigation of social aggression among children', *Developmental Psychology,* 33: 589–600.

Gilligan, C. (1993) *In a Different Voice: Psychological Theory and Women's Development*, Cambridge, MA: Harvard University Press.

Gruber, J. E. and Fineran, S. (2007) 'The impact of bullying and sexual harassment on middle and high school girls', *Violence Against Women*, 13: 627–643.

Jennifer, D. (2007) 'Understanding bullying in primary school: listening to children's voice', unpublished thesis, University of Surrey.

Jennifer, D., Cowie, H. and Bray, D. (2006), '"Bully Dance": animation as a tool for conflict resolution', *Pastoral Care in Education*, 24: 27–32.

Jennifer, D. and Williams, S. (2010) 'Inappropriate sexualised behaviours study report', unpublished manuscript.

Kehily, M. J., Mac An Ghail, M., Epstein, D. and Redman, P. (2001) 'Private girls and public worlds: producing femininities in the primary school', *Discourse*, 23: 167–177.

Lagerspetz, K. M. J., Björkqvist, K., Berts, M. and King, E. (1982) 'Group aggression among school children in three schools', *Scandinavian Journal of Psychology*, 23: 45–52.

Lagerspetz, K. M. J., Björkqvist, K. and Peltonen, T. (1988) 'Is indirect aggression typical of females? Gender differences in aggressiveness in 11- to 12-year-old children', *Aggressive Behavior*, 14: 403–414.

Lever, J. (1976) 'Sex differences in the games children play', *Social Problems*, 23: 478–487.

Lever, J. (1978) 'Sex differences in the complexity of children's play and games', *American Sociological Review*, 43: 471–483.

Ludwig, T. (2005) *My Secret Bully*, Berkeley, CA: Tricycle Press.

Maccoby, E. E. (1986) 'Social groupings in childhood: their relationship to prosocial and antisocial behavior in boys and girls', in D. Olweus, J. Block and M. Radke-Yarrow (eds), *Development of Antisocial and Prosocial Behavior: Research, Theories, and Issues*, Orlando, FL: Academic Press.

Meyer, A. (2007) 'The moral rhetoric of childhood', *Childhood*, 14: 85–104.

Morrison, B. (2006) 'School bullying and restorative justice: toward a theoretical understanding of the role of respect, pride, and shame', *Journal of Social Issues*, 62: 371–392.

Murray-Close, D., Ostrov, J. M. and Crick, N. R. (2007) 'A short-term longitudinal study of growth of relational aggression during middle childhood: associations with gender, friendship intimacy and internalizing problems', *Development of Psychopathology*, 19: 187–203.

Owens, L., Shute, R. and Slee, P. (2000). '"Guess what I just heard!": indirect aggression among teenage girls in Australia', *Aggressive Behavior*, 26: 67–83.

Papadopoulos, L. (2010) *Sexualisation of Young People Review*. Available at: http://webarchive.nationalarchives.gov.uk/+/homeoffice.gov.uk/about-us/news/sexualisation-young-people.html (accessed 16 May 2011).

Pellegrini, A. D. (2001) 'A longitudinal study of heterosexual relationships, aggression, and sexual harassment during the transition form primary school through middle school', *Applied Developmental Psychology*, 22: 119–133.

Pellegrini, A. D. and Long, J. D. (2002) 'A longitudinal study of bullying, dominance, and victimization during the transition from primary school through secondary school', *British Journal of Developmental Psychology*, 20: 259–280.

Pepler, D., Craig, W. M. and O'Connell, P. (1999) 'Understanding bullying from a dynamic systems perspective', in A. Slater and D. Muir (eds), *The Blackwell Reader in Developmental Psychology*, Oxford: Blackwell.

Renold, E. (2002) 'Presumed innocence (hetero)sexual, heterosexist and homophobic harassment among primary school girls and boys', *Childhood*, 9: 415–434.

Renold, E. (2006) '"They won't let us play … unless you're going out with one of them": Girls, boys and Butler's "heterosexual matrix" in the primary years', *British Journal of Sociology of Education*, 27: 489–509.

Rivers, I., Duncan, N. and Besag, V. E. (2007) *Bullying: A Handbook for Educators and Parents*, Westport, CT: Greenwood/Praeger.

Rogoff, B. (2003) *The Cultural Nature of Human Development*, Oxford: Oxford University Press.

Rutter, M. (2000) 'Psychosocial influences: critiques, findings, and research needs', *Development and Psychopathology*, 12: 375–405.

Salmivalli, C. (1999) 'Participant role approach to school bullying: implications for interventions', *Journal of Adolescence*, 22: 453–459.

Salmivalli, C. and Nieminen, E. (2002) 'Proactive and reactive aggression among school bullies, victims, and bully-victims', *Aggressive Behavior*, 28: 30–44.

Salmivalli, C., Lappalainen, M. and Lagerspetz, K. M. J. (1998) 'Stability and change of behavior in connection with bullying in schools: a two-year follow-up', *Aggressive Behavior*, 24: 205–218.

Seager, L. (2009) 'Staff understanding and response to sexual bullying between children and young people', unpublished thesis, Goldsmiths University of London.

Shaughnessy, J., and Jennifer, D. (2007) *Mapping the Statistics: Moving to a Shared Understanding of the Nature of Bullying and Violence in Schools Across Birmingham LA*, Birmingham: Report to Local Authority.

Shute, R., Owens, L. and Slee, P. (2008) 'Everyday victimization of adolescent girls by boys: sexual harassment, bullying or aggression?' *Sex Roles*, 58: 477–489.

Sippola, L. K., Paget, J. and Buchanan, C. M. (2007) 'Praising Cordelia: social aggression and social dominance among adolescent girls', in P. H. Hawley, T. D. Little and P. C. Rodkin (eds), *Aggression and Adaptation: The Bright Side to Bad Behaviour*, Mahwah, NJ: Lawrence Erlbaum Associates.

Smith, P. K., Cowie, H. and Blades, M. (2003) *Understanding Children's Development*, Oxford: Blackwell Publishing.

Spears, B., Jennifer, D. and Williams, S. (2011) 'Girls, inappropriate sexualised behaviours, harassment and bullying: implications for wellbeing', in R. Shute (ed.), *International Perspectives on Mental Health and Wellbeing in Education*, Adelaide: Shannon Research Press.

Tapper, K. and Boulton, M. J. (2004) 'Sex differences in levels of physical, verbal, and indirect aggression amongst primary school children and their associations with beliefs about aggression', *Aggressive Behavior*, 30: 123–145.

Timmerman, G. (2005) 'A comparison between girls' and boys' experiences of unwanted sexual behaviour in secondary schools', *Educational Research*, 47: 291–306.

Underwood, M. K., Galen, B. R. and Paquette, J. A. (2001) 'Top ten challenges for understanding gender and aggression in children: why can't we all just get along?' *Social Development*, 10: 248–266.

Wallis, A. and Van Every, J. (2000) 'Sexuality in the primary school', *Sexualities,* 3, 409–423.

Weare, K. (2004) *Developing the Emotionally Literate School*, London: Paul Chapman.

Witkowska, E. and Menckel, E. (2005) 'Perceptions of sexual harassment in Swedish high schools: experiences and school-environment problems', *European Journal of Public Health*, 15: 78–85.

World Health Organisation (1999) *Violence Prevention: An Important Element of a Health-Promoting School*, Author: Geneva.

World Health Organisation (2002) *World Report on Violence and Health*, Author: Geneva.

6 Sexual bullying in one local authority

Siân Williams

Introduction

Research into sexual bullying in the UK is limited. The first major study that engaged young people in conversations about sexual bullying was carried out over a decade ago (Duncan, 1999) and there has been little empirical work done since. This chapter sets out the experience of one London local authority where the author was involved in undertaking a vertically integrated research study into sexual bullying in two primary schools, two secondary schools (11–16 years of age) and the local further education (FE) college (16 years and older). This chapter presents the findings in relation to the secondary and FE college establishments and discusses their implications for policy and practice (see Table 6.1).

Table 6.1 English school system

Age of students	Year/Grade	Different school systems		
3	Nursery	Nursery		
4	Reception	Infant school	Primary school	First school
5	Year 1	Infant school	Primary school	First school
6	Year 2	Junior school	Primary school	First school
7	Year 3	Junior school	Primary school	First school
8	Year 4	Junior school	Primary school	First school
9	Year 5	Junior school	Primary school	Middle school
10	Year 6	Junior school	Primary school	Middle school
11	Year 7	Senior school	Secondary school with sixth form	Middle school
12	Year 8	Senior school	Secondary school with sixth form	Middle school
13	Year 9	Senior school	Secondary school with sixth form	Upper school with sixth form
14	Year 10	Senior school	Secondary school with sixth form	Upper school with sixth form
15	Year 11	Senior school	Secondary school with sixth form	Upper school with sixth form
16	Year 12	F.E. college/Sixth form	Secondary school with sixth form	Upper school with sixth form
17+	Year 13	F.E. college/Sixth form	Secondary school with sixth form	Upper school with sixth form

Before outlining the study, I want to explain the use of the term 'sexual bullying' in this chapter. Much of the literature on the subject uses slightly different terms such as 'sexual harassment', 'unwanted sexual behaviour', 'sexual violence' and 'sexual bullying' to describe similar behaviours. The decision here to use the term sexual bullying is based on earlier literature where discussions of the term 'bullying' argue that it needs to be understood within broader social and cultural factors (see for example Duncan, 1999; Pellegrini, 2002; Rivers et al., 2007; Gruber and Fineran, 2008; Ringrose and Renold, 2008) rather than the more traditional 'focus on the personal or psychological characteristics of bullies' (Gruber and Fineran, 2008: 522).

Rivers et al. (2007) neatly sum up this different way of looking at bullying, 'not as the sum of unpleasant behaviours that are owned by children, but the product of complex interactions within a system of social relationships that cannot be changed by simply removing bullies or reinforcing victims' (p. 35). This concept made sense in relation to our research as we came to see that the behaviours young people reported were multi-layered and more about group dynamics and identities than individual personalities. In this chapter the term sexual bullying encompasses bullying situations between individuals that incorporate sexual behaviour, and in behaviours that reflect a cultural/societal imbalance of power between various groups and exhibit repeated incidents of sexualised behaviour that are intended to harm. I have used the terms 'boys' and 'girls' to refer to gender throughout as these were used during the study as the most accessible terms for young people.

Finally, although this chapter refers to schools and colleges, similar issues have been found in young people's residential care homes (Barter, 2006; Kendrick, 2011). The conclusions presented below are therefore likely to have some relevance for other young people's settings.

Outline of the study

While rewriting the local authority's 'Children and young people's anti-bullying strategy' it became apparent that many school staff were concerned about what they saw as harmful relationships between boys and girls. In response to this, the local authority invited one of the editors of this volume, Neil Duncan, to talk about his work on gender conflict. This discussion generated further interest in the issue and enabled staff to talk more openly about the types of behaviours they were observing. Following the presentation, the local authority decided to find out more about such behaviours within the borough. We obtained funding for a small-scale research project and employed a professional researcher, Dawn Jennifer, to lead the study. The study took place during autumn 2009.

Our research had two aims. Firstly, as other research in the borough had already explored attitudes of more at-risk teenagers, we wanted to explore inappropriate sexualised behaviours between 'middle-of-the-road' boys and girls, young people who were not noted as exceptionally implicated in sexualised behaviours which caused physical or psychological harm. Secondly, in achieving the first aim, we then wanted to remain true to the borough's commitment to young people's participation and engage them meaningfully as active participants in the research, ensuring that their voices were clearly heard.

Following Duncan's (1999) study we employed a variant of 'Q' method card-sorting with group interviews. Q method asks participants to arrange a series of statements in response to an instruction. Outputs are then analysed statistically to reveal the range of various perceptions and positions. An advantage of Q method is that it can produce statistically robust data from a small sample of young people (Duncan and Owens, 2011). Our findings below present only one element of the card-sorting process, the simple ranking of the statements.

The statements we used were initially developed from previous research (Duncan, 1999; Gruber and Fineran, 2008; Timmerman, 2005; Witowska and Menckel, 2005). We then piloted and refined them in local schools. The statements reflected the behaviours of boys that girls found upsetting, and vice versa. The words 'sexual' and 'bullying' were deliberately excluded to avoid prejudicing the findings. The finalised statements (35 in total for each gender) were displayed on numbered cards; blank cards were added for young people to identify behaviours we had missed.

Volunteers from the three organisations involved were trained as lay researchers. Post-training they identified one middle-of-the-road student in each year group. If willing, this young person identified three or four more to the lay researcher. Once it had been ensured that there were no conflicting circumstances such as child protection issues and consent was granted from home (for school students only) the young people were invited to participate in the research and were fully briefed. In total, 40 young people volunteered to take part.

Ten hour-long, recorded, group sessions were conducted with between three and five students in each. In each of the two schools a male researcher conducted two sessions; one each for the Year 8 and Year 10 boy groups (four sessions). Similarly, in each school a female conducted two sessions for the Year 8 and Year 10 girl groups (four sessions). Two sessions were run in the FE college, one each for the Year 12 girl and boy groups.

During each session the lay researcher led a discussion based around the statements. This discussion ensured that the young people both understood the process and allowed a deeper exploration of their experiences, feelings and perceptions. At the end of the session young people were asked to carry out a card-sort individually, ranking the statements in terms of how frequently they experienced or witnessed the behaviours identified in each of the statements. Thirty-five card-sorts were satisfactorily completed across the ten groups. The individual scores for each statement were averaged across all the participants in each group. The average score provided an indication of the perceived prevalence for each behaviour for that group. Recordings of the sessions were transcribed for qualitative analysis.

Main findings

As noted above, card-sort scores provided an indication of the perceived prevalence of particular behaviours and should not be read as a measure of how often individuals experience them personally. For this reason and to improve overall readability the results of the statistical findings are presented here as headline findings. The main findings from both the analysis of the card-sort and the focus group discussions showed that for young people sexual bullying:

- was an everyday, public occurrence
- caused upset
- was experienced differently by girls and boys
- comprised a wide range of verbal and physical behaviour
- varied across the three settings, particularly for girls.

As in other studies (see Stein, 1999; Duncan, 1999; American Association of University Women – AAUW, 2001; Timmerman, 2005; Witowska and Menckel, 2005), young people reported a wide range of verbal, non-verbal and physical behaviour across a number of settings. Behaviours also differed in severity, from everyday sexual name-calling to extended rumour-spreading culminating in fights. These behaviours and their impacts are discussed in detail below.

When Year 10 girls were asked if boys ever called them names, they cited terms like 'ugly', 'butters' (a local term meaning ugly) or 'rude' which were used against them on a daily basis. Responses such as 'all the time, every day' and 'every minute of every day' were typical. The girls reported being asked if they were a virgin as the most frequent daily experience. Having their skirts pulled up and being touched by boys in the process was also very common.

One Year 10 girl described this as having its own name amongst boys in her school – 'Freeview' – after the set-top box that allows viewers to watch a large number of television channels without paying. A Year 8 girl talked about summertime in her school, which she said her male classmates refer to as, 'feel-up season'. Some girls talked about wearing shorts under their skirts, assuming that at some point during the day their skirt would be pulled up by a male classmate.

Boys 'pinging' girls' bra straps was widely reported in the girls' focus groups, with one Year 8 commenting, 'I think they like have dolls at home to be honest because they're actually training'. In the same Year 8 group, a particular type of physical harassment called 'daggering' was described as when a boy grabs a girl from behind and simulates sexual movements. One girl concluded that this is so frequent that, 'these days it's dangerous just to pick up stuff from the floor'.

Top of boys' card-sorts were verbal comments, for example being called 'waste man' (local term meaning 'waste of space') by girls: 'If a boy started to annoy them, after every sentence it would be "waste-man".' Being called 'ugly, butters or childish' was widely reported as being very frequent, as was being called 'Boom-ting' (local term meaning 'sexy') in schools. Having your perceived attractiveness publicly rated was also frequent, with one Year 10 group surmising that a girls' toilet in their school had been locked because of the amount of rating that was happening on its walls. Boys also stated that girls frequently made comments about their looks, body, clothes or private life (such as who they were going out with). One Year 8 boy stated 'if they don't like the couples, yeah ... they're just going to do everything just to split them up'. Another example of upsetting comments reported by boys was girls saying that a girl broke up with a boy when, in fact, he had ended it or by criticising a boy's sexual performance, usually by commenting on his 'small willy'.

A Year 8 boy referred to his precautions in making his tracksuit trousers very secure because of the possibility of a female classmate pulling them down in front of his peers: 'that's why in PE I always do my string tight'. There was a consensus among the school groups that PE lessons were a hotspot for unwanted touching. One Year 10 girl described the 'excited hands' of her male classmates. Perhaps surprisingly, public (for example classrooms), rather than private places was where most of the unwanted attention occurred. Year 10 girls talked about written public attractiveness ratings taking place in lessons and in registration. Both genders were reported to be taking part in these activities; however girls claimed boys pointed at girls and rated them out loud by number in front of the class. Both the Year 8 girls' groups talked about male classmates touching them 'by accident' in lessons under tables, and elsewhere around school. This experience was echoed by Year 10 girls in relation to the lunch queue:

> They try to make it accidental. Like in the lunch line we're all crammed up (...) and they'll lean against you, and you're like, 'what are you doing?' 'I'm just trying to move up'. They try and blag it out but we all ... we know what they're doing.

One theme from Year 10 and 12 boys' narratives was being 'eyed up' by girls, both around school/college and beyond. They also talked about girls using their bodies sexually in public, for example by 'shaking their arse' to gain boys' attention, with one boy in Year 10 commenting 'they try to ... try to just seduce you'. Another behaviour that these two boy groups specifically added to the set of statements was girls whispering in public: 'girls always whisper to their friend and then look over and start giggling and stuff a lot' (Year 12).

An unsurprising theme was the role of social networking sites in making sexual bullying – particularly rumour-spreading – public; this was reported by the Year 12 girls as being very frequent. Interestingly, a consensus emerged from across the genders – particularly the Year 10 groups – that it was mostly girls talking about girls on social networking sites, while boys generally made comments face to face.

In terms of frequency and location our findings were very similar to Duncan's 1999 research study in the Midlands of England. The finding that sexual bullying is mainly experienced in public spaces also supports evidence from other studies (for example Duncan, 1999; Stein, 1999; AAUW, 2001; Timmerman, 2005; Witowska and Menckel, 2005; Trotter, 2006). Due to the wider use of technology, the role of the internet and mobile phones were key differences from Duncan's earlier research.

Some girls spoke spontaneously about how strongly they felt about particular behaviours. Girls used words including, 'annoying', 'tiresome', 'really sad', 'uncomfortable' and 'paranoid' when describing how they felt about boys' behaviour, 'and it's really insulting and unappropriate [sic]'. Boys were less forthcoming, but did express feelings about girls trying to split couples up: 'that just gets on my nerves' (Year 8), and girls whispering: 'I fucking hate that' (Year 12).

Although research (see for example Duncan, 2002; Brown et al., 2007) has suggested that girls are more likely to leave schools as a result of sexual bullying, a Year 10 girls' group talked about a boy leaving their school as a result of a joke he instigated about the size of his penis. This went wrong after he used the wrong unit of measurement, resulting in him under-exaggerating rather than over-exaggerating as he had meant to. According to the girls, the ensuing level of bullying by both genders, verbal and gestural, direct and indirect, led him to leave the school.

The unprompted reports of hurt and upset from the young people, and the above example of the boy leaving school in shame, reinforce previous research about the impact of sexual bullying. Research shows there is impact on both genders (for example Duncan, 1999; AAUW 2001; Timmerman, 2005) but some researchers have suggested that heterosexual girls and lesbian, gay, bisexual and questioning young people are the most severely affected (Gruber and Fineran, 2005).

Analysis of the card-sorts indicated that sexual name-calling and the passing of sexual comments were experienced by both girls and boys, but with some key differences. In terms of physicality, girls reported being on the receiving end of more physical behaviour from boys, for example hitting and use of physical proximity. In terms of their use of the internet and mobile phones, girls (and in particular older girls) reported that they experienced sexual bullying more frequently via use of social networking sites and mobile phones. Year 12 girls identified this as most frequent. By way of contrast, boys reported denigration of their sexual reputations as a more frequent occurrence, mostly in relation to the size of their penis. Analysis of the qualitative data highlighted further differences between the genders as shown in Table 6.2.

Our evidence reinforces Duncan's (1999) study, and reveals gender differences and layers of complexity in peer relationships. Here are the 'complex interactions within a system of social relationships' identified by Rivers et al. (2007). Gaining insight into the system of social relationships and the complexity of interactions arising from them is vital for those wishing to tackle these behaviours.

Table 6.2 Further insights into gender differences from focus group narratives

Theme	Summary of young people's views
Threatening and forcing sexual behaviour	Boys did not threaten, 'they just do it' (Year 8 girl). Girls threatened sometimes but did not force boys to take part in sexual behaviour.
Attitude to sexual boundaries	Girls did not like the unwanted sexual attention they received; boys (Year 8) did not mind unsolicited hugging from girls and Year 12 said, 'you're not going to say no', if a girl says she is going to send a sexual picture to your mobile phone.
Boy to boy behaviour	Use of the word 'gay' was widely reported in the boys' focus groups to mean: • 'stupid' to describe a behaviour; • as a joke about boys in the room; • more seriously about boys not in the room – in particular girls' boyfriends who perceived themselves as 'hard'
Girl to girl behaviour	All groups noted the role of girls' in spreading sexual rumours, particularly online. Boys also expressed frustration and confusion about girls' shifting friendships and public falling-outs.
'Winding up' and retalliation	Boys 'winding up' girls and girls retaliating was a theme for all Year 10 and 12 groups. A typical interaction was a boy calling a girl a name and a girl hitting him or being verbally abusive back, but there were also examples of girls denigrating a boy's sexual reputation after he had cheated on her.
'There's no winning' if you're a girl	This sentiment was mentioned specifically by Year 8 and 10 girls in one of the secondary schools, in relation to virginity, clothing and friendship: 'if you hang around with girls, you're a lesbian. If you hang around with boys, you're a sket', 'f you hang around with both you're a bit of both'. (Year 10 girl)

Note: Sket is a term used to mean 'slag' or 'whore'.

The card-sort analysis highlighted differences across three settings (two secondary schools and one FE college), particularly so for girls. In one school the behaviour was more explicitly physical and sexual and resulted in girls reporting more unwanted sexual attention. The girls in the FE college reported experiencing more cyber sexual bullying. This finding suggests that there are local cultural factors at work in relation to sexual bullying, for example in the level of its acceptance and/or the range of responses to it, which can influence its prevalence and severity. This has far-reaching implications for policy and practice.

Future directions for policy and practice

The findings above support and build on the previous study by Duncan (1999) and together these offered directions for the development of policy and practice. These directions are provided below.

Firstly, it is important to acknowledge the specific sexualised forms of bullying, and assess its presence in all schools, colleges and other young people's settings. There is strong evidence that sexual bullying can cause significant harm to individuals, yet research suggests school staff are often unwilling either to acknowledge these behaviours (Stein, 1999). The first step, then, must be to acknowledge – as with racist and homophobic bullying – that sexual bullying exists at varying levels in our educational institutions. Raising awareness of any new concept needs the right leadership and strategic approach. As a first step it may be useful to involve those with in-depth knowledge of sexual bullying to highlight and initiate a discussion of the issues. Following this, doing research at a local level would not only help to maintain a focus on the issues but would provide greater insight into the particular types of behaviour to be addressed. Such research would also help to widen a very narrow UK evidence base. Local authorities should encourage and coordinate such research across their boroughs.

Secondly, it is important to increase practitioners' understanding of sexual bullying, its nature, prevalence and impact. Researchers have been calling for increased knowledge and understanding of this area for over ten years (for example Stein, 1999; Pellegrini, 2002; Meraviglia et al., 2003; Maxwell and Aggleton, 2009; Stanley et al., 2011). Experience of training lay researchers indicates a full day is needed to: clarify definitions; understand the characteristics of sexual bullying learning from existing research; understand the role of the internet and mobile phones; explore inherent socio-cultural factors: gender; power; organisational culture; society's views; explore the possible consequences of sexual bullying, including links to domestic violence; become familiar with the legal requirements in the field; challenge pre-existing assumptions; start to discuss how to respond to and support young people; and identify appropriate people to comprise a local 'core team' to develop practice and policy (Stein, 1999; Eisenbraun, 2007).

It is also important to develop a core specialist team that would be equipped to provide more targeted, specialist support. The core team would need more input and time to develop higher-level expertise in support for young people involved in sexual bullying and violence (note: staff working with serious incidents also need support) and have the in-depth knowledge to facilitate sessions with young people

Given the status of Personal Social and Health Education (PSHE) in the curriculum, adding work about sexual bullying to initial teacher training would present a major challenge. But as Maxwell and Aggleton assert, it is vital to 'ensure adequate investment in teacher training so that teachers of

Sex and Relationships Education are competent to address gender, power and relationships issues in their work' (Maxwell and Aggleton, 2009: 21)

Informal education sessions for parents and carers are increasingly common; to add the topic of sexual bullying to a parent/carer programme would be a natural progression. Given the limited time available for such sessions, it would seem sensible to cover a basic level of information and spend more time discussing concerns and questions. The main outcome should be to give parents/carers the language and confidence to talk with their children about peer relationships and sexual bullying.

It is of course recognised that there are a number of challenges to overcome in achieving the above, and PSHE is seen as 'low status often taught by non-specialists and generally considered a burdensome appendix to the crowded "real" curriculum' (Duncan, 1999: 57). The expectation for staff to learn about socio-cultural concepts and consequently change culture 'places the burden of change on the adults and the institutions rather than on the students' (Rivers et al., 2007: 36), and this might well meet resistance from already pressed managers of such institutions.

A final challenge lies with the economic constraints on schools and colleges in relation to funding staff training, particularly in little-known areas. Budget cuts mean there are fewer local authority staff available to search out examples of best practice to develop in their home boroughs, and support schools with the hard task of culture change. However there are still some opportunities. Coupled with national on-going concern around bullying generally, there are a number of recent reports and guidance relating to sexuality, sexualisation, and sexual bullying and violence (for example Papadopoulous, 2010; Department of Children, Schools and Families, 2009; Bailey, 2011; End Violence Against Women, 2011). These factors, combined with the possibility of increased freedom for schools in relation to learning and teaching, may provide the grounds for more open discussion of, and learning about, sexual bullying.

Thirdly, there is a need to develop a range of strategies to address sexual bullying and gender conflict in schools and colleges. As there is no UK research into the effectiveness of strategies to address sexual bullying, this section draws on literature from the fields of anti-bullying, sexual harassment, violence reduction and behaviour management. Figure 6.1 presents a three tier model based on research into restorative approaches (Morrison, 2007), sexual harassment (Stein, 1999) and my own experience with schools and colleges.

Given the diverse range of sexual bullying, schools need to respond with a range of effective strategies (Thompson and Smith, 2011; Hewitt et al., 2002). Anti-bullying research (Olweus, 2011; Smith and Sharp, 1994; Thompson and Smith, 2011) also suggests that a whole-school/college approach needs to be taken to maximise effectiveness, which involves everyone and pervades all areas of school/college life. Schools/colleges should consider the following ideas:

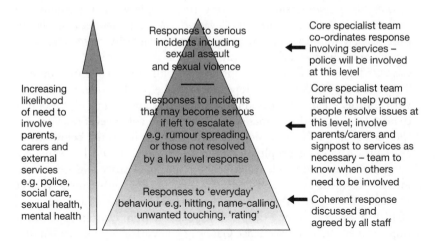

Figure 6.1 Three-tier model of restorative approaches

- *Integration within the wider school/college curriculum.* Sexual bullying sessions need to be part of the mainstream curriculum and be revisited throughout the year (Taylor et al., 2010). Personal, Social and Health Education (PSHE) lessons are the obvious place for sessions, as long as these are delivered effectively. Where this is not the case, alternatives such as drama lessons may be suitable.
- *Time to talk.* Time to talk needs to be built into sexual bullying sessions (AAUW, 2001; Trotter, 2006; Maxwell and Aggleton, 2009), as illustrated by a young woman in a sexual harassment survey: 'Instead of popping in a video and exploring the problem to be solved, teachers need to take the time out and TALK to us. It's a problem that one video can't fix' (AAUW, 2001).
- *Single or mixed gender groups?* Our research study worked with boys and girls separately. Following the project the FE College developed their practice, bringing mixed gender groups together after single gender sessions. Anecdotal feedback indicates this worked well as young people could: a) have their behaviour reflected back to them; b) begin to understand the other gender's views; c) develop language to engage in thoughtful discussion; and d) have their assumptions challenged. Single sex schools may wish to work with a partner school to facilitate mixed gender sessions.
- *Facilitation.* Stanley et al. (2011) suggest that having the confidence of the group may be a more important factor than a facilitator's gender. Most schools and colleges have staff capable of delivering sexual bullying sessions with the appropriate training (see learning for adults above). External facilitators can be used but this raises questions about sustainability of sessions and long-term embedding of new ideas.

- *Style, relevance and resourcing.* Anecdotal feedback from the study and further FE college sessions indicate young people want discussions and active learning which is directly relevant to their experiences. Schools and colleges may want to supplement their own sexual bullying sessions with, for example, drama workshops run by specialist companies.

- *Content.* There is little research into sexual bullying curriculum content. The following ideas were developed with the help of FE college staff. Start with broader themes to introduce key concepts and language. Resources covering these broader themes are widely available. However resources for specific sexual bullying sessions are rare, but are indicated below where available. All young people's learning in this area should be evaluated. Suggested themes include: relationships; personal space – external and internal boundaries; gender conflict (see Duncan, 1999 and Rivers et al., 2007 for activities); understanding sexual bullying ('Linking Lies', 2011 film made by young people downloadable from Learning and Skills Improvement Service Excellence Gateway – www.lsis.org.uk, see Jennifer and Williams, 2011; Theatre in Education companies, Brook Sexual Bullying Project – www.sexualbullying.org.uk); individual and group roles in sexual bullying (using the resources above); gender stereotypes; the role of the media; group influence and conformity; the law; and the evaluation of young people's learning.

It is important that schools and colleges are supported in reviewing the nature and role of their own organisational culture in relation to sexual bullying. Individual behaviour is often entrenched and hard to change (Rivers et al., 2007). While not an easy option, changing the wider school/college culture may be the more effective way to raise awareness of the issue and thereby begin to challenge sexual bullying behaviours. Research suggests that school staff have sometimes exacerbated sexual harassment and bullying by: trivialising incidents (Stein, 1999; Ringrose, 2008); adopting male-dominated methods of managing young people (Duncan, 1999); missing the complex context of incidents (Ringrose, 2008), and; having less concern for victims as they become more experienced (Meriviglia et al., 2003).

Research into zero tolerance and other punishment-focused policies has deemed them ineffective and proposes that they may even cause further damage (Skiba and Knesting, 2001; Stein, 2005; Morrison, 2007), as they can cause confusion, anger and long-term resentment. Stein (1999) warns against other 'draconian' approaches, for example banning all physical contact as these practices remove responsibility from young people, thus burdening staff whose job it becomes to police rather than educate young people. She also advocates against involving peer mediators or tribunals in sexual bullying incidents.

Finally, in a meta-study on school violence reduction, counselling and psychotherapy were identified as one of the least effective strategies (Lipsey, 1991). This is not to say that these methods do not benefit specific individuals but in a strategy for whole-institution change they form only a small part of the jigsaw.

The evidence of what might work points to a combination of two main strategies. The first is to have clear and specific rules about acceptable behaviours that are perceived as fair by all (Hewitt et al., 2002). The second recommends relationship-building by involving young people in communicating effectively and taking responsibility for their school or college community (Hewitt et al., 2002; Eisenbraun, 2007; Thompson and Smith, 2011). Hewitt et al. (2002: 6) described the best practice they saw in schools as being where there was:

> The most attention to talking to pupils about incidents, listening to pupils' accounts, mediating and ensuring good communication between pupils, staff and parents/guardians – and having a strong philosophy of respect for pupils' accounts.

Although staff talked about time needed to resolve incidents in this way, they also saw a clear pay-off as minor incidents did not escalate. These strategies do not preclude use of sanctions. In the course of my work helping schools to embed restorative justice practices (which may be one way of unpicking and resolving some of the issues inherent in sexual bullying) it was apparent that sanctions were still applied but were done so within the framework of thoughtful and effective communication described above, not as a first option.

Finally, it is essential that practice is formalised into policy. At the level of schools and colleges, policies should: have clear definitions of sexual bullying and identified the range and level of behaviour in the establishment; make explicit mention of sexual bullying in the anti-bullying policy; as practice develops, record effective strategies in the policy; link the anti-bullying policy with other relevant policies which will need to be added to as practice develops e.g. Gender Equality Duty; Sex and Relationships; Teaching and Learning, as well as the School or College Improvement Plan; and contribute to local authority policy development.

At the local authority level, officers should: make explicit mention of sexual bullying and gender conflict within the anti-bullying policy; coordinate research projects across the borough to raise awareness and assess the nature of the issue; work with partners to raise awareness and identify the right people to develop policy; support settings to develop effective practice and policy; record and disseminate effective practice and policy; refine the local authority anti-bullying policy as necessary; and contribute to national policy development.

Ultimately at national government level there should be a commitment to: fund research involving young people that gives a national picture of sexual bullying – this should include primary schools; consider revising, or adding to, the current guidance on sexual bullying to include socio-cultural factors in relation to sexual bullying – this vital aspect is currently missing; and work with, or commission, academics, local authorities and school/college staff to begin to capture and evaluate good practice, then record findings for dissemination.

Conclusion

In this chapter I have presented findings from a small London-based research study which has added to a limited UK research base. The findings from the study reinforce those from previous research: that sexual bullying is frequent and potentially damaging and can have far-reaching impacts on the lives of young people into adulthood. This chapter has provided some recommendations for developing a response to sexual bullying. There is a need for further research into the nature and scale of sexual bullying in young people's settings. However, most urgent is the need for research that enables us to identify best practice, develop more effective responses and add to the 'what works' evidence base.

References

American Association of University Women – AAUW (2001) *Hostile Hallways: Bullying, Teasing and Sexual Harassment in Schools*, Washington, DC: Author.

Bailey, R. (2011) *Letting Children be Children. Report of an Independent Review of the Commercialisation and Sexualisation of Childhood*, London: Department for Education.

Barter, C. (2006) 'Discourse of blame: deconstructing (hetero)sexuality, peer sexual violence and residential children's homes', *Child and Family Social Work*, 11: 347–356.

Brown, M., Chesney-Lind, M. and Stein, N. (2007) 'Patriarchy matters: toward a gendered theory of teen violence and victimization', *Violence Against Women*, 13: 1249–1273.

Department of Children, Schools and Families – DCSF (2009) *Guidance for Schools on Preventing and Responding to Sexist, Sexual and Transphobic Bullying*, London: Author.

Duncan, N. (1999). *Sexual Bullying: Gender Conflict in Pupil Culture*, London: Routledge.

Duncan, N. (2002) 'Girls, bullying and school transfer', in T. V. Sunnari, J. Kangasvuo, and M. Heikkinen (eds), *Gendered and Sexualised Violence in Educational Organisations*, Oulu: University of Oulu Press.

Duncan, N. and Owens, L. (2011) 'Bullying, social power and heteronormativity: girls' constructions of popularity', *Children and Society*, 25: 306–316.

Eisenbraun, K. (2007) 'Violence in schools: prevalence, prediction and prevention', *Aggression and Violent Behaviour*, 12: 459–469.

End Violence Against Women – EVAW (2011) *A Different World is Possible: A Call for Long-Term and Targeted Action to Prevent Violence Against Women and Girls*, London: Author.

Gruber, J. E. and Fineran, S. (2008) 'Comparing the impact of bullying and sexual harassment victimization on the mental and physical health of adolescents', *Sex Roles*, 59: 1–13.

Hewitt, R., Epstein, D., Leonard, D. and Watkins, C. (2002) *The Violence-Resilient School: A Comparative Study of Schools and Their Environments*. Available at: http://www.esrc.ac.uk/my-esrc/grants/L133251041/read/reports (accessed 9 June 2011).

Jennifer, D. and Williams, S. (2011). *Linking Lies: Resource Pack for Staff*, London: Learning and Skills Improvement Service.

Kendrick, A. (2011) 'Peer violence in provision for children in care', in C. Barter and D. Berridge (eds) *Children Behaving Badly? Peer Violence Between children and Young People*, Chichester: Wiley.

Lipsey, M. (1991) 'The effect of treatment of juvenile delinquents: results from meta-analysis', in F. Losel, D. Bender and T. Bliesener (eds), *Psychology and Law*, New York: Walker De Gruyter.

Maxwell, C. and Aggleton, P. (2009) *Young Women and Their Relationships – Power and Pleasure: Key Issues for Practitioners and Policy-Makers*, London: Institute of Education (Thomas Coram Research Unit).

Meriviglia, M., Becker, H., Rosenbluth, B., Sanchez, E. and Robertson, T. (2003) 'The Expect Respect Project: creating a positive elementary school climate', *Journal of Interpersonal Violence*, 18: 1347–1360.

Morrison, B. (2007) *Restoring Safe School Communities: A Whole School Response to Bullying, Violence and Alienation*, Leichhardt, NSW: Federation Press.

Olweus, D. (2011) *Bullying Prevention Program*. Available at: http://www.olweus.org/public/bullying_prevention_program.page (accessed 18 May 2011).

Papadopoulos, L. (2010) *Sexualisation of Young People Review*. Available at: http://www.wrc.org.uk/includes/documents/cm_docs/2010/s/sexualisationyoungpeople.pdf (accessed 16 May 2011).

Pellegrini, A. (2002) 'Bullying, victimization and sexual harassment during the transition to middle school', *Educational Psychologist*, 37: 151–163.

Rivers, I. Duncan, N. and Besag, V. (2007) *Bullying: A Handbook for Educators and Parents*, Westport, CT: Greenwood/Praeger.

Ringrose, J. (2008) '"Just be friends": exposing the limits of educational bully discourses for understanding teen girls' heterosexual friendships and conflicts', *British Journal of Sociology of Education*, 29: 509–522.

Ringrose, J. and Renold, E. (2008) 'Normative cruelties and gender deviants: the performative effects of bully discourses for girls and boys in school', *British Educational Research Journal*, 36: 573–596.

Skiba, R. J. and Knesting, K. (2001) 'Zero tolerance, zero evidence: an analysis of school disciplinary practice', in R. J. Skiba and G. G. Noam (eds), *Zero Tolerance: Can Suspension and Expulsion Keep Schools Safe?* San Francisco, CA: Jossey-Bass.

Stanley, N., Ellis, J. and Bell, J. (2011) 'Delivering preventative programmes in schools: identifying gender issues', in C. Barter and D. Berridge (eds), *Children Behaving Badly? Peer Violence Between Children and Young People,* Chichester: Wiley.

Smith, P. and Sharp, S. (1994) (eds) *School Bullying: Insights and Perspectives,* London: Routledge.

Stein, N. (1999) *Classrooms and Courtrooms: Facing Sexual Harassment in K-12 schools*, New York: Teacher's College Press.

Stein, N. (2005) 'A rising pandemic of sexual violence in elementary and secondary schools: locating a secret problem', *Duke Journal of Gender Law and Policy*, 12: 33–52.

Taylor, B., Stein, N. and Burden, F. (2010) 'The effects of gender violence/harassment prevention programming in middle schools: a randomized experimental evaluation', *Violence and Victims*, 25: 202–223.

Thompson, F. and Smith, P. (2011) *The Use and Effectiveness of Anti-Bullying Strategies in Schools*, London: Department of Children, Schools and Families.

Timmerman, G. (2005) 'A comparison between girls' and boys' experiences of unwanted sexual behaviour in secondary schools', *Educational Research*, 47: 291–306.

Trotter, J. (2006) 'Violent crimes? Young people's experiences of homophobia and misogyny in secondary schools', *Practice: Social Worker in Action*, 18: 291–302.

Witowska, E. and Menckel, E. (2005) 'Perceptions of sexual harassment in Swedish high schools: experiences and school-environment problems', *European Journal of Public Health*, 15: 78–85.

7   Homophobic bullying

V. Paul Poteat, Ethan H. Mereish,
Craig D. DiGiovanni and Jillian R. Scheer

Introduction

Bullying remains a ubiquitous part of many students' experiences as they progress through school. This is especially the case for students from marginalised groups in society. It is well-established that lesbian, gay, bisexual, transgender, or questioning youth (LGBTQ) experience more frequent victimisation than heterosexual youth (Berlan *et al.*, 2010; Poteat *et al.*, 2009; Williams *et al.*, 2005), that racial and minority ethnic youth face hostility and discrimination in schools (Fisher *et al.*, 2000; Flores *et al.*, 2010; Grossman and Liang, 2008; Rosenbloom and Way, 2004), and that students with disabilities (Rose *et al.*, 2009) and immigrant youth (Perreira *et al.*, 2010) are frequent targets of victimisation. Additionally, students experience victimisation on account of their gender or gender expression, religious beliefs and other minority social identities (Grossman and D'Augelli, 2006; Russell *et al.*, in press; Stein, 1995).

For a number of these students, the bullying they experience reflects blatant prejudice on the part of the aggressor and is discriminatory. Until recently, however, there has been little attention to the discriminatory nature of bullying. This subsequently has masked the fact that much of the way in which prejudice and discrimination are expressed among youth is through behaviours typically conceived as bullying. Yet, it is critical to note that bias-based discriminatory bullying carries more elevated consequences for victimised youth compared to bullying absent of bias (Russell *et al.*, in press). Greater attention to this form of bullying is warranted, as it carries significant implications for programming and social policies.

In this chapter, we cover several issues related to bias-based bullying and more specifically homophobic bullying. First, we discuss the prevalence of homophobic and other forms of bias-based bullying and note various ways it is expressed. We also note how homophobic victimisation is experienced by LGBTQ and heterosexual youth. Further, we discuss emerging findings on the development of this behaviour over time. Next, we provide an overview of factors that motivate individuals' engagement in homophobic bullying. In this section we note individual characteristics as well as social contextual factors that predict this behaviour. We then give attention to the range of psychological, social and educational outcomes associated with homophobic victimisation. Moreover, we describe several key factors that serve as buffers against the negative effects normally connected to homophobic victimisation. Finally, we discuss implications for research, practice and policy.

The consistent and common occurrence of bias-based bullying and victimisation

Prevalence of bias-based bullying

As more studies explore the connection between bullying and discrimination, the emerging findings provide several indicators of the prevalence of bias-based bullying. One of the most recent and largest scale studies to assess this was a population-based study of over 600,000 middle school (11–14 years of age) and high school (14–18 years of age) students in California, USA. Among those who reported victimisation in the last year, approximately 40 per cent considered at least some of these experiences to be based on their gender, sexual orientation, race or ethnicity, religion, or physical or mental disability (Russell *et al.*, in press). This same paper reported rates of approximately 36 per cent among a separate population-based sample of over 17,000 middle school and high school students in Wisconsin, USA. These rates underscore that bullying is frequently discriminatory.

Data specific to homophobic bullying are consistent with those for bias-based bullying in general. Furthermore, when focusing directly on the experiences of LGBTQ youth as opposed to the general student population, the data clearly indicate that the large majority of LGBTQ youth experience some form of school-based peer victimisation. Of the many forms of victimisation experienced by LGBTQ youth, name-calling, rumour-spreading, teasing and assault tend to be the most common (Rivers, 2001). Data from the most recent national school climate survey conducted by the US Gay, Lesbian and Straight Education Network (GLSEN) found that nearly 85 per cent of LGBT students were verbally harassed and 40 per cent were physically harassed at school (Kosciw *et al.*, 2010). Notably, the rates of victimisation of LGBTQ youth have changed little over the past several decades during which data have been collected (Kosciw *et al.*, 2010; Pilkington and D'Augelli, 1995; Rivers, 2001).

Data from the perspective of students who actually engage in homophobic bullying provide additional indicators of the frequency of this behaviour. Higher levels of bullying are strongly associated with more frequent use of homophobic epithets toward other students (Poteat and Espelage, 2005; Poteat and DiGiovanni, 2010). In fact, students who take on a variety of roles as part of bullying episodes (e.g. assisting, reinforcing or supporting the primary bullying individual) all report more frequent use of homophobic epithets (Poteat and Rivers, 2010). This finding converges with reports from LGBT youth who indicate that the victimisation they experience is often perpetrated by groups of youth as opposed to single individuals (Rivers, 2001). In addition, the use of homophobic epithets toward other students is strongly associated with other forms of aggression, such as fighting and relational aggression (e.g., rumour-spreading or group exclusion; Poteat and Espelage, 2005). These findings reflect again the substantial overlap between bulling and discrimination.

Although LGBTQ youth face more frequent victimisation than heterosexual youth, heterosexual youth are often targets of victimisation that is homophobic in nature. Heterosexual boys are called these epithets for varying reasons such as gender non-conformity (Epstein, 2001; Pascoe, 2007; Phoenix *et al.*, 2003). In general, boys tend to use and be called homophobic epithets more often than girls (Poteat and Espelage, 2005; Poteat and Rivers, 2010). Also, the association between bullying and homophobic epithet use, as well as the association between victimisation and being called homophobic epithets, tends to be larger for boys than girls (Poteat and DiGiovanni, 2010; Poteat and Espelage, 2005; Poteat and Rivers, 2010). This suggests homophobic expressions are more commonly a part of bullying episodes among boys than among girls. To date, the extant research has focused largely on this behaviour and its underlying motivations among boys. Little is known about the conditions under which or why girls use homophobic epithets toward other students or engage in homophobic behaviour more generally. Yet, it is important to note that these associations are significant among girls and thus there is a need to examine and remain aware of this behaviour as it occurs among both boys and girls. While these behaviours among girls may be motivated in part by similar factors as for boys (e.g., to enforce gender norms), this behaviour also may be motivated by a unique set of factors or circumstances that have yet to be identified.

Homophobic bullying across the educational experience

Homophobic bullying occurs throughout students' educational experience. Heterosexual and sexual minority adult men recalled that the homophobic bullying they experienced began in elementary school (Plummer, 2001). Even when the meaning of certain homophobic epithets was not initially understood or connected to sexuality, they later were, and the use of these epithets was intentional and intensified the effect of bullying (Plummer, 2001). LGBTQ youth also have recalled that they experienced homophobic victimisation early in elementary school, and this has been documented among those in middle school and high school (Kosciw *et al.*, 2010; Pilkington and D'Augelli, 1995; Rivers, 2001). These findings point to the need for anti-bullying programmes to be implemented at all levels of education in order to address issues of diversity and promote welcoming and respectful schools.

From these data, there has been an implicit assumption that homophobic bullying and victimisation are relatively stable. There has been little empirical data, however, to indicate whether there are increases, decreases or stability in how frequently students engage in or are targets of homophobic bullying over the course of their educational experience. Some retrospective reports suggest that such victimisation is indeed chronic for a number of LGBTQ youth (Plummer, 2001; Rivers, 2001). Nevertheless, are there certain periods during which these experiences are particularly elevated relative to others? For instance, findings in the general bullying literature have documented increases in bullying following the transition from elementary school to middle school (Pellegrini and Long, 2002). Similar information with respect to homophobic bullying could greatly inform targeted prevention and intervention efforts.

In a recent longitudinal study among a general student population, we documented significant changes in students' use of and being called homophobic epithets as they progressed through high school (Poteat *et al.*, 2011c). On average, boys reported an increase in using and being called homophobic epithets as they progressed through high school whereas girls reported relatively low and stable levels over time. Further, fluctuations in students' bullying or victimisation over time coincided with fluctuations in their engagement in or being the target of homophobic epithets. These significant co-occurring changes, over and above those connected to progressive grade-related changes, further underscore how many of the homophobic epithets frequently heard by students are a part of bullying. Notably, in the findings there remained a substantial degree of variability in these trajectories, even after accounting for these factors. In effect, students' experiences with homophobic bullying and victimisation were quite diverse.

These findings point to the dynamic and complex nature of homophobic bullying and the need to identify other factors that explain the different experiences reported across students. For example, why do some LGBTQ and heterosexual youth experience chronic homophobic victimisation while others do not? Also, why do some students increase while others decrease in their engagement in homophobic bullying? With regard to the latter question, individual factors such as perspective-taking, empathy or attitudes related to masculine norms or dominance could potentially account for these differences. Additionally, social factors such as peer group norms and socialisation processes within these groups could account for different patterns of change (Poteat, 2007). Also, as a greater number of sexual minority youth are coming out at earlier ages (Grov *et al.*, 2006) this, too, could lead some students to reconsider their engagement in this behaviour. Finally, under optimal conditions, intergroup contact can lead to decreases in prejudice (Allport, 1954; Pettigrew and Tropp, 2006), which in turn could lead to decreases in homophobic bullying. In sum, although there is strong evidence of the frequency of homophobic bullying and victimisation among LGBTQ and heterosexual students, there remain a number of limitations to our understanding of how this behaviour develops and how it is experienced differently among students.

Why do students engage in homophobic bullying?

Despite the growing attention to homophobic bullying, few studies have actually considered why students engage in this behaviour. Is such behaviour purely an expression of prejudice, or are there other contributing factors? Emerging findings suggest that students engage in homophobic bullying for a number of interrelated reasons. Further, both individual and social contextual factors contribute to this behaviour.

Individual correlates of homophobic bullying

Homophobic bullying, specifically in the form of homophobic epithet use toward other students, is indeed associated with sexual prejudice among boys (Poteat and DiGiovanni, 2010), as is sexual prejudice and general bullying behaviour (Pleck *et al.*, 1994). Of interest, however, these associations are not particularly large. As suggested by other studies (Plummer, 2001), students, especially those younger in age, do not always have a clear awareness of how this behaviour relates to prejudice and discrimination at a broader societal level. Thus, many students' use of homophobic language may not align with their specific attitudes toward sexual minorities. Some young people describe such behaviour as a form of joking or banter and downplay its seriousness (Korobov, 2004; Phoenix *et al.*, 2003). Nevertheless, the significant association between prejudice and homophobic bullying does point to the need to address issues of prejudice and diversity specifically within the context of anti-bullying efforts. Also, it is possible that other more serious forms of homophobic bullying (e.g. physical aggression or assault) are more strongly associated with prejudice. Indeed, studies among adults have documented strong associations between aggressive homophobic behaviour and sexual prejudice (Bernat *et al.*, 2001; Parrott *et al.*, 2002).

In addition to prejudice, several other key factors are associated with homophobic bullying. Among them include gender normative beliefs and enforcement. Children and adolescents use homophobic language or engage in other forms of homophobic bullying as one way to enforce gender norms among peers (Kimmel, 1997; Phoenix *et al.*, 2003; Poteat *et al.*, 2011b). Boys who engage in gender non-conforming behaviour often are targets of homophobic bullying (Eder *et al.*, 1995; Epstein, 2001). Other studies find that individuals who more strongly endorse traditional masculine ideology beliefs also report more frequent engagement in homophobic bullying (Pleck *et al.*, 1994; Poteat *et al.*, 2011b). Many students consider homophobic bullying a form of sexual harassment (American Association of University Women, 2001; Fineran, 2002). The link between homophobic bullying and gender expression provides one explanation for why heterosexual youth report experiencing homophobic victimisation.

The role of homophobic bullying in the establishment and maintenance of dominance hierarchies also has received some attention. Dominance behaviour can include attempts to achieve greater status or influence over other peers

(Hawley, 1999). These attempts do not necessarily have to be antagonistic or overtly aggressive. Nevertheless, students who engage in behaviours intended to establish dominance over their peers do report more frequent use of homophobic epithets (Poteat and DiGiovanni, 2010). Moreover, these findings applied to both boys and girls. In some ways this may relate to the marginalised status of sexual minorities at the broader societal level. Because of the societal marginalisation of sexual minorities, referring to a student as a sexual minority in a disparaging manner, regardless of whether the student identifies as LGBTQ, symbolically places that student in a subordinate position. Similar to the findings for gender norm enforcement, the connection between homophobic behaviour and dominance also offers an explanation for why heterosexual youth are targets of homophobic behaviour.

The social dynamics of homophobic bullying

A full understanding of homophobic bullying cannot be attained without attention to the broader context in which it occurs. Certain characteristics of the social environment contribute to the perpetuation of this behaviour. We review several of these factors in this section.

Peer groups have a significant role in the perpetuation of homophobic bullying. Earlier findings have noted how homophobic bullying involves multiple aggressors (Rivers, 2001). Recent findings have documented that individuals within the same peer group report similar rates of homophobic bullying, and moreover, that peers socialise and influence these behaviours among group members over time (Poteat, 2007). Several implications follow from this knowledge. First, these findings suggest that the homophobic bullying experienced by many students is likely perpetrated by select groups of students. Second, interventions directed at specific students who engage in this behaviour may be ineffective because the student will likely be resocialised by his or her peers to reengage in this behaviour. Consequently, interventions must be more expansive and address the social norms within peer groups that perpetuate this behaviour.

Other social norms also describe groups of students who engage in this behaviour more often than others. For instance, homophobic banter between students is more likely to occur within homophobic peer groups than non-homophobic peer groups (Poteat, 2008). In this case, students who are called homophobic epithets are more likely to use these epithets if they are members of homophobic peer groups. Because of the negative attitudes toward sexual minorities held by their peers, these students may feel a greater sense of threat or hostility from being called a sexual minority and may feel greater pressure to respond in a homophobic manner.

Chesir-Teran (2003) outlined a number of factors at the school level that could contribute to hostile school climates for sexual minority youth, and these should be examined empirically in future research. Attention to factors such as enumerated anti-bullying policies that extend explicit protection to

LGBTQ students, the presence of a Gay-Straight Alliance (GSA) in the school, representation of LGBTQ individuals within the standard course curriculum, the overall diversity within the school, and a range of other factors could represent key characteristics of schools in which LGBTQ youth are safer and in which homophobic bullying is less frequent. Research of this scale that includes multiple schools is critical in the effort to identify individual and contextual factors that promote the health and wellbeing of LGBTQ youth.

The effects of homophobic victimisation and factors that promote resilience

Bullying, in general, has deleterious effects on the mental health and academic performance of all youth (Juvonen *et al.*, 2000; Rigby, 2000; Poteat *et al.*, 2011b; Schwartz *et al.*, 2005). Among LGBTQ youth in particular, victimisation is associated with a range of factors such as suicidality, posttraumatic stress and depression symptoms, various externalising behaviours, and risky health behaviours (Bontempo and D'Augelli, 2002; D'Augelli *et al.*, 2002; Friedman *et al.*, 2006; Hershberger and D'Augelli, 1995; Williams *et al.*, 2005). Further, homophobic bullying has added negative effects on the mental health, psychosocial concerns and distress, and academic functioning of both LGBTQ and heterosexual youth (Poteat and Espelage, 2007; Poteat *et al.*, 2011b; Swearer *et al.*, 2008). Students who experience victimisation that is homophobic evidence greater risk on these indices compared to those whose victimisation experiences are not homophobic (Poteat *et al.*, 2011b; Swearer *et al.*, 2008). Moreover, homophobic victimisation has long-term consequences. Students' experiences with homophobic victimisation predicted poorer psychological outcomes (e.g. depression, distress, school belonging) for boys and predicted greater social withdrawal for girls even after controlling for their mental health and social functioning from the previous year (Poteat and Espelage, 2007).

The effects of homophobic bullying are especially harmful for LGBTQ youth relative to heterosexual youth. This can be understood within the framework of the minority stress model (Meyer, 2003). This model posits that sexual minorities experience unique, chronic and adverse stressors (e.g., prejudice, victimisation) specific to their sexual minority identity and in turn these stressors have negative effects on their mental health (Meyer, 2003). For instance, the effects of homophobic bullying on depressed and suicidal feelings as well as on drug use are greater for sexual minority youth than heterosexual youth (Espelage *et al.*, 2008). Furthermore, homophobic bullying is associated with greater risk for depression, isolation, drug use, emotional distress and truancy for sexual minority youth (Almeida *et al.*, 2009; Birkett *et al.*, 2009; Hershberger *et al.*, 1997). Chronic experiences of homophobic bullying at school are also related to symptoms of posttraumatic stress in adulthood for sexual minorities (Rivers, 2004). Moreover, homophobic victimisation is associated with suicidal ideation and attempts as well as self-harm ideation (Hershberger *et al.*, 1997; Huebner *et al.*, 2004; Rivers, 2000).

Among racially diverse sexual minority youth, victimisation also has significant and unique effects on mental health. Sexual minority youth of colour experience multiple forms of discrimination related to their multiple minority social identities (Balsam *et al.*, 2004; Rosario *et al.*, 2004), as well as poorer mental health and academic concerns related to discrimination and bullying (Poteat *et al.*, 2011c; Russell *et al.*, 2009a; Wong *et al.*, 2010). For example, among an ethnically diverse sample of young sexual minority men, homophobic discrimination was significantly associated with illicit drug use in the past three months (Wong *et al.*, 2010). More research is needed, however, to better understand their experiences as the literature is mixed in understanding their victimisation and resilience experiences.

Promoting resilience

The literature has elucidated several factors that promote resilience and buffer against the harmful effects of bullying for LGBTQ youth. Parent and peer support as well as positive school climates and resources consistently have been documented as protective factors. Additionally, school-based interventions and prevention programs are key factors to promote resilience.

Family and peer acceptance and support are critical for resilience among sexual minority youth. These are related to positive mental health and a positive sense of sexual orientation identity among LGBTQ youth and young adults (Anderson, 1998; Doty *et al.*, 2010; Hershberger and D'Augelli, 1995; Ryan *et al.*, 2009; Willoughby *et al.*, 2008). Family acceptance, affirming reactions to sexual minority youth's LGBT identity and connectedness all buffer against depression as well as suicidal ideation and attempts (Eisenberg and Resnick, 2006; Ryan *et al.*, 2010).

Family support not only promotes overall mental health but it also can buffer against the negative effects connected to homophobic victimisation. Parental support buffered against the effects of homophobic victimisation on depression and drug use for LGBTQ youth in one study (Espelage *et al.*, 2008). However, it did not buffer against the effects of homophobic victimisation on suicidality and school belonging for LGBTQ youth in another study (Poteat *et al.*, 2011b). The effects of parent support may themselves be dependent on a range of other factors. These factors could include whether LGBTQ youth are out to their parents or the extent to which parents feel equipped to provide support specific to homophobic bullying. Much greater attention is needed to identify how the positive effects of parent support can be magnified.

Positive school climates also buffer against the effects of homophobic victimisation for LGBTQ youth (Birkett *et al.*, 2009; Espelage *et al.*, 2008). In relation to this, sexual minority youth are less likely to report victimisation, suicidality and mental health concerns, and are more likely to report feeling safe at school when they attend schools with GSAs, anti-bullying and anti-harassment policies, supportive school staff and schools with clear and consistent rules and expectations (Goodenow *et al.*, 2006; Hatzenbuehler *et al.*, 2011; O'Shaughnessy *et al.*, 2004; Sandfort *et al.*, 2010).

School-based programmes are critical for addressing the insidious effects of homophobic victimisation. These can include providing school-based psychotherapy services, developing broader programmatic efforts (e.g. empowerment programmes, programmes that raise cultural sensitivity awareness, promote positive identity development or intergroup dialogues), and fostering interpersonal relationships that promote resilience (e.g. peer, family or teacher support). Furthermore, social justice efforts are critical in addressing homophobic bullying. These efforts include advocating for anti-bullying legislation and protective school policies, diversifying school curriculum to reduce the invisibility of sexual minority youth, as well as addressing and countering prejudice and stereotypes.

Current challenges and implications

The ongoing and harmful nature of homophobic bullying presents a number of challenges and implications for educators, policy advocates and practitioners. Further, the expansive nature of homophobic bullying underscores that approaches to address this serious concern must be taken at multiple levels that extend beyond the immediate individual or interpersonal level. In this final section, we note several issues related to social policy and programming.

Implications for anti-bullying policies and programming

As we noted previously, several efforts at the school level have included protective policies, inclusivity of LGBTQ issues within the curriculum, and support for GSAs and other school-based diversity resources. These efforts also extend beyond the school. For instance, most states have passed anti-bullying legislation. Although the content and intent of these policies vary significantly across states, often they stipulate requirements for schools to document and report bullying incidents and to develop approved procedures for addressing such incidents. Few of these policies specifically address the discriminatory and homophobic nature of bullying. Indeed, these policies are often contentious when they specify the protection of sexual minority youth. Whereas supporters of these policies view enumeration as a step toward raising awareness and reducing victimisation of those groups of youth who traditionally have been disproportionately victimised, opponents are either sceptical of its effectiveness or believe it infringes on religious and cultural beliefs (Horn, 2007; Nairn and Smith, 2003). Nevertheless, studies indicate that, at least among students, individuals are capable of separating their individual beliefs about sexual minorities from how they believe their LGBTQ peers at school should be treated (Horn *et al.*, 2008).

In general, school-based anti-bullying programmes have produced mixed results (Frey *et al.*, 2009; Merrell *et al.*, 2008; Vreeman and Carroll, 2007). This lack of strong or consistent outcomes may be expected due to the complexity of victimisation in schools as well as the variability in how consistently policies are enforced and the fidelity with which interventions are implemented. Alternatively, it may reflect the need for new approaches and techniques to address this issue. Regardless, most programmes do not give attention to diversity issues in their materials (Espelage and Poteat, 2012). At minimum, anti-bullying policies and programmes should ensure that diversity issues are represented and addressed, given the discriminatory nature that underlies many bullying experiences. In tandem, research should evaluate the potential added benefit of including such materials.

A focus on Gay–Straight Alliances in the USA

While school policies and general anti-bullying programs play a vital role in combating homophobic bullying, student-led organisations such as GSAs also have gained support as an effective resource that can serve as an intervention against homophobic bullying and homophobic school climates. Since the first GSA originated in Massachusetts in 1988, the number of GSAs has increased dramatically over the past two decades (GLSEN, 2011). GSAs provide a safe environment for LGBTQ and heterosexual students to discuss sexual orientation issues, to receive support from experiences of discrimination and to participate in advocacy work to address these issues at various systemic levels (Griffin *et al.*, 2004).

Inherent in the goals of GSAs is the inclusion of students of all sexual orientations. Notably, heterosexual youth also benefit from these groups (Szalacha, 2003). We suspect that their membership can provide opportunities for intergroup dialogue to foster mutual understanding. These positive intergroup relations may then extend beyond the GSA, as members can share their learned perspectives with non-GSA friends and their family in an effort to educate them on LGBTQ issues. Additional research is needed to test whether this process does indeed occur, and if so, what factors foster and promote this process.

GSAs exhibit benefits to both members and non-members of these groups. Student directly involved report positive peer socialisation and greater support (Griffin *et al.*, 2004). Membership also promotes youth empowerment and leadership through advocacy initiatives that address inequality (Russell *et al.*, 2009b). Additionally, the mere presence of GSAs in schools is associated with lower suicidality, truancy, drug use and sexual health risk behaviour (Poteat *et al.*, 2011a). This suggests that the preence of GSAs may benefit the entire school regardless of membership. Building on these findings, there is a continued need to examine conditions that may magnify the positive effects of GSAs, such as students' level of involvement in their GSA, GSA size or visibility, or how strongly school administrators support the GSA. Overall, GSAs have the potential to serve as a validating presence for LGBTQ and heterosexual youth and thus warrant our greater attention and support.

Concluding remarks

Many challenges remain in our ongoing efforts to counter homophobic bullying. Indeed, homophobic bullying, albeit particularly prominent and harmful to all students, constitutes one of many forms of bias-based bullying. This highlights an even broader need to address issues of prejudice and intergroup relations among children and adolescents that includes, but also extends beyond, anti-bullying efforts. Within this broader domain, many scholars have called attention to the importance of addressing stereotypes and prejudices earlier in development and prior to their reinforcement during adulthood (Bigler and Liben, 2006; Fishbein, 1996; Horn, 2006; Poteat, 2007). As we do so, we must expand the scope of our efforts to promote diversity-affirming attitudes and positive intergroup relations. This represents an important extension beyond the immediate reduction of bullying and prejudice. However, this represents an important and shared goal in both areas. Ultimately, it is one that should involve the combined efforts of educators, parents, those responsible for creating social policies, as well as researchers and practitioners across disciplines invested in promoting positive youth development.

References

Allport, G. W. (1954) *The Nature of Prejudice*, Cambridge, MA: Perseus Books.

Almeida, J., Johnson, R. M., Corliss, H. L., Molnar, B. E. and Azrael, D. (2009) 'Emotional distress among LGBT youth: the influence of perceived discrimination based on sexual orientation', *Journal of Youth and Adolescence*, 38: 1001–1014.

American Association of University Women. (2001) *Hostile Hallways: Bullying, Teasing, and Sexual Harassment in School*, Washington, DC: Author.

Anderson, A. L. (1998) 'Strengths of gay male youth: an untold story'. *Child and Adolescent Social Work Journal*, 15: 55–71.

Balsam, K. F., Huang, B., Fieland, K. C., Simoni, J. M. and Walters, K. L. (2004) 'Culture, trauma, and wellness: a comparison of heterosexual and lesbian, gay, bisexual, and two-spirit Native Americans', *Cultural Diversity and Ethnic Minority Psychology*, 10: 287–301.

Berlan, E.D., Corliss, H. L., Field, A. E., Goodman, E. and Austin, S. B. (2010) 'Sexual orientation and bullying among adolescents in the Growing Up Today study', *Journal of Adolescent Health*, 46: 366–371.

Bernat, J. A., Calhoun, K. S., Adams, H. E. and Zeichner, A. (2001) 'Homophobia and physical aggression toward homosexual and heterosexual individuals', *Journal of Abnormal Psychology*, 110: 179–187.

Bigler, R. S. and Liben, L. S (2006) 'A developmental intergroup theory of social stereotypes and prejudice', in K. Robert (ed.), *Advances in Child Development and Behavior*, San Diego, CA: Elsevier Academic Press.

Birkett, M., Espelage, D. L. and Koenig, B. (2009) 'LGB and questioning students in schools: the moderating effects of homophobic bullying and school climate on negative outcomes', *Journal of Youth and Adolescence*, 38: 989–1000.

Bontempo, D. E. and D'Augelli, A. R. (2002) 'Effects of at-school victimization and sexual orientation on lesbian, gay, or bisexual youths' health risk behavior', *Journal of Adolescent Health,* 30: 364–374.

Chesir-Teran, D. (2003) 'Conceptualizing and addressing heterosexism in high schools: a setting-level approach', *American Journal of Community Psychology*, 31: 269–279.

D'Augelli, A. R., Pilkington, N. W. and Hershberger, S. L. (2002) 'Incidence and mental health impact of sexual orientation victimization of lesbian, gay, and bisexual youths in high school', *School Psychology Quarterly*, 17: 148–167.

Doty, N. D., Willoughby, B. L. B., Lindahl, K. M. and Malik, N. M. (2010) 'Sexuality related social support among lesbian, gay, and bisexual youth', *Journal of Youth and Adolescence*, 39: 1134–1147.

Eder, D., Evans, C. C. and Parker, S. (1995) *School Talk: Gender and Adolescent Culture*, New Brunswick, NJ: Rutgers University Press.

Eisenberg, M. E. and Resnick, M. D. (2006). 'Suicidality among gay, lesbian and bisexual youth: the role of protective factors', *Journal of Adolescent Health*, 39: 662–668.

Epstein, D. (2001) 'Boyz' own stories: masculinities and sexualities in schools', in W. Martino and B. Meyenn (eds), *What About the Boys? Issues of Masculinity in Schools*, Philadelphia, PA: Open University Press.

Espelage, D. L., Aragon, S. R., Birkett, M. and Koenig, B. W. (2008) 'Homophobic teasing, psychological outcomes, and sexual orientation among high school students: what influence do parents and schools have?', *School Psychology Review,* 37: 202–216.

Espelage, D. L. and Poteat, V. P. (2012) 'Counseling psychologists in schools', in N. Fouad and L. Subich (eds), *APA Handbook of Counseling Psychology*, Washington, DC: American Psychological Association.

Fineran, S. (2002) 'Sexual harassment between same-sex peers: intersection of mental health, homophobia, and sexual violence in schools', *Social Work,* 47: 65–74.

Fishbein, H. D. (1996) *Peer Prejudice and Discrimination: Evolutionary, Cultural, and Developmental Dynamics*, Boulder, CO: Westview Press.

Fisher, C. B., Wallace, S. A. and Fenton, R. E. (2000) 'Discrimination distress during adolescence', *Journal of Youth and Adolescence*, 29: 679–695.

Flores, E., Tschann, J. M., Dimas, J. M., Pasch, L. A. and de Groat, C. L. (2010) 'Perceived racial/ethnic discrimination, posttraumatic stress symptoms, and health risk behaviors among Mexican American adolescents', *Journal of Counseling Psychology*, 57: 264–273.

Frey, K. S., Hirschstein, M. K, Edstrom, L. V. and Snell, J. L. (2009) 'Observed reductions in school bullying, nonbullying aggression, and destructive bystander behavior: a longitudinal evaluation', *Journal of Educational Psychology*, 101: 466–481.

Friedman, M. S., Koeske, G. F., Silvestre, A. J., Korr, W. S. and Sites, E. W. (2006) 'The impact of gender-role nonconforming behavior, bullying, and social support on suicidality among gay male youth', *Journal of Adolescent Health*, 38: 621–623.

Gay, Lesbian, and Straight Education Network (GLSEN) (2011) *Background and Information About Gay-Straight Alliances.* Available at: http://www.glsen.org/cgi-bin/iowa/all/library/record/2336.html (accessed 22 September 2011).

Goodenow, C., Szalacha, L. and Westheimer, K. (2006) 'School support groups, other school factors, and the safety of sexual minority adolescents', *Psychology in the Schools,* 43: 573–589.

Griffin, P., Lee, C., Waugh, J. and Beyer, C. (2004) 'Describing roles that Gay-Straight Alliances play in schools: from individual support to school change', *Journal of Gay and Lesbian Issues in Education,* 1: 7–22.

Grossman, A. H. and D'Augelli, A. R. (2006) 'Transgender youth: invisible and vulnerable', *Journal of Homosexuality,* 51: 111–128.

Grossman, J. M. and Liang, B. (2008) 'Discrimination distress among Chinese American adolescents', *Journal of Youth and Adolescence,* 37: 1–11.

Grov, C., Bimbi, D. S., Nanin, J. E. and Parson, J. T. (2006) 'Race, ethnicity, gender, and generational factors associated with the coming-out process among gay, lesbian, and bisexual individuals', *Journal of Sex Research,* 43: 115–121.

Hatzenbuehler, M. L., Wieringa, N. F. and Keyes, K. M. (2011) 'Community-level determinants of tobacco use disparities in lesbian, gay, and bisexual youth', *Archives of Pediatrics and Adolescent Medicine,* 165: 527–532.

Hawley, P. H. (1999) 'The ontogenesis of social dominance: a strategy-based evolutionary perspective', *Developmental Review,* 19: 97–132.

Hershberger, S. L. and D'Augelli, A. R. (1995) 'The impact of victimization on the mental health and suicidality of lesbian, gay, and bisexual youths', *Developmental Psychology,* 31: 65–74.

Hershberger, S. L., Pilkington, N. W. and D'Augelli, A. R. (1997) 'Predictors of suicide attempts among gay, lesbian, and bisexual youth', *Journal of Adolescent Research,* 12: 477–497.

Horn, S. S. (2006) 'Heterosexual adolescents' attitudes and beliefs about homosexuality and gay and lesbian peers', *Cognitive Development,* 21: 420–440.

Horn, S. S. (2007) 'Adolescents' acceptance of same-sex peers based on sexual orientation and gender expression', *Journal of Youth and Adolescence,* 36: 363–371.

Horn, S. S., Szalacha, L. A. and Drill, K. (2008) 'Schooling, sexuality, and rights: an investigation of heterosexual students' social cognition regarding sexual orientation and the rights of gay and lesbian peers in school', *Journal of Social Issues,* 64: 791–813.

Huebner, D. M., Rebchook, G. M. and Kegeles, S. M. (2004) 'Experiences of harassment, discrimination, and physical violence among young gay and bisexual men', *American Journal of Public Health,* 94: 1200–1203.

Juvonen, J., Nishina, A. and Graham, S. (2000) 'Peer harassment, psychological adjustment, and school functioning in early adolescence', *Journal of Educational Psychology,* 92: 349–359.

Kimmel, M. S. (1997) 'Masculinity as homophobia: fear, shame, and silence in the construction of gender identity', in M. M. Gergen and S. N. Davis (eds), *Toward a New Psychology of Gender,* Florence, KY: Taylor and Frances.

Korobov, N. B. (2004) 'Inoculating against prejudice: a discursive approach to homophobia and sexism in adolescent male talk', *Psychology of Men and Masculinity,* 5: 178–189.

Kosciw, J. G., Greytak, E. A., Diaz, E. M. and Bartkiewicz, M. J. (2010). *The 2009 National School Climate Survey: The Experiences of Lesbian, Gay, Bisexual and Transgender Youth in our Nation's Schools,* New York: GLSEN.

Merrell, K. W., Gueldner, B. A., Ross, S. W. and Isava, D. M. (2008) 'How effective are school bullying intervention programs? A meta-analysis of intervention research', *School Psychology Quarterly*, 23: 26–42.

Meyer, I. (2003) 'Prejudice, social stress, and mental health in lesbian, gay, and bisexual populations: conceptual issues and research evidence', *Psychological Bulletin*, 129: 674–697.

Nairn, K. and Smith, A. B. (2003) 'Taking students seriously: their rights to be safe at school', *Gender and Education*, 15: 133-149.

O' Shaughnessy, M., Russell, S., Heck, K., Calhoun, C. and Laub, C. (2004) *Consequences of Harassment Based on Actual or Perceived Sexual Orientation and Gender Non-Conformity and Steps for Making schools Safer*, California Schools Coalition and 4-H Center for Youth Development, University of California.

Parrott, D. J., Adams, H. E. and Zeichner, A. (2002) 'Homophobia: personality and attitudinal correlates', *Personality and Individual Differences*, 32: 1269–1278.

Pascoe, C. J. (2007) *'Dude, You're a Fag': Masculinity and Sexuality in High School*, Los Angeles, CA: University of California Press.

Pellegrini, A. D. and Long, J. (2002) 'A longitudinal study of bullying, dominance, and victimization during the transition from primary to secondary school', *British Journal of Developmental Psychology*, 20: 259–280.

Perreira, K. M., Fuligni, A. and Potochnick, S. (2010) 'Fitting in: the roles of social acceptance and discrimination in shaping the academic motivations of Latino youth in the U.S. Southeast', *Journal of Social Issues*, 66: 131–153.

Pettigrew, T. F. and Tropp, L. R. (2006) 'A meta-analytic test of intergroup contact theory', *Journal of Personality and Social Psychology*, 90: 751–783.

Phoenix, A., Frosh, S. and Pattman, R. (2003) 'Producing contradictory masculine subject positions: narratives of threat, homophobia, and bullying in 11–14 year old boys', *Journal of Social Issues*, 59: 179–195.

Pilkington, N. W. and D'Augelli, A. R. (1995) 'Victimization of lesbian, gay, and bisexual youth in community settings', *Journal of Community Psychology*, 23: 34–56.

Pleck, J. H., Sonenstein, F. L. and Ku, L. C. (1994) 'Attitudes toward male roles among adolescent males: a discriminant validity analysis', *Sex Roles*, 30: 481–501.

Plummer, D. C. (2001) 'The quest for modern manhood: masculine stereotypes, peer culture and the social significance of homophobia', *Journal of Adolescence*, 24: 15–23.

Poteat, V. P. (2007) 'Peer group socialization of homophobic attitudes and behavior during adolescence', *Child Development*, 78: 1830–1842.

Poteat, V. P. (2008) 'Contextual and moderating effects of the peer group climate on use of homophobic epithets', *School Psychology Review*, 37: 188–201.

Poteat, V. P. and DiGiovanni, C. D. (2010) 'When biased language use is associated with bullying and dominance: the moderating effect of prejudice', *Journal of Youth and Adolescence*, 39: 1123–1133.

Poteat, V. P. and Espelage, D. L. (2005) 'Exploring the relation between bullying and homophobic verbal content: the Homophobic Content Agent Target (HCAT) Scale', *Violence and Victims*, 20: 513–528.

Poteat, V. P. and Espelage, D. L. (2007) 'Predicting psychosocial consequences of homophobic victimization in middle school students', *Journal of Early Adolescence*, 27: 175–191.

Poteat, V. P. and Rivers, I. (2010) 'The use of homophobic language across bullying roles during adolescence', *Journal of Applied Developmental Psychology*, 31: 166–172.

Poteat, V. P., Aragon, S. R., Espelage, D. L. and Koenig, B. W. (2009) 'Psychosocial concerns of sexual minority youth: complexity and caution in group differences', *Journal of Consulting and Clinical Psychology*, 77: 196–201.

Poteat, V. P., Kimmel, M. S. and Wilchins, R. (2011b) 'The moderating effects of support for violence beliefs on masculine norms, aggression, and homophobic behavior during adolescence', *Journal of Research on Adolescence*, 21: 434–447.

Poteat, V. P., Mereish, E. H., DiGiovanni, C. D. and Koenig, B. W. (2011a) 'The effects of general and homophobic victimization on adolescents' psychosocial and educational concerns: The importance of intersecting identities and parent support', *Journal of Counseling Psychology*, 58, 597–609.

Poteat, V. P., O'Dwyer, L. M. and Mereish, E. H. (2011c). 'Changes in how students use and are called homophobic epithets over time: Patterns predicted by gender, bullying, and victimization status', *Journal of Educational Psychology*, 104, 393–406.

Rigby, K. (2000) 'Effects of peer victimization in schools and perceived social support on adolescent well-being', *Journal of Adolescence*, 23: 57–68.

Rivers, I. (2000) 'Social exclusion, absenteeism, and sexual minority youth', *Support for Learning*, 15: 13–18.

Rivers, I. (2001) 'The bullying of sexual minorities at school: its nature and long-term correlates', *Educational and Child Psychology*, 18: 32–46.

Rivers, I. (2004) 'Recollections of bullying at school and their long-term implications for lesbians, gay men, and bisexuals', *Crisis: The Journal of Crisis Intervention and Suicide Prevention*, 25: 169–175.

Rosario, M., Schrimshaw, E. W. and Hunter, J. (2004) 'Ethnic/racial differences in the coming-out process of lesbian, gay, and bisexual youths: a comparison of sexual identity development over time', *Cultural Diversity and Ethnic Minority Psychology*, 10: 215–228.

Rose, C. A., Espelage, D. L. and Monda-Amaya, L. E. (2009) 'Bullying and victimization rates among students in general and special education: a comparative analysis', *Educational Psychology*, 29: 761–776.

Rosenbloom, S. R. and Way, N. (2004) 'Experiences of discrimination among African American, Asian American, and Latino adolescents in an urban high school', *Youth & Society*, 35: 420–451.

Russell, S. T., Clarke, T. J. and Laub, C. (2009a) *Multiple forms of bias-related harassment at school* (California Safe Schools Coalition Research Brief No. 8). San Francisco, CA: California Safe Schools Coalition.

Russell, S. T., Muraco, A., Subramaniam, A. and Laub, C. (2009b) 'Youth empowerment and high school gay-straight alliances', *Journal of Youth and Adolescence*, 38: 891–903.

Russell, S. T., Sinclair, K. O., Poteat, V. P. and Koenig, B. W. (in press) 'Adolescent health and harassment based on discriminatory bias', *American Journal of Public Health*.

Ryan, C., Huebner, D., Diaz, R. M. and Sanchez, J. (2009) 'Family rejection as a predictor of negative health outcomes in White and Latino lesbian, gay, and bisexual young adults', *Pediatrics*, 123: 346–352.

Ryan, C., Russell, S. T., Huebner, D., Diaz, R. and Sanchez, J. (2010) 'Family acceptance in adolescence and the health of LGBT young adults', *Journal of Child and Adolescent Psychiatric Nursing*, 23: 205–213.

Sandfort, T. G., Bos, H. M., Collier, K. L. and Metselaar, M. (2010) 'School environment and the mental health of sexual minority youths: a study among Dutch young adolescents', *American Journal of Public Health*, 100: 1696–1700.

Schwartz, D., Gorman, A. H., Nakamoto, J. and Toblin, R. L. (2005) 'Victimization in the peer group and children's academic functioning', *Journal of Educational Psychology*, 97: 425–435.

Stein, N. (1995) 'Sexual harassment in school: the public performance of gendered violence', *Harvard Educational Review*, 65: 145–162.

Swearer, S. M., Turner, R. K., Givens, J. E. and Pollack, W. S. (2008) '"You're so gay!" Do different forms of bullying matter for adolescent males?' *School Psychology Review*, 37: 160–173.

Szalacha, L. A. (2003) 'Safer sexual diversity climates: lessons learned from an evaluation of Massachusetts Safe Schools Program for gay and lesbian students', *American Journal of Education*, 110: 58–88.

Vreeman, R. C. and Carroll, A. E. (2007) 'A systematic review of school-based interventions to prevent bullying', *Archives of Pediatrics and Adolescent Medicine*, 161: 78–77.

Williams, T., Connolly, J., Pepler, D. and Craig, W. (2005) 'Peer victimization, social support, and psychosocial adjustment of sexual minority adolescents', *Journal of Youth and Adolescence*, 34: 471–482.

Willoughby, B. L., Doty, N. D. and Malik, N. M. (2008) 'Parental reactions to their child's sexual orientation disclosure: A family stress perspective', *Parenting: Science and Practice*, 8: 70–91.

Wong, C. F., Weiss, G., Ayala, G. and Kipke, M. D. (2010) 'Harassment, discrimination, violence, and illicit drug use among young men who have sex with men', *Aids Education and Prevention*, 22: 286–298.

8 Mapping the boundaries of homophobic language in bullying

Mark McCormack

Introduction

A large body of research documents how homophobia has traditionally pervaded educational institutions (Epstein *et al.*, 2003; Rivers 2011), and that one of the key mechanisms by which this occurs is through the use of homophobic language (Ellis and High 2004; Plummer 1999). Through this 'anti-gay' abuse, lesbian, gay, bisexual, trans and questioning/queer (LGBTQ) students have been the victims of social marginalisation and bullying (D'Augelli *et al.*, 2002; Rivers, 2001; Warwick *et al.*, 2001). It is perhaps unsurprising, therefore, that research documents fewer LGBTQ youth continue into further and higher education (college and university) compared to their heterosexual peers and that these students also have elevated levels of absenteeism (Ryan and Rivers 2003; Wilkinson and Pearson, 2009).

However, a central component of understanding the use of homophobic language is the recognition that it is not only directed that those who are LGBTQ. It is also targeted at those who *are perceived* to be LGBTQ (in particular), but also includes those boys who do not 'measure up'. Indeed, scholarship on masculinities has highlighted the centrality of homophobia in the construction of masculinities in general (Anderson, 2009; Kimmel, 1994; Richardson, 2010). Heterosexual male students have been shown to use homophobic language and proclaim anti-gay attitudes as a way of demonstrating their own heterosexuality; something required in order to avoid the stigma of homosexuality (Connell, 1995; Epstein, 1997). The violence, aggression and emotional illiteracy of heterosexual boys and men has been attributed to the fear of being thought 'gay' (Anderson, 2009; Mac an Ghaill, 1994; McCormack, 2012). Furthermore, while homophobia has regulated both boys and girls (Duncan, 1999; Epstein *et al.*, 2003), it has been most instrumental in policing acceptable forms of masculinity (Connell, 1995; Plummer, 1999).

Recent years have seen an increased awareness of the deleterious effects of homophobic language, both in academia (see Rivers, 2011) and in the broader culture (Cowan, 2007). And while this cultural consciousness of the problem of homophobia in schools may be most evident in the UK, there are increasing attempts to combat this social issue in the USA as well (Miceli, 2005; Russell *et al.*, 2009). In addition to the successful campaigning of gay rights groups in both countries (most notably *Stonewall* in the UK and *GLSEN* in the USA), this is also attributable to a decrease in homophobia in the wider culture as evidenced by both qualitative and quantitative studies (Anderson, 2009; Savin-Williams, 2005; Pryor *et al.*, 2011; Weeks, 2007).

In this chapter, I contextualise the use of homophobic language as part of a broader use of language; what I call 'homosexually themed language' (see McCormack, 2011a). While homophobic language must be combatted where it persists, I also argue that the use of words such as 'gay' and 'fag' are not necessarily homophobic: thist depends on how they are used, with what intent, and how such language is interpreted. I further argue that such language may privilege heterosexuality without necessarily being homophobic, but that it can also be used to bond heterosexual and gay students together. The model of language I provide should enable academics, educators and parents to better understand the changing meanings of language, and therefore be in a better position to educate young people about the negative effects of such language when they are present.

Homphobic language

Although a multitude of social forces construct and regulate hierarchies of gender and sexuality, language is central in their re/production (Cameron and Kulick, 2003; Kiesling, 2007). Foucault (1979) argued that discourse 'literally' creates the rules and identities by which we live, suggesting that people inhabit the 'real world', but that their experience, thoughts and desires can only be understood through the discursive tools available to them. The use of language therefore has a direct and material effect on peoples' identities and lives. Social constructionist scholars of gender have supported this view. They examine how discourse works in the regulation of masculinities (Anderson, 2002; Plummer, 1999), and how homophobic discourse reflects and reproduces homophobia among its users (Burn, 2000).

While a diverse body of literature exists on the topic (McCormack and Anderson, 2010a; Pascoe, 2007; Rasmussen, 2004), understanding and debate about the use of homosexually-themed language in academic, media and educational circles remains all-too-frequently based on a simplistic conceptualisation of whether language is or is not homophobic. This can lead to an exaggeration of the prevalence of homophobia because many people have been brought up in a culture where almost all colloquial language relating to homosexuality has been homophobic; increasing the perception that homophobia exists in language regardless of the context in which a word or phrase is uttered. This is problematic because fear of homophobia (even when this fear is unwarranted) can cause gay people to stay hidden (Anderson, 2002).

In order to clarify what makes language homophobic, I argue that the literature documents two requisite features: 1) it is said with pernicious intent; and 2) it has a negative social effect. The first requirement of homophobic language – pernicious intent – recognises that the speaker is intending to degrade or marginalise a person or behaviour by using a word or phrase that has an association with homosexuality. Thurlow (2001) highlighted the use of intent by examining *intensifiers* or words in a phrase that evidence a desire to wound a person (e.g. saying 'you fucking queer' rather than 'you queer'). Thurlow found that homophobic language was accompanied by intensifiers more frequently than any other form of insult. Further evidence of the mal-intent of homophobic language is provided by considering its role in bullying. Rivers (1996) found that verbal abuse was the most common form of bullying practice levelled at lesbians, gay men and bisexuals (LGBs), and that homophobic language has also been frequently used by bullies of heterosexual students (Epstein, 1997).

Bullying also evidences the second component of homophobic language: that it maintains negative social effect. Gay and lesbian adults often speak of the emotional trauma caused by homophobic bullying in their youth (Flowers and Buston, 2001; Plummer, 1999) and research also highlights the socio-negative impact this has on students: this includes elevated rates of absenteeism, social isolation and higher drop-out rates in school (Warwick *et al.*, 2001). Furthermore, homophobic bullying has led to elevated levels of suicide among LGB youth (D'Augelli *et al.*, 2001), although more recent research suggests that LGBTQ suicide rates are in fact comparable to urban heterosexual young people (Mustanski *et al.*, 2010).

Even when homophobic language is intended to marginalise a behaviour or action rather than a person, it still reproduces homophobia because users intend to stigmatise same-sex desire (Hillier and Harrison, 2004; Rubin, 1984). For example, using explicitly anti-gay epithets to regulate heterosexual student-athletes who do not conform to orthodox gender stereotypes reproduces the hierarchical stratification of all masculinities, as well as harming the recipient of the abuse. Accordingly, homophobic language can contribute to a hostile educational culture for all youth (Hekma, 1998; Vicars, 2006).

While pernicious intent and negative social effect are the two key factors that have been used to determine if language is homophobic or not, implicit in most of the academic research is an assumption that this homophobic language is said within a homophobic environment. That is, homophobic language has occurred in schools where students have homophobic attitudes and gay students are 'closeted' or marginalised. Some scholars have documented the homophobic culture (Mac an Ghaill, 1994), while others assumed its presence (Thurlow, 2001).

The assumption of a homophobic environment is understandable given that the vast majority of the research on homophobic language occurred between 1980 and 2000, when UK and US cultures were to all intents and purposes overtly homophobic (Anderson, 2009; Loftus, 2001). Yet the marked decrease in levels of homophobia of recent years necessitates that this assumption be made explicit and for the cultural context to be recognised. Accordingly, I propose an additional factor for analysing homophobic language – namely that of a homophobic environment. In Figure 8.1 I provide a pictorial framework for understanding the components of homophobic language.

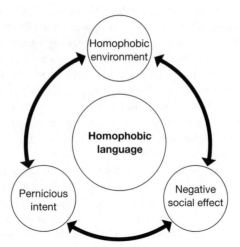

Figure 8.1 The traditional framework for understanding homophobic language.

This linking of environment with effect and intent helps to historically contextualise the conceptualisation of homophobic language that so accurately captured the social dynamics of the 1980s and 1990s (see Phoenix *et al.*, 2003). However, more recent research on the use of homosexually-themed language has highlighted complexities which do not readily fit into this framework of homophobic language.

The changing use of language

In 2005, C. J. Pascoe introduced the concept of 'fag discourse' into discussions of homophobic language. Building on Thorne and Luria's (1986) earlier notion of 'fag talk', fag discourse conceptualised a sexualised form of gender regulation. Here, the purpose was not necessarily to regulate sexuality, but instead to regulate boys' behaviours (and the word 'fag' was primarily aimed at boys). Importantly, Pascoe distinguished the use of the word fag from the use of anti-gay pejoratives such as 'queer' and 'poof' because fag no longer had explicit associations with sexuality for many of the participants in her study.

While the observation about the gendered nature of homophobia built on the work of British scholars of masculinity (Epstein, 1997; Mac an Ghaill, 1994), an important difference was that Pascoe (2005, 2007) documented the ways in which fag was used as a pernicious insult that regulated gender without intending to marginalise same-sex identities. For example, Pascoe (2005) highlighted that, 'some boys took pains to say that "fag" is not about sexuality' (p. 336).

Pascoe (2007) also highlighted that the intent was not necessarily pernicious. She commented that 'fag talk and fag imitations serve as a discourse with which boys discipline themselves and each other through joking relationships' (p. 54). This makes the notion of intent far more complex than with overtly homophobic language. While there is always intent within fag discourse to regulate something – be it sexuality or gender, a person or a behaviour – the precise intention varies. For example, it can be used to wound someone, but it can also be used to castigate a behaviour or even just competitively joke with friends. Indeed, the use of the word fag seems almost habitual or a 'compulsive' (p. 86) part of boys' interactions.

While Pascoe's work does have evidence for decreasing homophobia, it can be read as arguing that high levels of homophobia persisted in the school where she completed her ethnography. This is why, I suggest, most academics failed to appreciate the significance of her work in documenting the changing nature of homosexually-themed language. Because pernicious intent was still sometimes evident, and because the social effect was often extremely negative, researchers overlooked the changes in the use of language that fag discourse conceptualises. Accordingly, despite the subtle changes in intent and effect, scholars continued to label fag discourse as part of the traditional framework of homophobic language (Bortolin, 2010; Kimmel, 2008). While this is appropriate for research conducted in the 1980s and 1990s when the word fag was used to demonstrate disgust of homosexuality, in a broader culture of extreme homophobia, it does not accurately capture use of the word in a different cultural context (see Figure 8.2).

It is easy to read high levels of homophobia in the school where Pascoe (2005) collected data, yet there were also several openly gay students, as well as heterosexual students who maintained pro-gay attitudes. Indeed, Pascoe (2007) also documented that many students elected not to use homophobic language or fag discourse. She wrote, 'I was stunned at the myriad opportunities to levy the epithet and the seeming refusal by these boys, gay and straight, to invoke it' (p. 79). This is something not documented in previous research (see Mac an Ghaill, 1994) and in this context is likely to be illustrative of a less homophobic environment.

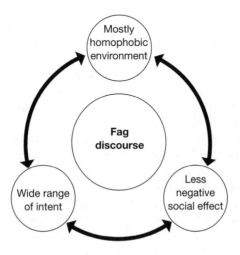

Figure 8.2 A framework for understanding fag discourse.

Pascoe's work has not been the final development in understanding homosexually-themed language. This is because homophobia has continued to decrease since Pascoe's study (McCormack, 2012; Weeks, 2007). While many researchers acknowledge this (Swain, 2006), my own research examined how homosexually-themed language operates in a pro-gay environment (McCormack and Anderson, 2010a; McCormack, 2011a). In an attempt to address this lack of engagement with changing cultural attitudes and working collaboratively with Eric Anderson, I sought to understand how the effect of homosexually-themed language varied according to the social context (McCormack and Anderson, 2010a). We developed the concept of 'gay discourse' to understand the use of language that had a homosexual theme but was not homophobic as described by the framework above. This concept emerged from our ethnographic data with heterosexual rugby players who espoused pro-gay attitudes and had openly gay friends but nonetheless used phrases like 'don't be gay' and 'that's so gay'. They asserted that this position was consistent because gay had two meanings: (1) it referred to sexuality in some contexts and (2) it meant 'rubbish' in others (see Lalor and Rendle-Short, 2007). The rugby players also argued that the two meanings were wholly independent of each other.

While some scholars continue to argue that the phrase 'that's so gay' is homophobic in a period of decreasing cultural homophobia (see DePalma and Jennett, 2010; Sanders, 2008) they tend to do this without critical investigation of the attitudes of those using the language. As a result, they may misattribute a phrase as homophobic because they do not engage with those they study or fully understand their attitudes toward homosexuality (Adams *et al.*, 2010 and Lalor and Rendle-Short, 2007, can be viewed as notable exceptions).

In our rugby research, Anderson and I explained this use of language by viewing the phenomenon through Ogburn's (1950) lens of 'cultural lag'. Cultural lag occurs when two related social variables become dissociated because their meanings change at different rates. In this case, young people employ this language without consideration of or even knowledge about its previous use. In other words, the language of the rugby players in our study fell behind their pro-gay attitudes. Accordingly, we felt the need to develop a new way of understanding their language; one that did not position the participants as implicitly homophobic. Our concept – gay discourse – ameliorated this issue by arguing that while implicitly privileging heterosexuality, the language did not have the negative social effects of either homophobic language or fag discourse. Figure 8.3 conceptualises this in a way that draws out the difference from homophobic language. With a more inclusive environment and an absence of pernicious intent, the social effects of this language are far less negative.

This framework was useful in understanding the dynamics and implications of a phrase such as 'that's so gay'. In order to understand the limited extent of this negative effect, it is important to recognise that the word gay has been used as an expression of displeasure without intent to reflect or transmit homophobia in many contemporary youth settings (Adams *et al.*, 2010; Lalor and

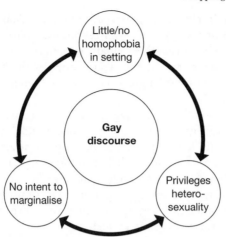

Figure 8.3 A new framework for understanding gay discourse.

Rendle-Short, 2007; McCormack and Anderson, 2010b; McCormack 2011b). Thus, when young people hear the phrase 'that's so gay' they do not automatically associate it with homosexuality. Furthermore, it is not necessarily the case that the expression of dissatisfaction translates to negative feelings about same-sex desires or LGBTQ people.

'Pro-gay' language

While gay discourse is a powerful concept to understand use the prevalence of 'that's so gay' and other similar phrases, it is less effective in explaining another use of homosexually-themed language. In our study of rugby players (McCormack and Anderson, 2010a) many of the players used homosexually-themed language as a form of social bonding. In greeting one another, they would often say, 'hey gay boy', or 'hey sister', with such language used between friends in a welcoming manner. And, we argued, that this continued to privilege heterosexuality. Unfortunately, we observed that we were falling back on the same assumptions of context that we accused others of doing in labelling 'that's so gay' as homophobic – a position that was aided by the fact that there were no openly gay athletes to judge this use of language.

In a more recent study (McCormack, 2012), I conceptualised 'pro-gay language' as a way of understanding homosexually-themed language which has a *positive* social effect. I defined it as, 'the use of homosexually-themed language that is used to bond people together in socio-positive ways or to demonstrate pro-gay attitudes'. In research in sixth forms (16–18 years) in the UK, I documented that both gay and straight male students used pro-gay discourse as a way of bonding. One example of this occurred in an English lesson, when openly gay student, Max, was working with his heterosexual friends, Cooper and James. While Cooper was doodling in his book, he looked up and asked John, 'Is this really gay what I'm doing?' Max started laughing, and said, 'Yeah, it's pretty gay.' This was just one example of pro-gay discourse not only bonding students together, but also expunging some of the negativity from these words. Interestingly, this again supports the heterosexual rugby players' contention that their language use was not homophobic (McCormack and Anderson, 2010a).

A second form of pro-gay language was also documented – one where heterosexual male students casually call their close friends 'lover' or 'boyfriend'. Students enacted this language out of homosocial affection, without any discernible attempt to consolidate their heterosexual standing. Proclaiming close friends as 'boyfriends' was understood by the students as a way of demonstrating emotional intimacy. Importantly, these students did not think that labeling each other this way would 'homosexualise' them. The ability for boys to express their emotions in such an open way is clearly a positive development. Moreover, just as homophobic language once contributed to a homophobic school environment, this form of pro-gay language now helps promote gay friendly cultures of inclusivity.

A model of homosexually-themed discourse

In this section, I present an empirically-grounded model for conceptualising all forms of homosexually-themed language (see McCormack 2011a). To highlight the differences in meaning and effect, 'gay discourse' is conceptualised as distinct from 'homophobic language'. As noted previously, homophobic language is well documented in the academic literature (Plummer, 1999), and is defined by pernicious intent, a homophobic environment and having negative social effect. In contrast, gay discourse lacks any intent to marginalise or wound and as a result has little if any negative social effect. However, some scholars may argue that it continues to promote heteronormativity.

In addition to the use of gay discourse, I also discussed male students using homosexually themed language in ways that have a socio-positive effect, calling this 'pro-gay language'. First, this form of language was used as a way of bonding heterosexual and gay students. Second, it was used by heterosexual friends as a way of demonstrating their emotional intimacy. Neither of these forms of pro-gay language were accompanied by homophobia, and it always occurred in gay friendly settings.

In the following new model of homosexually themed language, the importance of the cultural context in understanding language comes to the fore. This is because the social environment is pivotal in discerning the intent of language, how it is interpreted and the social effects it has. Thus, no phrase is necessarily part of a particular category. For example, a few years ago, if a 'closeted' young man heard the phrase 'that's so gay' at school frequently, it more than likely confirmed the safety of staying 'in the closet' because the phrase was interpreted as deeply homophobic, and thus resulted in a negative emotional response. This would be particularly the case if that the phrase was heard alongside homophobic pejoratives such as 'poof', 'shirtlifter' and 'bender'. However students attending the sixth forms where I conducted my ethnographic research heard the same phrase differently (McCormack, 2012). Today, 'that's so gay' is not necessarily homophobic, nor does it have to be part of pro-gay language, and the categorisation of language will depend on the cultural context. In order to explore the importance of context in more depth, Anderson's (2009) concept of homohysteria was used (see Chapter 10 of this book).

Briefly, homohysteria is defined as the cultural fear of being 'homosexualised'. Two key factors affect the level of homohysteria: (1) the homophobia with a culture; and (2) the awareness that any member of the population can be gay. Anderson (2009) argues that as homohysteria declines, boys no longer care about being socially perceived as gay and they are afforded a greater range of gendered behaviours. In this contexnt, homohysteria is a useful concept here because it explains how homophobia is central to constructions of masculinity in particular historical times and social contexts.

Relating the model to homohysteria

In Figure 8.4, cultural context is central to understanding and categorising types of homosexually-themed language. First, in cultures or subcultures with high levels of homohysteria, boys use homophobic language to consolidate their own heterosexual identity and masculine standing (see Plummer, 1999). In this stage, homosexually-themed language is indeed homophobic, as it is used with pernicious intent and has a very negative social effect.

The second framework – fag discourse – occurs in settings where there is less homohysteria. Here, it is likely that many gay people have negative educational experiences, and the setting is homophobic; but it is also likely that there will be people who support gay rights. In this stage, some young men who use fag discourse will insist that it is not meant to stigmatise homosexuality, while others will use it with pernicious intent. It will continue to have negative social effects, however, including the regulation and restriction of acceptable masculine behaviours, because the intent of language use is not always clear (Anderson, 2002).

In the third framework gay discourse occurs in settings where young men are not particularly concerned about whether they are socially perceived as gay. In these settings of low homohysteria, boys say phrases like 'that's so gay' as expressions of dissatisfaction and frustration. Importantly, there is no intent to marginalise or wound people with this use of language. And while this is not necessarily pro-gay, young men maintain that the word gay does not connote same-sex desire in this context.

Finally, in gay-friendly cultures such as the sixth forms where I conducted my research, the young men with whom I worked were not part of a homohysteric culture. While they might have preferred to be thought heterosexual,

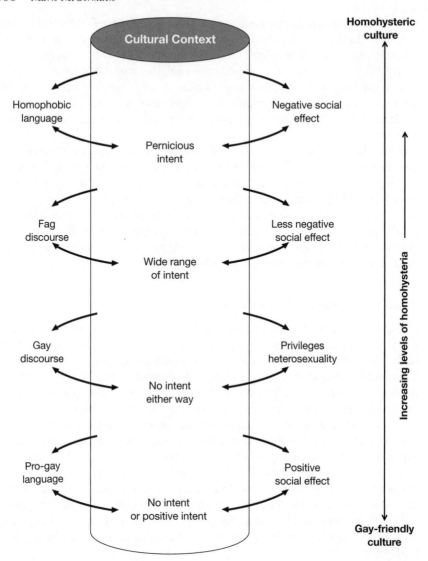

Figure 8.4 A model for homosexually-themed language.

they did not police their behaviours to live up to a heteromasculine ideal. Here, homosexually-themed language was used in a way that had positive social effects. Sometimes pro-gay language was said without any specific intention, but it was also used as a mechanism for bonding by demonstrating emotional intimacy or inclusion of openly gay students.

It is worth emphasising that use of language is always complex and tricky. There will be some overlap between types of language, as well as exceptions to the framework. For example, while a person can use homophobic language in a gay friendly setting, this would be an anomalous result and would not fit with general conceptualisations of homophobic language in the wider literature. For example, if a student were to shout 'you fucking poof' at another boy on a gay-friendly sports team, it is highly likely that the athlete would be reprimanded by his fellow teammates and his coach; and apart from the impact it would have on the recipient, it would be unlikely if it had any negative social effect on the broader culture. Likewise, saying 'that's so gay' in a highly homophobic setting would probably be interpreted as homophobic, while it would not in a gay friendly one. In understanding this form of language, context is all-important (see Davies, 1999; McCormack and Anderson, 2010a).

It should also be noted that Figure 8.4 does not provide an exhaustive list of words or phrases with a homosexual theme. I suggest that this would be impossible to do as language is constantly changing. It does, however, provide a framework by which to judge other forms of language. One example of this is the phrase 'no homo'. 'No homo' is used when men transgress traditional heteromasculine boundaries as a way of consolidating their heterosexual identities – defined as 'heterosexual recuperation' (see McCormack and Anderson, 2010b). In Figure 8.4, 'no homo' is akin to gay discourse. There is no actual intent to stigmatise feminine behaviours or homosexuality; there is just recognition that a particular behaviour might code a person as gay. One could argue whether it is homosexually-themed at all; that it is not instead just a statement of one's own heterosexuality (McCormack, 2011a). While 'no homo' privileges heterosexuality, and quite possibly regulates gender somewhat, it is hard to see it as necessarily homophobic. Accordingly, this model may be used as a framework to understand new manifestations of homosexually-themed language as they arise.

Concluding remarks

In this chapter, I have attempted to map out the changing dynamics of how young people use homosexually themed language today. This chapter is driven from an underlying dissatisfaction with how the existing literature misconceptualises certain types of language as homophobic. I have been spurred on to talking to the young people in my research, and trainee teachers with whom I currently work because they do not recognise 'that's so gay' as homophobic, and realise that their understandings are at odds with the dominant discourse. For trainee teachers, strategies such as telling students not to say 'that's so gay' are not working. This chapter goes some of the way to explaining why this might be the case, and it is important or anyone working with young people to recognise the nuance within homosexually-themed language. Without question, it is vital that we all condemn homophobia and find ways to stamp it out, but it may be counterproductive to do the same with gay language and pro-gay language. We should, instead, view these instances as learning experiences both for ourselves and the young people with whom we work.

References

Adams, A., Anderson, E. and McCormack, M. (2010) 'Establishing and challenging masculinity: the influence of gendered discourses in organized sport', *Journal of Language and Social Psychology*, 29: 278–300.

Anderson, E. (2002) 'Openly gay athletes: contesting hegemonic masculinity in a homophobic environment', *Gender & Society*, 16: 860–877.

Anderson, E. (2009) *Inclusive Masculinity: The Changing Nature of Masculinities*, New York: Routledge.

Bortolin, S. (2010) '"I don't want him hitting on me": the role of masculinities in creating a chilly high school climate', *Journal of LGBT Youth*, 7: 200–223.

Burn, S.M. (2000) 'Heterosexuals' use of "fag" and "queer" to deride one another', *Journal of Homosexuality*, 40: 1–11.

Cameron, D. and Kulick, D. (2003) *Language and Sexuality*, Cambridge: Cambridge University Press.

Connell, R. W. (1995) *Masculinities*, London: Polity.

Cowan, R. (2007) *Living Together: British Attitudes to Lesbian and Gay People*, London: Stonewall.

D'Augelli, A., Hersheberger, S.L. and Pilkington, N.W. (2001) 'Suicidality patterns and sexual orientation-related factors among lesbian, gay, and bisexual youths', *Suicide and Life-Threatening Behavior*, 31: 250–264.

D'Augelli, A. R., Pilkington, N. W. and Hershberger, S. L. (2002), 'Incidence and mental health impact of sexual orientation victimization of lesbian, gay, and bisexual youths in high school', *School Psychology Quarterly*, 17, 148–167.

Davies, C. (1999) *Reflexive Ethnography*, London: Routledge.

DePalma, R. and Jennett, M. (2010) 'Homophobia, transphobia and culture: deconstructing heteronormativity in English primary schools', *Intercultural Education*, 21: 15–26.

Duncan, N. (1999) *Sexual Bullying: Gender Conflict in Pupil Culture*, London: Routledge.

Ellis, V. and High, S. (2004) 'Something more to tell you: gay, lesbian or bisexual young people's experience of secondary schooling', *British Educational Research Journal*, 30: 213–225.

Epstein, D. (1997) 'Boyz' own stories: masculinities and sexualities in schools', *Gender and Education*, 9: 105–115.

Epstein, D., O'Flynn, S. and Telford, D. (2003) *Silenced Sexualities in Schools and Universities*, Stoke-on-Trent: Trentham Press.

Flowers, P. and Buston, K. (2001) '"I was terrified of being different": exploring gay men's accounts of growing-up in a heterosexist society', *Journal of Adolescence*, 24: 51–65.

Foucault, M. (1979) *The History of Sexuality: Volume 1*, London: Penguin.

Hekma, G. (1998) '"As long as they don't make an issue of it…": gay men and lesbians in organized sports in the Netherlands', *Journal of Homosexuality*, 35: 1–23.

Hillier, L. and Harrison, L. (2004) 'Homophobia and the production of shame: young people and same-sex attraction', *Culture, Health & Sexuality*, 6: 79–94.

Kiesling, S. F. (2007) 'Men, masculinities, and language', *Language and Linguistics Compass*, 1: 653–673.

Kimmel, M. S. (1994) 'Masculinity as homophobia: fear, shame, and silence in the construction of gender identity', in H. Brod & M. Kaufman (eds), *Theorising Masculinities*, London: Sage.

Kimmel, M. S. (2008) *Guyland: The Perilous World Where Boys become Men*, New York: Harper Collins.

Lalor, T. and Rendle-Short, J. (2007) '"That's so gay": a contemporary use of *gay* in Australian English', *Australian Journal of Linguistics*, 27: 147–173.

Loftus, J. (2001) 'America's liberalization in attitudes towards homosexuality, 1973–1998', *American Sociological Review*, 66: 762–782.

Mac an Ghaill, M. (1994) *The Making of Men: Masculinities, Sexualities and Schooling*, Buckingham: Open University Press.

McCormack, M. (2011a) 'Mapping the terrain of homosexually-themed language', *Journal of Homosexuality*, 58: 664–679.

McCormack, M. (2011b) 'The declining significance of homohysteria for male students in three sixth forms in the south of England', *British Educational Research Journal,* 37: 337–353.

McCormack, M. (2012) *The Declining Significance of Homophobia: How Teenage Boys are Redefining Masculinity and Heterosexuality*, New York: Oxford University Press.

McCormack, M. and Anderson, E. (2010a) 'The re/production of homosexually-themed discourse in educationally-based organised sport', *Culture, Health & Sexuality*, 12: 913–927.

McCormack, M. and Anderson, E. (2010b) '"It's just not acceptable any more": the erosion of homophobia and the softening of masculinity in an English state school', *Sociology*, 44: 843–859.

Miceli, M. (2005) *Standing Out, Standing Together: The Social and Political Impact of Gay–Straight Alliances*, London: Routledge.

Mustanski, B. S., Farofalo, R. and Emerson, E.M. (2010) 'Mental health disorders, psychological distress, and suicidality in a diverse sample of lesbian, gay, bisexual, and transgender youths', *American Journal of Public Health*, 100: 2426–2432.

Ogburn, W. F. (1950) *On Culture and Social Change*, Chicago: Chicago University Press.

Pascoe, C. J. (2005) '"Dude, you're a fag": adolescent masculinity and the fag discourse', *Sexualities,* 8: 329–346.

Pascoe, C. J. (2007) *Dude, You're a Fag*, London: University of California Press.

Phoenix, A., Frosh, S. and Pattman, R. (2003) 'Producing contradictory masculine subject positions: narratives of threat, homophobia and bullying in 11–14 year old boys', *Journal of Social Issues*, 59: 179–195.

Plummer, D. (1999) *One of the Boys: Masculinity, Homophobia and Modern Manhood*, New York: Harrington Park Press.

Pryor, J. H., DeAngelo, L., Palucki Blake, L., Hurtado, S. and Tran, S. (2011) *The American Freshman: National Norms Fall 2011*, Los Angeles, CA: University of California Los Angeles, Higher Education Research Institute.

Rasmsussen, M. L. (2004) '"That's so gay!": a study of the deployment of signifiers of sexual and gender identity in secondary school settings in Australia and the United States', *Social Semiotics*, 14: 289–308.

Richardson, D. (2010) 'Youth masculinities: compelling male heterosexuality', *British Journal of Sociology*, 61: 737-756.

Rivers, I. (1996) 'Protecting the gay adolescent at school', *Medicine, Mind and Adolescence,* 11: 15–24.

Rivers, I. (2001) 'The bullying of sexual minorities at school: its nature and long-term correlates,' *Educational and Child Psychology*, 18: 32–46.

Rivers, I. (2011) *Homophobic Bullying: Research and Theoretical Perspectives*, New York: Oxford University Press.

Rubin, G. (1984) 'Thinking sex: notes for a radical theory of the politics of sexuality', in C. Vance (ed), *Pleasure and Danger: Exploring Female Sexuality*, Boston: Routledge.

Russell, S. T., Muraco, A., Subramaniam, A. and Laub, C. (2009) 'Youth empowerment and high school gay-straight alliances', *Journal of Youth and Adolescence*, 38: 891–903.

Ryan, C. and Rivers, I. (2003) 'Lesbian, gay, bisexual and transgender youth: victimization and its correlates in the USA and UK', *Culture, Health and Sexuailty*, 5: 103–119.

Sanders, S. (2008) 'Tackling homophobia, creating safer spaces', in R. dePalma and E. Atkinson (eds) *Invisible Boundaries: Addressing Sexualities Equality in Children's Worlds*, Stoke-on-Trent: Trentham.

Savin-Williams, R. C. (2005) *The New Gay Teenager*, Cambridge, MA: Harvard University Press.

Swain, J. (2006) 'Reflections on patterns of masculinity in school settings', *Men and Masculinities*, 8: 331–349.

Thorne, B. and Luria, Z. (1986) 'Sexuality and gender in children's daily worlds', *Social Problems*, 33: 176–190.

Thurlow, C. (2001) 'Naming the "outsider within": homophobic pejoratives and the verbal abuse of LGB high-school pupils', *Journal of Adolescence*, 24: 25–38.

Vicars, M. (2006) 'Who are you calling queer? Sticks and stones may break my bones but names will always hurt me', *British Educational Research Journal*, 32: 347–361.

Warwick, I., Aggleton , P. and Douglas, N. (2001) 'Playing it safe: addressing the emotional and physical health of lesbian and gay pupils in the U.K.', *Journal of Adolescence*, 24: 129–140.

Weeks, J. (2007) *The World We have Won*, London: Routledge.

Wilkinson, L. and Pearson, J. (2009) 'School culture and the well-being of same-sex-attracted youth', *Gender & Society*, 23: 542–568.

9   Disability, sexuality and bullying

Neil Duncan

Introduction

This chapter aims to examine the intersection of three related but problematic concepts: disability, sexuality and bullying. Each of these concepts has a huge canon of research behind it, but very little work examines overlaps between these areas and even fewer studies attempt to synthesise them. The chapter first describes relevant issues in the lives of typical non-disabled young people at school and revisits the theory that sexuality underpins much of what is considered typical bullying. Then the common notion of disabled people as a monolithic and desexualised group is deconstructed to enable better understanding of their diverse experiences. The social model of disability is then explored in relation to the multiple forms of social oppression that disabled people experience to understand how, and more importantly, why the latter group is disproportionately affected by bullying.

Sameness and difference

One of the abiding themes of research on bullying is that of difference. It is often posited that the actors have an obvious difference that engenders some form of aggression, for example, ethnic background, sexual orientation, appearance or behaviours. Sometimes the differences are deemed to be more subtle transgressions of homogeneity, such as withdrawnness or non-mainstream interests (Frisen *et al.*, 2008). But despite the commonsense nature of this widely accepted belief, surely it is not just any differences between people that cause the bullying or conflict? If it were so, then everyone would be bullying everyone else, as one could find differences between any two persons if one looked closely enough. The germane issue here is the reason why, under certain conditions, particular differences trigger aggression that we describe as bullying. It is the meanings ascribed to those differences that precipitate hostility, and these may be motivated by competition, jealousy, disgust, fear, or any one of a hundred variations of response to difference.

In a great deal of research power is based upon numerical superiority. For example, minority ethnic groups are considered more at risk from bullying by the majority ethnic group (Connolly and Keenan, 2002), and the same applies to sexuality. In school, the relatively small numbers of students deemed to have minority sexualities such as lesbian, gay, bisexual, transgender and questioning youth (Varjas *et al.*, 2008), are much more likely to be targeted by demonstratively heteronormative students who constitute the majority. Similarly, students defined or read as 'disabled' are more likely to be bullied than their non-disabled peers (Carter and Spencer, 2006).

In most schools, even in single-sex schools, the sexuality of peers is a topic of great import and the site of many bullying encounters – mainly non-physical, but not always. Sexual bullying can often be quite devastating in terms of its effects, drawing as it does on hate codes of misogyny (Rahimi and Liston, 2011) and homophobia (Rivers, 2002). The centrality of a healthy sexuality to human wellbeing is well recognised (World Health Organisation, 2012) and is a core component of identity that people endeavour to achieve and maintain.

In this chapter I use the term sexual identity to mean a person's conception and expression of their sexual self. Although I use the term in the singular, I accept the multiple and changing nature of sexual identities. In earlier work I argued that sexual identity had replaced the social class and religious sectarian identifiers that had been so taken-for-granted in the nineteenth century: sexual identity had become the prime site for personal status in schools (Duncan, 1999). My evidence for this was, in part, based upon the near monopoly of sexual hate-words used in conflict between students in live exchanges and as graffiti. This, I maintain, indicates a preoccupation with sexual identity and attempts to hurt one's targets by derogation of their sexual reputation.

Figure 9.1 Graffito.

The graffito in Figure 9.1 illustrates this point. In this photograph of a shutter at a children's centre in a rural location in England, the sexual reputation of the target of abuse is clearly the main aspect of the identity being attacked. Deploying the language of sex-hate, the attacker brings masturbation, homophobia and bestial imagery into the mix, and also attacks the victim's girlfriend, all in a handful of words. Showing this to hundreds of my undergraduate students over the years, almost all of them deduce that the defamation was written for reasons of jealousy and revenge by a girl aged between 13 and 15. In other words, when this phenomenon of sexual aggression is presented to young adults, they recognise it readily even though they may not have considered it previously. Whilst they deplore the language and sentiments, my students say it seems very natural to them that sexuality would be the focus of attack: apart from serious physical assault how else would you really hurt someone without an attack on their precious asset of sexual reputation?

Sexual reputation in this context refers to the perception, interpretation and evaluation of a person's sexual identity by others. As Bragg *et al.* (2011: 281) put it:

> Little attention is paid here to research on the social and cultural contexts of sexuality, how sexual meanings are established and negotiated, or how children and young people interpret and use sexual content. None of the reports even recognizes the existence of wider debates within feminist cultural theory and research around the 'sexualization of culture'.

'Ordinary' bullying: its socio-sexual substrate and its links to popularity

Whilst there is undoubtedly a psycho-sexual dimension to the struggle for an esteemed sexual reputation, the social context, the school climate and the wider community culture play a decisive role in how the struggle for a high status sexual reputation manifests itself in forms of bullying. Sometimes those forms appear quite removed from sexuality and appear to be 'ordinary' bullying, but conceal homophobic or misogynistic motivation. Recently, Guerra *et al.,* (2011: 308) supported this theory: 'In all of the middle school and high school focus groups, bullying was linked to both popularity and sexuality, albeit in somewhat different ways for boys and girls.' Their research describes in detail how young people's sexuality is patrolled by the peer group, and how esteemed sexuality, in other words what passes for an ideal boy or girl for that particular age in that particular school, bestows power and popularity.

The relationships between sex, gender, sexuality and sexual identity are a matter of ongoing theoretical dispute, and my addition to them of sexual reputation only complicates matters. But the idea of sexual reputation is vital because it presents itself as a contested prize of social power inasmuch as it affords those who are exalted as desirable (on whatever basis) to be worthy of admiration and emulation.

To be popular in school has at least two very different meanings (Eder, 1985; Eder *et al.*, 1995). Firstly, the received understanding of being popular means to be 'well-liked by many', often evidenced by sociometric peer-nominations. It is associated with pro-sociality, pleasantness and admiration. In this sense of the term, one might desire popularity as it confers the approval and friendliness of one's peers. To be well liked by many is obviously protective against abuse and maltreatment from peers, as, logically, there would be fewer to want to harm you and more to support you.

A second meaning of popularity in this context is more complex, and draws upon Machiavellian discourses of strategic alliances, subterfuge and coercion (Sutton and Keogh, 2000). To be popular here means to be aloof, conspicuously socially powerful, to give or withhold approval of others and to have that approval matter. This kind of high peer-group status is not so much about being well-liked by many, rather that the many want you to like them because they fear you. Again, it is logical that this is a desirable position in relation to protection against bullying as others are likely to be careful not to antagonise you, but either to avoid you or fawn over you.

In schools, to be 'popular and nice' does not sit easily with being 'popular and scary', indeed, as Hoff *et al.* (2009: 397) explain:

> Youth who are liked by the majority of peers (i.e. sociometrically popular) are not necessarily the same youth that peers will nominate as cool, popular or socially powerful; rather, a moderate correlation exists between sociometric popularity and perceived popularity constructs.

Mayeux and Cillesen (2008) among others, found that both these forms of popularity were associated with aggression, but more strongly with relational aggression, which in the field of bullying research is sometimes referred to as indirect bullying and includes name-calling, teasing and social exclusion (Owens *et al.*, 2000). This strain of bullying is linked to the need for group identity and cohesion: inclusivity is inimical to this purpose as one cannot vaunt oneself and one's group if it is open to everyone. The exclusivity of a group protects its prestige, and this group exclusivity can often be detected by the public display of carefully managed personal appearance and the 'othering' of those who don't belong.

Francis, Skelton and Read (2009) describe the very strong association between appearance and popularity, in that study popularity meaning both high achieving and popular with peers (HAP). The descriptions given in peer nominations are exquisitely detailed, showing a fine appreciation of the aesthetics of being popular:

> the overwhelming tendency for HAP pupils to be noted as both 'good looking' and fashionable. Indeed, all of the 'alpha' pupils bar one were specifically noted as physically attractive (...) Billy (Winterfell):'Tall white boy with gelled up dark hair, quite good-looking, cocky, loose tie'; Michael (Saltcliffe): 'White, quite small, short dark hair, dark eyes, quite good looking, a few freckles, looks just like Just William. Friendly and confident'; Kennedy (Highgarden): 'Tall, slender, white, long blondy-brown hair in a feathery cut. Middle-class accent. Pretty. Fashionable.

Wearing braces. Is wearing a short pleated skirt and black tights, and lots of thin silver bangles'.

(Francis *et al.*, 2009: 323)

Along with many other feminist and masculinities studies, Francis *et al.*'s work emphasises the gendered nature of popularity, in fact of the whole peer culture, contained as it is within school walls. To be a 'proper' boy needs a skill or at least a keen interest in sports or gaming and other typically male pursuits, while 'doing girl' requires being interested in fashion, make-up, celebrities, heterosexual relationships and emotional/social engagement with friends (Renold and Allen, 2006).

A highly refined knowledge is needed to avoid the *faux pas* that lie in wait for the ignorant wannabe. Signifiers impenetrable even to the experienced gender studies researcher are of huge importance, as Bragg *et al.* (2011: 289) exemplify in their work on early sexualisation of children:

> One spirited 13 year-old argued that her own style of make-up, bleached-blond hair and piercings marked her not as a 'Barbie' (signifying vacuous, man-pleasing artificiality) but a 'bimbo' (whose roleplaying was more conscious and thus 'authentic') – a crucial distinction that might pass undetected by those with less investment in such differences.

Not only does fashion promote the person, but the body does too. In recent years, the body has become an issue of great interest for social scientists as they speculate on its uses in creating, presenting and transforming identities. There is growing evidence of the increase in body dissatisfaction within both male and female adolescents, the latter showing greater discontent. Figures from numerous studies show a fairly stable rate of around 40 per cent of girls and 20 per cent of boys expressing dissatisfaction (Knauss *et al.*, 2007), with factors influencing this including the media representation of ideal gendered bodies and pressure to conform to that type.

Once the domain of small deviant subcultures, the burgeoning popularity of body piercing and tattooing over the last two decades (DeMello, 2000) gives credence to the theory that the body can be seen as a palimpsest on which the ordinary person can write and re-rewrite themselves; an expression of agency over the only thing the person really owns. Swami's recent study links these fashion practices to young people's attempts to reduce their body dissatisfaction (Swami, 2011).

How one looks and how one behaves is of central importance to school students whose physical appearance is changing radically during adolescence, and whose desires are acted out in new behaviours of adult sexual expression. Irrespective of cultures and communities, sexual preferences or practices, these sexual desires are one of the most widely shared human traits, but in each community young people are variously oppressed in their sexual expression. In some cases the policing is to discourage sexual activity, while in others it is to encourage it, but in every case it is patrolled somehow by those interested and powerful enough to do so (see Sauerteig and Davidson, 2009, for an excellent account of these practices).

The resistance of young people to the adult policing of their sexualities can be seen in the breaking of school uniform codes, their clandestine sexual experiences recorded on social networking sites, and the number of under-age sexual contacts that are evidenced by pregnancy and STIs. Indeed, adult society expects there to be resistance to their policing, because that is just what they did when they themselves were younger. The resistance is not too much of a problem because most young people find a way around it. But some young people, perhaps from strict religious backgrounds, for example, or those with minority sexual interests, find it harder than others to escape this control and therefore to join in the competition for an esteemed sexual reputation.

Problematising the disabled student

At the start of this chapter I noted the research that indicated the higher levels of risk of being bullied that young disabled people endure, but also that the literature provides a mosaic picture of the issue without many certainties. It might seem that the disproportionate bullying of disabled children is to some degree based upon obvious, though morally repugnant, reasons, namely a) they are in a minority, and b) that simply by being disabled they must be weaker and more vulnerable to attacks than their non-disabled peers. While this might be true in part, it is an unproblematised area that requires more thought than it is usually afforded.

Firstly, terminology covering disabled children is ambiguous in that it is often conflated with special educational needs (cf. the Special Educational Needs and Disability Act, 2001). Sometimes a child with autism is described as having SEN, other times she may be described as disabled. In addition to this, educational inclusion has an inherent social justice project that transcends educational opportunities (United Nations Educational, Scientific and Cultural Organisation, 1994), but this can be overlooked by research into bullying. Most relevant surveys are carried out in an educational context where the precise organisation of the school will be very important but not interrogated in the research. An example of these important factors is where children in a mainstream school, but placed in a special unit, will be viewed by mainstream peers very differently from those who are fully included in all regular classes. Likewise, students from a special school who are in casual contact with mainstream students from a neighbouring school will be perceived as more different, more alien, than if they had closer, managed, contact opportunities on the same campus (Griffiths, 2007).

Disability theory has grown away from the medical model in which the individual is seen as abnormal and 'wrong', a flawed entity that should be a scientific object of work for the medical and psychological professions. In the medical model, the whole agenda was based upon the premise that the abnormal individual must be changed or removed, cured or segregated by experts who were not themselves disabled (Finkelstein, 1980). Unfortunately the medical model has not been eradicated fully. Whilst professionals can cover their true colours with 'politically correct' terminology, many still subscribe to an expert-led, top-down paradigm of scientific objectivity without really attempting any empowerment of the individual at the centre. Residual medical models notwithstanding, since the 1980s there has been a steady improvement in the sensitive study of disability.

One model that has gained purchase, the social model of disability, regards disability as socially constructed (Oliver, 1996). The physical, cognitive or sensory impairment or difference is accepted for what it is, but the disability is the reduction of social opportunity imposed by society. For example, a child who uses a wheelchair can learn perfectly well, but if the school has no ramps, only steps, then that child is disabled by the school. In the terms of the social model of disability, that child is now learning disabled. This conceptualisation of learning disability turns previous paradigms of disability on their heads and opens up a new discourse of entitlement, human rights and diversity to replace the discourse of objectification, Otherness and abnormality (Morgan, 2012). Where society chooses not to include wheelchair users in the design and operation of its school systems it disables that group from learning. However, a wheelchair user in a school that has ramps and elevators continues to have an impairment (loss of ambulatory function) but is not disabled, as her needs for the social opportunity of learning have been included in the provision.

The distinction between 'being disabled' rather than 'having a disability' is core to the social model of disability: impairment is a part of natural human diversity, but disability is something that the powerful impose upon the weak because of their minority needs. Disability activists see a strong association between the oppression of people with impairments and the oppression of gays and lesbians, non-whites and females (Vernon, 1999). In the social model of disability, the research concern is emancipation of the individual from socially oppressive practices such as segregated schooling, negative mass media representation and discrimination at work. One can easily determine the legacy of the aforementioned social groups in the disability agenda, but if young disabled people are different from the majority of other young people then there are just as many profound and important differences between young disabled people themselves.

Unfortunately for disabled people, there are crucial differences between their 'community' and those minorities described above, principally in the internal differences between their constituents. In other words, a young Black woman may share similar experiences with other Black women, but the experiences of a bright dyslexic boy are very different to those of a learning disabled deaf-blind girl. Moreover, each person defined as disabled also has a gender, and an ethnicity, a social class and other characteristics that may lay first claim to their identity. As Vernon (1999: 394) explains:

The stigma of being impaired, and of a minority ethnic status, and/or female, and/or gay, and/or older, and/or working-class interact in variable and complex ways in shaping their daily experience so that they do not only experience the simultaneity of institutional discrimination prevalent in our society against all oppressed groups.

In addition to this problem of diversity is the matter of capability. By virtue of the impairments by which they are described as disabled, many such people are less able to communicate, organise and defend themselves as a collective. Finally, at least for this argument, is the issue of the essence of disability: its corporeal fact. The impairment, the loss, limitation or dysfunction of a part of the body is a painful reality that transcends social construction. Being a young lesbian might be emotionally difficult (perhaps) and limit one's social life (perhaps), but not in the same way as deafness, or of paraparetic cerebral palsy. Life is very hard for the young lesbian who is deaf or who has cerebral palsy and is subsequently doubly disabled by social stigmata and oppressive practices (Corbett, 1994). To discuss the entire population of disabled children as a single community is to completely miss the importance of the hierarchical categories within that classification and their relationship with social attitudes and mistreatment by peers (Deal, 2003). Indeed, peer bullying between pupils with special needs in special schools is a problem just like it is in mainstream schools (Hollomotz, 2009).

Same school, different experience

Whatever type or severity of special need, young people with physical, sensory or cognitive impairments are more likely to be over-protected by their parents or carers and therefore less likely to be as independent as their non-disabled peers (Black, 2005). There is a natural drive for many parents to be reluctant to see their offspring enter the tough world of adulthood, but for parents of disabled children the fear is amplified. In some cases there is still a need, and always will be, for care and support beyond what is usual. Certain impairing conditions make independent travel impossible, and typical adolescent employment such as milk or paper deliveries, fast food service and so on, might be beyond the reach of young people with, for instance, epilepsy or visual impairment (Hughes *et al.*, 2005).

These lacunae for social inclusion are further-reaching than might be imagined, and reduce the social skills and circles of friends that are protective of victimisation. Not only do young disabled people lose out on the self-esteem that paid employment can bring, but also the money it provides for further independent adventure. In addition, they represent a missed opportunity for a vital rite of passage travelled by millions of young people in the transition from childhood to adulthood, and, by their absence, consolidate the belief that disabled people are not part of mainstream society: they are alien and 'Other'. It is this state of affairs that enabled the President of the United

States of America to joke that his bowling action is 'like something from the Special Olympics' (Spillius, 2009). Although President Obama apologised to disabled athletes for his comments, the lesson is that deep down, just like regular folks, he makes jokes that assume only those who are not touched by disability will hear them: they are 'Other'. He would never have dreamed of offending a sexual or ethnic minority group in the same way, and this is a clear reinforcement of the vulnerable status of disabled people as an exceptionally marginalised, non-mainstream group.

The disabled sexuality

The increasing inclusion of disabled children in mainstream schools has brought many benefits for their social inclusion as adults in later life. However, it brings us back to the issues outlined above, of the trials and tribulations of schooling for 'typical' young people, and then adds some that are unique to the disabled experience. The benefits of being educated alongside one's peers bring a number of challenges, not least in the area of sexual reputation. Sexuality and schooling are not comfortable partners, and when disability is part of the mix things can get difficult and dangerous. The close scrutiny of young people by their peers means that even the smallest changes in appearance can be noted and exaggerated, and then subjected to comments, criticism and ridicule. When children are brought together in such tightly age-stratified groupings these differences are more conspicuous. The peer group during puberty is intensely interested in, perhaps obsessed with, normality (Duncan, 1999). For disabled children who are conspicuously different, this poses great hazards.

In a student subculture that is preoccupied with being normal and which equates normality with being safe or good, diversity is not to be valued, but relates closely to Erving Goffman's concept of 'spoiled identity' (Goffman, 1963). Even those differences which might be later deemed desirable attributes, for example early development of breasts for females, or tallness in boys, are a source of worry for pubescent youth and the source of a lot of teasing from both genders, even though it is a temporary difference. This anxiety in early maturers created by peer pressure can lead to drug misuse and self harm (Petersen and Shibley Hyde, 2009). Exceptional children with greater, permanent, differences such as muscular dystrophy or spina bifida are much more likely to be viewed as abnormal and undesirable by the peer-group and far removed from the all-important mainstream peer culture. How does a pubescent girl with spinal scoliosis join in a group discussion on the worry of split ends, or the nuisance of acne? The beauty magazines' depiction of the body beautiful, straight and true has little resonance with physically impaired youngsters (Blackburn, 2002).

The 'abnormal' bodies of disabled children are objectified from birth by the medical profession, but are discounted as sexual by peers. They are dislocated from the discourse of sex and romance which is such an enjoyable part of being human and takes up so much adolescent time. The discourse of adolescent body dissatisfaction takes a quantum leap when the body in question has a severe or conspicuous impairment (Franko and Streigel-Moore, 2002).

Earlier in this chapter, I suggested that appearance and behaviour were the vehicles of sexual identity and reputation, and have now touched upon the former in relation to disabled children in the school setting, but not all disabled children have visible or conspicuous differences. The largest number of children classified as having special needs are categorised as having learning difficulties (Department for Education, 2009). This term, like all the others in this field, is not fixed, not exclusive but is interchangeable with others depending upon time, place and professional practice. Here, I use it to mean those students who are seen by the school to be functioning well below expected levels for their chronological age in one or more important areas of learning or behaviour. Discrete conditions include dyslexia, autism, social, emotional and behavioural difficulties, Tourette's syndrome and general cognitive impairment.

Often children with severely impairing conditions can go unnoticed until set amongst their peers, when behaviour and conduct reveal their differences in a dramatic way. Autistic spectrum condition (ASC) is a good example of this. Frequently, young people with ASC appear physically no different to their peers, but their aloofness, their oddness and their different understanding of personal space or feelings of others can cause peers to react very negatively to them. Where a child with a missing limb might be viewed as unusual by the peer-group, they can compensate if they have good social skills. With ASC, a major hurdle is the very lack of those social skills and the group reaction is less sympathetic.

However, people with ASC have needs and desires too, and the difficulties of navigating mainstream schooling while trying to manage sexual development is a challenge too much for many professionals and parents. As Tissot puts it:

> It is this apparent mismatch – the desire for a sexual identity set against limitations in the ability to learn as well as limited social skills (which are often necessary to define that identity) – that creates tension.
>
> (Tissot, 2009: 139)

The finer points of what one can reveal to peers or adults about one's sexual state is so high-risk and so high-stakes, that many students with ASC are bullied for their disclosures, for example, inconvenient erections or masturbatory behaviour in class. Control of the sexual self is a problem for millions of 'normal' people who attract disapproval for their slightly excessive or mildly unusual behaviour, even when they are aware of the prevailing social norms. Unlike most students, children with ASC have an inherent disadvantage in not being able to learn from observing others, and are therefore far more prone to making mistakes in developing a sexual reputation than their peers, and, as explained above, more likely to pay the penalty for those mistakes.

Schools do not do much to address this issue; indeed they make it more of a problem by their focus on sex education as a moral issue with a discourse of social responsibility and personal safety rather than mutual pleasure or self-fulfilment. From the school's point of view, the pleasure and fulfilment aspects of sexual knowledge are tacitly expected to come from the peer group itself, from older siblings and friends, and from cultural experiences of film, music and magazines.

It is this demi-monde of vital information that is often missing from the lives of disabled children and which leaves a gap in social knowledge that lets them become prey to bullying and rejection (Koller, 2000). Children with this type of special need not only have bullying to contend with, but are also very vulnerable to sexual abuse and exploitation, with reports finding 'twice the frequency' compared to non-ASC children (Murphy and Young, 2005: 643).

Many children with severe impairing conditions are placed in residential schools where sexual contact is not allowed even if the individuals consent and are over 18 years of age. This legislation further pathologises the sexuality of an already socially oppressed group: it would be more convenient if young disabled people were simply nonsexual (Allen, 2007). On the one hand, young disabled people's sexuality is infantilised by over-protective parents, disavowed by schools prioritising a moral sexual order, and ignored by peers as undesirable; on the other hand it is hyper-inflated as predatory or excessive and sets them up as dysfunctional targets for marginalisation and abuse.

In a student culture where appearance and behaviour are the signifiers of the competition for a desired sexual reputation, which in turn is a core component of personal identity, disabled young people are at a serious disadvantage: 'Youth signifies beauty, hope, potency, vigour, and strength. (...) Disability is a signifier of ugliness, tragedy, asexuality, invalidity and frailty' (Hughes *et al.*, 2005: 12). The carefully policed boundaries of gendered and sexualised appearance and behaviour don't apply to most young disabled people. They are absent from the social and cultural scene, written off in case they damage the appeal of consumer products and services (Murray, 2002).

The effect of this marginalisation is apparent in the way that young people express their understanding of disability. In one of my research projects, I interviewed groups of adolescent high school girls and asked what characteristics made a girl popular or unpopular. The card marked 'Is disabled' was the first to go into the 'Most Unpopular' pile. The discussions usually centred on their perceptions that disabled girls would not be interested in boys, nor boys in them, so what was the point in having someone like that as a friend? On one occasion a girl asked me if disabled people 'had a sex', because, as she put it, they do not use male or female toilets, they all use a third type (Duncan, 2004). To be viewed by one's peers as asexual is a dreadful assault on one's identity, more so if the identity is already stigmatised in other ways due to physical, cognitive or sensory impairment.

As young people progress through puberty and adolescence their struggle for an esteemed reputation often lapses into bullying in order to achieve or maintain that status, propelled by the competitive ethos for popularity within the peer-culture. However, what motivates the victimisation of some disabled children is perhaps different from the motivation for bullying more similar peers. In this case, it is not that they are viewed as competitors for the desired popular status, but instead they are used as symbols of 'the Other': that which the subject fears because of contamination, infection or association. By pointing out the difference in the object (the young disabled person) as negative/abnormal, the subject (the aggressor) defines herself as positive/normal, and gains esteem from the Other's loss. Students with low popularity ratings might single out those with special needs as 'Other' in order to highlight the differences between good (themselves) and bad (the disabled student). In support of this theory one might observe that many of the aggressors against disabled people are insecure and unhappy themselves, already unpopular with their own peer group – as happy, confident and successful people are not so inclined to destroy others.

By examining bullying in schools as related to popularity, and popularity in turn being related to establishing a high status sexual reputation, we can see how the differences presented by some disabled young people become hostages in that competition. This chapter has analysed the relationship between disability, sexuality and bullying from a range of theoretical perspectives in order to explore the issues lying behind the high numbers of disabled targets of bullying. The diversity of disabled young people has been shown to confound easy categorisation, and even with this careful analysis there are uncomfortable generalisations. Thankfully many disabled young people are happy, vibrant and fulfilled, and become socially esteemed individuals; and of course not all non-disabled children have a negative view of their disabled peers. However the disproportionately high levels of bullying of disabled children should be a priority for further research, in the hope that by looking beyond the obvious we can develop school-based strategies that are genuinely inclusive.

References

Allen, L. (2007) 'Denying the sexual subject: schools' regulation of student sexuality', *British Educational Research Journal*, 33: 221–34.

Black, K. (2005) 'Disability and sexuality: holistic care for adolescents', *Paediatric Nursing*, 17: 34–37.

Blackburn, M. (2002) *Sexuality and Disability*, Oxford: Butterworth Heinemann.

Bragg, S., Buckingham, D., Russell, R. and Willett, R. (2011) 'Investigating young people's sexual cultures. Too much, too soon? Children, 'sexualization' and consumer culture,' *Sex Education: Sexuality, Society and Learning*, 11: 279–292.

Carter, B. B. and Spencer, V. G. (2006) 'The fear factor: bullying and students with disabilities', *International Journal of Special Education*, 21: 11–23.

Connolly, P. and Keenan, M. (2002) 'Racist harassment in the white hinterlands: minority ethnic children and parents' experiences of schooling in Northern Ireland', *British Journal of Sociology*, 23: 341–355.

Corbett, J. (1994) 'A proud label: exploring the relationship between disability politics and gay pride', *Disability and Society*, 9: 343–357.

Deal, M. (2003) 'Disabled people's attitudes toward other impairment groups: a hierarchy of impairments', Disability and Society, 18: 897–910.

DeMello, M. (2000) *Bodies of Inscription: A Cultural History of the Modern Tattoo Community*, Durham, NC: Duke University Press.

Department for Education (2009) 'Prevalence of pupils with special educational needs', Available at: http://www.education.gov.uk/rsgateway/DB/STA/t000851/Chapter1.pdf (accessed 16 February 2012).

Duncan, N. (1999) *Sexual Bullying: Gender Conflict and Pupil Culture in Secondary Schools*, London: Routledge.

Duncan, N. (2004) 'It's important to be nice, but it's nicer to be important. Girls, popularity and sexual competition', *Sex Education Sexuality Society and Learning*, 4: 137–152.

Eder, D. (1985) 'The cycle of popularity: interpersonal relations among female adolescents', *Sociology of Education*, 58: 154–165.

Eder, D., Evans C. and Parker, S. (1995) *School Talk: Gender and Adolescent Culture*, Rutgers University Press: New Jersey.

Finklestein, V. (1980) *Attitudes and Disabled People*, New York: World Rehabilitation Fund.

Francis, B., Skelton, C. and Read, B. (2009) 'The simultaneous production of achievement and popularity', *British Educational Research Journal*, 36: 317–340.

Franko, D. L. and Streigel-Moore, R. H. (2002) 'The role of body dissatisfaction as a risk factor for depression in adolescent girls: are the differences Black and White?' *Journal of Psychosomatic Research*, 53: 975–983.

Frisen, A., Holmqvist, K. and Oscarsson, D. (2008) '13-year-olds' perception of bullying: definitions, reasons for victimisation and experience of adults' response', *Educational Studies*, 34: 105–117.

Goffman, E. (1963) Stigma: *Notes on the Management of Spoiled Identity*, Harmondsworth: Penguin Books.

Griffiths, E. (2007) '"They're gonna think we're the dumb lot because we go to the special school": a teacher research study of how mainstream and special school pupils view each other', *Research in Education*, 78: 78–87.

Guerra, N. G., Williams, K. R. and Sadek, S. (2011) 'Understanding bullying and victimization during childhood and adolescence: a mixed methods study. *Child Development*, 82: 295–310.

Hoff, E. H., Reese-Weber, M., Schneider, W. J., and Stagg, J. W. (2009) 'The association between high status positions and aggressive behavior in early adolescence' *Journal of School Psychology*, 47: 395–426.

Hollomotz, A. (2009) *Learning Difficulties and Sexual Vulnerability: A Social Approach*, London: Jessica Kingsley Publishers.

Hughes, B., Russell, R. and Paterson, K. (2005) 'Nothing to be had "off the peg": consumption, identity and the immobilization of young disabled people', *Disability & Society*, 20: 3–17.

Knauss, C., Paxton, S. J. and Alsaker, F. D. (2007) 'Relationships amongst body dissatisfaction, internalisation of the media body ideal and perceived pressure from media in adolescent girls and boys', *Body Image*, 4: 353–360.

Koller, R. (2000) 'Sexuality and adolescents with autism', *Sexuality and Disability*, 18: 125–35.

Mayeux, L. and Cillessen, A. H. N. (2008) 'It's not just being popular, it's knowing it, too: the role of self-perceptions of status in the associations between peer status and aggression', *Social Development*, 17: 871–888.

Morgan, H. (2012) 'The social model of disability as a threshold concept: troublesome knowledge and liminal spaces in social work education', *Social Work Education: The International Journal*, 31: 215–226.

Murphy, N. and Young, P. (2005) 'Sexuality in children and adolescents with disabilities', *Developmental Medicine and Child Neurology*, 47: 640–644.

Murray, P. (2002) *Disabled Teenagers' Experiences of Access to Inclusive Leisure*, York: Joseph Rowntree Foundation.

Oliver, M. (1996) '*Defending impairment and disability*', in C. Barnes and G. Mercer (eds), *Exploring the Divide*, Leeds: Disability Pres.

Owens, L., Slee P. and Shute, R. (2011) '"It hurts a hell of a lot ...": the effects of indirect aggression on teenage girls', *School Psychology International*, 21: 359–376.

Petersen, J.L. and Shibley Hyde, J. (2009) 'A longitudinal investigation of peer sexual harassment victimization in adolescence', *Journal of Adolescence*, 32: 1173–1188.

Rahimi, R. and Liston, D. (2011) 'Race, class and emerging sexuality: teacher perceptions and sexual harassment in schools', *Gender and Education*, 23: 799–810.

Renold, E. and Allen, A. (2006) 'Bright and beautiful: high achieving girls, ambivalent femininities and the feminization of success in the primary school', *Discourse: Studies in the Cultural Politics of Education*, 27: 457–73.

Rivers, I. (2002) 'Developmental issues for lesbian and gay youth', in A. Coyle and C. Kitzinger (eds), *Lesbian and Gay Psychology: New Perspectives*, Oxford: Blackwell.

Sauerteig, L. and Davidson, R. (2009) *Shaping Sexual Knowledge: A Cultural History of Sex Education in Twentieth Century Europe*, Abingdon: Routledge.

Spillius, A. (2009) 'Barack Obama apologises for disabled gaffe', The Telegraph, 20 March. Available at: http://www.telegraph.co.uk/news/worldnews/barackobama/5023848/Barack-Obama-apologises-for-disabled-gaffe.html (accessed 16 February 2012).

Sutton, J. and Keogh, E. (2000) 'Social competition in school: relationships with bullying, Machiavellianism and personality', *British Journal of Educational Psychology*, 70: 443–456.

Swami, V. (2011) 'Marked for life? A prospective study of tattoos on appearance anxiety and dissatisfaction, perceptions of uniqueness, and self-esteem', *Body Image*, 8: 237–244.

Tissot, C. (2009) 'Establishing a sexual identity. Case studies of learners with autism and learning difficulties', Autism, 13: 551–566.

United Nations Educational, Scientific and Cultural Organisation (1994) *Salamanca Statement and Framework for Action on Special Needs Education*. Available as: http://unesdoc.unesco.org/images/0009/000984/098427eo.pdf (accessed 13 February 2009).

Varjas, K., Dew, B., Marshall, M., Graybill, E., Singh, A., Meyers, J. and Birkbircher, L. (2008) 'Bullying in schools towards sexual minority youth', *Journal of School Violence*, 7: 59–86.

Vernon, A. (1999) 'The dialectics of multiple identities and the disabled people's movement', *Disability and Society*, 14: 385–395.

World Health Organisation (2012) *Sexual Health*. Available at: http://www.who.int/topics/sexual_health/en/ (accessed 13 February 2012).

10 Masculinity and homophobia in high school and college sports

A personal journey from coach to researcher

Eric Anderson

Coming out

I took delight in the 1993 presidential election of Bill Clinton over George Bush. Clinton had advocated for gays and lesbians to openly serve in the United States Armed Forces and sparked national debate around the issue. Although he failed to secure a safer space for America's gay and lesbian soldiers (something that would not occur until 2010) the discourse regarding the gays in the military issue proved beneficial for gay liberation politics in general, and for gay male athletes in particular.

I was not a sociologist at the time, and I had no idea of the shifting cultural attitudes on the issue. All I knew was that, as a closeted high school coach, for the first time I began to hear discussions of homosexuality around me. Not only was the issue of gays in the military important for raising general discussion about homosexuality, but the discussion also made Americans aware that gay men *did* exist in the highly masculinised arena of war making. And while I doubt most people thought of this in more complex terms, the mere fact that the question was raised also meant to me that homosexuality was compatible not only with masculinity, but with hypermasculinity. As a closeted athlete, and as a closeted athletics coach, this gave me hope: it meant that if gay men could exist within the highly masculinised and homophobic armed forces, they might also exist in other highly masculinised institutions – like the institution I had devoted my life to as a way of hiding my sexuality from others – sport.

1993 was also the year that I 'came out of the closet' as an openly gay distance running coach at a rather conservative high school in Southern California. Here, I experienced just how important sexuality is in America. Whereas before I was a privileged white, middle class, athletic and (some would say) good looking young, ostensibly heterosexual male, things changed after coming out of the closet. Overnight I had gone from being known as the hilarious teacher, and revered coach, to the faggot teacher and the faggot coach. My athletes, once the pride of the school, became the shame of the school – affected by a guilt-by-association process relating to my stigma. In other words, because their coach was gay, they too were considered gay. My athletes and I began to face the discrimination that went hand in hand with the stigma of the time. New athletes ceased to join my team, and those remaining found themselves immersed in daily battles with ignorance. Some that even threatened their safety.

My status as the first publicly recognised gay male coach in the USA went relatively unnoticed until 1996, when a football player brutally assaulted one of my athletes who he assumed to be gay because he was on my team. We had several problems with the football team before; we had been moved from one locker room to the next, in order to protect my team from harassment. In fact, after a near fight, in which several football players decided that we could no longer use 'their' locker room, we finally ended up moving into a small, locked bathroom, effectively segregated away from the rest of the athletic community. The brutal attack saw the football player knock my runner to the ground, where he sat atop him and began pounding at his face. The assailant even tried to gouge my athlete's eyes out and when a bystander begged him to stop the beating he proclaimed, 'It ain't over until the faggot's dead'. My runner knew that he had to escape.

Although his vision was bloodied, my heterosexual athlete managed to squirm from beneath the large football player, and run away. He climbed a fence that the pursuing football player was too large to scale, and got away. He was left with four broken facial bones, and for the rest of his life will have two screws through his pallet. The police reported the incident as 'mutual combat' not a hate crime or even aggravated assault; the assailant received no time behind bars, no legal penalty whatsoever.

In addition to a predicable anger that lingered for years, I was also left with an intellectual angst over the issue. I was not satisfied with the 'boys will be boys' or 'people hate what they don't understand' rationalisations. It was clear to me that the incident did not 'just happen'. Such homophobia is not surprising especially when one considers that the assailant had been socialised into the homophobic language of masculinity embedded in combative team sports. I suspected his training served as a powerful socialisation into the norm of violent masculinity. It is this socialisation, and America's blind-obsession for sports, that I maintain is responsible for most of America's social ills. Masculinity (at that time in America), I maintained was a public health crisis.

Wanting to understand the relationship between men, masculinities, sport and homophobia better, I left my job as a high school science teacher and athletics coach, and I attended the University of California, Irvine to earn a doctorate in sociology. As a sociologist, I now better understand the near-seamless manner in which groups of people can maintain power by policing ideologies through the threat of force and the willing compliance of those oppressed. I have grown to understand the complex role that sport plays in society; particularly in the production of a violent, homophobic form of masculinity. I now have a much better understanding of the unfortunate circumstances by which the structure of sport in society influences many boys to develop such a narrow sense of masculinity, as well as a strong hatred for homosexuality. I understand the role sport plays in teaching boys to accept risk, to out-group others, and to use violence in order to gain masculine capital by physically subjugating other men.

Accordingly, in this chapter, I use my unique position of having first been an openly gay male coach, and then being the only openly gay male sport sociologist to study the changing relationship between homophobia in sport. Fortunately, since returning to do my PhD in 1998, much has changed. It seems that in the new millennium US citizens, and even more so, the British, are increasingly less tolerant of both institutional and cultural homophobia. Thus, after tracing the beginnings of sport in order to explain how we began to value sport, and why we created sport as a homophobic enterprise in the first place, I explain how school cultures, including physical education, adopted the masculinity of sports. I show that schools, particularly in the 1980s, became places with rigid masculine hierarchies, before showing how decreasing homophobia of the 1990s and the greatly diminished homophobia of the first decade of the new millennium has positively impacted upon youth. Embedded in my findings is the claim that decreased cultural homophobia not only has a very positive effect on the lives of gay males in sport and physical education (where my work shows that they are widely accepted onto their teams with open arms) but that it also has a profound impact on heterosexual boys and men, too.

Placing sport within historical context

Although today competitive, organised team sports take on religious fervour in Western cultures, they were not so popular until the dawn of the twentieth century. There were multiple reasons for the promotion of sport: 1) the sacrifice required was thought capable of preparing youth for industry and factory work; 2) the socialisation into a sex-segregated, 'macho' institution was thought necessary to develop proper heterosexual and masculine boys; and 3) it followed the same corporal procedures of ranks and obedience to authority and complicity within masculine peer culture as the military, thus assuring a military-ready youth culture. Decades later, particularly the 1980s, competitive organised sport (whether played as part of physical education or within youth leagues or school teams) served the function of reproducing hegemonic masculinity by distancing heterosexual boys from the spectre of homosexuality.

It was during this time that researchers began studying homophobia and masculinity in sport; and researchers who did so largely agreed that organised sports have been and are portrayed as being highly homophobic. Messner (1992: 34) wrote, 'The extent of homophobia in the sports world is staggering. Boys (in sports) learn early that to be gay, to be suspected of being gay, or even to be unable to prove one's heterosexual status is not acceptable'. Hekma (1998: 2) stated that, 'Gay men who are seen as queer and effeminate are granted no space whatsoever in what is generally considered to be a masculine preserve and a macho enterprise'. Finally, Pronger (1990: 26) agreed, saying, 'Many of the (gay) men I interviewed said they were uncomfortable with team sports ... orthodox masculinity is usually an important subtext if not the *Leitmotif* in team sports'. Matters were reported as being no better for students compelled to take physical education in schools (see Gill et al., 2006).

Sports (particularly contact sports), whether inside or outside of physical education, have been, and oftentimes remain, described as a place in which a dominant and dominating (or hegemonic) form of masculinity is reproduced and defined (i.e. a male athlete represents the ideal of what it means to be 'a man') and this definition contrasts markedly with what it means to be gay and/or feminine (Messner, 1992). As women have increasingly gained access to once masculine-dominated institutions, sport has become an increasingly contested terrain in which men try to validate masculine privilege through their ability to physically out-perform women, thus symbolically dominating women, eschewing aspects of femininity or non-masculinity (Connell, 1995). However, as Griffin (1998) suggests, if gay male athletes, who are stigmatised as being feminine, can be as strong and competitive as heterosexual male athletes, they then, by implication, threaten the perceived distinctions between 'gay' and 'straight', and thus the perceived differences between men and women as a whole.

Bourdieu (2001) agreed. He maintained that gay men are uniquely situated to undermine masculine orthodoxy because of their unique ability to invisibly gain access to masculine privilege before 'coming out' (disclosing) as gay. Because of this ability, gay men may be uniquely positioned to align with feminists in a terrain of progressive coalition politics to symbolically attack male dominance. Thus, gay male athletes (who are seen as a paradox because they comply with the gendered script of being a man through the physicality involved in sports, but who violate another masculine script through the existence of same-sex desires) may threaten sport as a prime site of hegemonic masculinity and masculine privilege. Homophobia, therefore, has traditionally presented itself in the form of resistance against the intrusion of a gay sub-culture within organised sports and, pertinently, physical education: it serves as a means to maintaining the rigidity of orthodox masculinity and patriarchy.

The establishment of masculine hierarchies (1980s and 1990s)

Although the primary purpose of homophobia in male-dominated sport might have been to marginalise gay men, there are ancillary consequences for heterosexual men as well during these decades. Heterosexual men, and particularly boys, rigidly policed their gendered behaviours to best approximate orthodox masculinity in order to ward off suspicion of being thought 'gay'. This is something I came to describe as 'homohysteria': the cultural fear of being 'homosexualised' for acting or associating with symbols of homosexuality (see Anderson, 2011a).

Two key factors affect the level of homohysteria: 1) the homophobia of a culture (in this case organised sports and physical education) and; 2) the awareness that homosexuality exists within the culture. More specifically, in highly homohysteric cultures there exists a cultural awareness that anyone can be gay. In homohysteric settings, the stigma attached to homosexuality therefore results in men using homophobia in an attempt to prove their heterosexuality. However homohysteria can also decline, often with age or through cultural shifts in perceptions of masculinity, so that boys no longer care about being socially perceived as gay. Here, they are afforded a greater range of gendered behaviours (see Anderson, 2009, 2011b).

A culture where homohysteria exists (such as the UK and USA in the 1980s and 1990s) is damaging not only to the boys who are marginalised, but even to those who privilege from the masculine hierarchy. Exemplifying the damage caused by such a culture, Pollack (1998) suggested that, in an attempt to displace homosexual suspicion, boys at a very young age learned not to ask for help, hide weakness, and disguise fear or intimidation. They learned that they must fight when challenged and that they must sacrifice their bodies for the sake of the team. Pollack calls these mechanisms a 'boy code,' which he maintained puts boys and men into a gender straightjacket that constrains not only them but everyone else. He argued that this reduces us all as human beings, and eventually makes us strangers to ourselves and to one another.

This was very much the environment that my adolescence was saturated in. Growing up in the 1980s, I was perpetually afraid of doing something, saying the wrong thing, or in some other way not acting straight enough to pass. But it was not just gay men who had to do this, it was all men. Homosexuality is not readily visible, thus any man interested in avoiding suspicion had to act opposite of whatever was thought to be 'gay'.

For example, McGuffey and Rich (1999) showed that those who cross the boundary (especially boys who move into female space) risked being ostracised and accused of being a sissy or like a girl, or being accused directly of homosexuality. Thus, transgression is met with the violent language of homophobic and misogynistic discourse. Terms like 'fag' were employed to police and pressure the individual to devalue their behaviours and return to conventional masculinised space and/or behaviours, thereby securing men's privilege over women as a whole.

Athleticism was (and may still be in many locales) the primary axis of masculine stratification among school-aged boys, even though athleticism has little practical value in modern society outside the athletic arena. Here, the most athletic boys occupy the top positions within the masculine hierarchy and the least athletic are at the bottom. At school every male knew that the more athletic they are, the more popular they will be. Supporting this, Rivers (2011) has shown with the body of his work collected over two decades that the principle cause of bullying in schools was not sexual orientation, but one's sporting abilities.

This hierarchy continues (or at least used to continue) beyond high school, into university. Here, boys with the most masculine capital are provided with many social privileges, including near immunity from homosexual suspicion. Another way to examine this is to say that the better the athlete is and the more masculine the sport he plays, the less homosexual suspicion there is about him. Consequently, within college and universities for example, American Football players are provided near immunity from homosexual suspicion, while band members are inundated with it. From the top of the hill, the male is able to marginalise others, by using homonegative discourse, and his derision is legitimated because he has earned the respect of peers. It is here that the discursive bullying begins. Even without escalation into violence, the fear of being labelled gay polices the behaviours of men, even within the educational system.

Ironically, boys at the top of the masculine hierarchy are provided much more leeway in terms of their ability to transgress rigid gender boundaries, often because few other boys would be willing to challenge their sexuality for fear of social or physical reprisal. This phenomenon is also found when it comes to what may be described as 'homoerotic' activities: the more masculine capital a man possesses the more homoerotic activity he is able to engage in without having his sexuality questioned. This homoerotic play is expressed at a number of levels, such as towel-snapping and wrestling.

Although athleticism has little practical value for men once they disengage from the sporting arena (particularly as masculinity becomes more scripted in professional occupations in later stages of life), the 'jock' identity is often maintained where an individual may publicly recall his youthful sporting accomplishments in order to influence his level of masculine capital. Thus, even in adulthood, the masculine glory of one's youth can be tapped to influence perceptions among adult peers.

While the masculine hierarchy is mainly built via athleticism, consistent associations with femininity or things considered to be consistent with gay males are important determinants in the downgrading of one's masculine capital too, whether the association is real or perceived. Sociologist David Plummer (1999) points out that an accusation of homosexuality is the primary manner in which to verbally marginalise another man. He maintains that homophobic terms come into currency in primary/elementary school, even though the words may not yet have sexual connotations. Yet, despite this, he posits that these terms are far from indiscriminate as they tap a complex array of meanings that he says are precisely mapped in peer cultures.

Some young boys who slip out of their bounded zones may be able to recoup some of their masculinity and be reabsorbed back into the masculine arena by deflecting the suspicion of homosexuality onto another boy. A higher status boy, for example, who transgresses gender boundaries and may not have as much masculine capital as he thinks he has, might call a lower status boy a fag in attempt to displace suspicion. Thus, by negatively talking about and excluding members who are presumed to be gay, boys are delineating their public heterosexuality, while collectively endorsing hegemonic masculinity. As a researcher, I saw that in a game of 'tag, you're it' the marginalised attempted to gain power and control by marginalising one or more others (Anderson, 2005a). However, in certain highly masculinised social locations, such as sports, it seems that demonstrating one's heterosexuality may not be sufficient enough to maintain an unambiguous heterosexual masculinity and I have argued that it becomes important to show opposition and intolerance toward homosexuality (see Anderson, 2005b).

For boys particularly, the stigma of homosexuality brings with it a guilt-by-association fear that the stigma will rub off onto those not already marginalised, Goffman (1963) described this as 'courtesy stigma'. Here homosexuality is looked upon as a contaminant. For example, after I came out of the closet as an openly gay high school coach in 1993 my student athletes were frequently perceived as gay because they had a gay coach (Anderson, 2009). Making boys contaminated in this way sends a strong warning to the other boys not to act similarly or associate with 'those' boys or they will be isolated and ostracised by their male peers. In my case, students stopped joining my team.

Hegemonic masculinity in 'jock-ocratic' school cultures

The USA might be more susceptible to having school cultures controlled by jocks. This is because, unlike the UK, sports are structured into the schools themselves. Much like the game 'King-of-the-Hill' where the most dominant male occupies the top of the hill and physically pushes weaker boys down it, the contest for masculine stratification is played out through compulsory physical education. In the US high schools, and indeed many universities, are stratified around and place significant emphasis upon athletics. In such a 'jock-ocracy', boys that score the most touchdowns, goals, or baskets symbolically occupy the top of the hierarchy, and they often naturalise their status by marginalising other men through homophobic and misogynistic discourses. Those who are perceived to be 'softer', weaker, or more feminine are thus regarded as homosexual and are relegated to the bottom of the stratification or, more often than not, cast out from the masculine terrain altogether. As mentioned before, a continuous process of homosocial patrolling occurs by both self and others, as boys who deviate are routinely chastised for their aberrant behaviours through homophobic and misogynistic discourse. Michael Kimmel (1994: 122) describes these processes:

> Masculinity must be proved, and no sooner is it proved that it is again questioned and must be proved again – constant, relentless, unachievable, and ultimately the quest for proof becomes so meaningless than it takes on the characteristics, as Weber said, of a sport.

A high school 'jock-ocracy' provides a clear understanding of the process of masculinity as hegemonic oppression because ancillary players (those possessing subordinated forms of masculinity) keep this volatile framework in place by lauding social merits onto the 'kings-of-the-hill', and literally cheer them on. Girls, other marginalised boys and some adults can often be seen to pay tribute to these 'kings' by supporting them in the very arena where they demonstrate their power – athletic competitions. Within US schools and colleges, this can be demonstrated in multiple ways. For example it can be demonstrated by the fervent cheers female students give for their school or college male athletes thus relegating themselves to symbolic subservience, or when a student body votes a football player as 'homecoming king'. The public celebration of masculine domination makes this form of masculinity a popular identity to adopt and therefore ensures compliance by other males seeking such admiration.

The praise of these kings by individuals and their institutions naturalises and legitimates the power of those who control the jock-ocracy. But an important question is who controls this jock-ocracy? Hegemonic processes are often 'dressed up' in the myths and discourse that surrounds the notions of school pride. Subordinated members of a school culture do not view their cheering as praise for the so-called elite and powerful men who dominate them; rather they view it as cheering for or taking pride in the success of 'our school'. In effect, hegemonic oppression is tacitly supported by school or college hierarchies, and alumni associations that choose to value one form of performance over another.

Being 'gay' and playing sport: shifting sands

By the end of the first decade of the twenty-first century, I began to report a noticeable decrease in levels of homophobia in sporting cultures, and especially in men's team sports (Anderson, 2005a; Kian and Anderson, 2009; Southall et al., 2011). Supporting this, a poll in *Sports Illustrated* magazine (27 February 2006) found that of 1,401 professional team sport athletes contacted, the majority (and 80 per cent of those in the National Hockey League) said that they would welcome a gay teammate. Signs that there has been a reduction in homophobia has implications for the theory we use to examine the relationship between men, homophobia and masculinity; and it has significant implications for our understanding of research on homophobic bullying conducted in the 1980s and 1990s and the 'jock-ocratic' nature of school culture.

Inclusive masculinity theory: a changing world for boys

Inclusive masculinity theory explains the stratification of men alongside their social dynamics in times of lower homohysteria. Here, in the second decade of the new millennium, heterosexual boys are permitted to engage in an increasing range of behaviours that once led to homosexual suspicion, including 'homoerotic horseplay', without the threat to their publicly perceived heterosexual identity. For example in various studies I have conducted with fraternity members in US universities (Anderson, 2008), rugby players in UK universities (Anderson and McGuire, 2010), boys attending UK schools

(McCormack and Anderson, 2010), and even the young men on a Catholic College soccer team in the US Midwest (Anderson, 2011b) have shown that they maintain close physical and emotional relationships with each other – something unheard of a decade ago.

In the UK, Mark McCormack has demonstrated that, among students attending three sixth-forms in schools (16–18 years of age), boys were able to not only able to engage in physical touch with one another, but that homophobia (including homophobic language) was stigmatised (McCormack, 2012). Another study (Anderson et al., 2012) has shown that nine out of ten heterosexual male students attending two universities and one sixth form college (16–18 years of age) in the United Kingdom felt able to kiss their male friends on the lips as a form of non-sexual, homosocial bonding (similar findings were reported in a study of US university undergraduates who were also soccer players). Significant for schools, in a three-month ethnographic study of teaching in a sixth form (high school) in the UK, I discovered that students believed homophobia was unacceptable, and especially within physical education (see Anderson, forthcoming). Collectively, these studies highlight the fact that as cultural homophobia diminishes, it offers up opportunities for masculinity to be reshaped in ways that would once have been perceived to be more 'feminine' or more suggestive of indicative of homosexuality. While not all students will exist within this type of inclusive culture, researchers argue there are positive implications resulting from this, including the erosion of discursive bullying and particularly homophobic bullying. Thus, I have increasingly argued that homophobia aligns various masculinities vertically. However, in the absence of homophobia multiple and varied masculinities can flourish.

There is increasing evidence that team sport athletes are 'coming out' in greater numbers. For example, I reported on the experiences of 26 openly gay US high school and university athletes (Anderson, 2011c). Compared to an earlier study I conducted (Anderson, 2002), these athletes did not fear coming out in the same way or to the same degree as their predecessors in 2002. Specifically, they were not afraid that coming out would result in physical hostility, marginalisation or social exclusion by peers, coaches or teachers (either on or off the field).

Neil was an openly gay soccer player attending a small, Catholic college in a rural Midwestern state in the USA who said, 'My teammates are very supportive'. He went on to say:

> I think it's good that we played together for a long time. So they got to know me before I came out. But they have been amazing. Absolutely nothing has changed since I came out … I should have come out earlier.

While the young athletes in the 2011 study were more diverse in terms of the split between team sports and individual athletics, they were not able to use sporting capital as a shield against homophobia as much as other athletes because they were not ranked as highly. Nevertheless, these young men were widely accepted by their teammates. In fact, they reported that their teammates were 'closer' at the time of the interviews than before they came out. It seems as if disclosure of something personal engenders further disclosure, and team mates demonstrated that rather than a player's disclosure of his sexuality being used as a means of denigration, it was taken as a mark of trust and enhanced relationships among players..

Remarkably, openly gay high school and college athletes evade the culture of *'Don't Ask, Don't Tell'* (DADT) that characterised many of the experiences of the young athletes in my study. Nearly a decade on, young gay athletes talked about their sexualities frequently, and no one reported that their teammates tried to publicly or privately humiliate them or make them feel uncomfortable. They were asked about the types of 'guys' they liked, and even asked about which teammates they thought were attractive. 'Of course we talk about my sexuality,' Mark said. 'We talk about it all the time.' He added:

> I think it's fair to say that I'm known as 'the gay hockey player' at my high school. I'm the only gay athlete who is out, even though I suspect a few more … It's funny, I'll be at a party, and meet someone new and they will be like, 'hey, I heard of you. You're the gay hockey player, huh?'

The young athletes in this study were not bullied by their teammates, or by other teams. This highlights the salience of the argument that a culture of homohysteria structures homophobic discursive bullying, while a culture free of homohysteria makes bullying unnecessary and undesirable. Much of boys' bullying occurs as a result of perceptions about what it is to be masculine – it is a form of social survival – it may not be a deep-seated aggression.

Concluding thoughts

Whereas Rivers' (2011) work from the early 2000s found that the primary source of bullying in secondary and high school was the inability to perform at sport, it is likely that this was the case because school sports promoted heteromasculinity. However, my research suggests that with increasingly positive attitudes toward homosexuality, particularly among older students, not only should bullying against LGBT young people decrease, so should bullying against those who are less adept at sport.

From my perspective, inclusive masculinity theory suggests that in an Anglo-US culture of diminishing homohysteria, a homophobic discourse is also lost or, at least, the meanings associated with it no longer have a 'homosexualising' utility. In a wider context, the esteemed attributes of men will no longer rely on control and domination, thus intentional homophobic stigmatisation should cease, even among boys and young men. Hopefully this means that friendships will increasingly develop from a baseline of social inclusion instead of exclusion.

As noted earlier, this is likely to have a profound effect on bullying. Exemplifying this, Mark McCormack (Chapter 8) indicates that as a by-product of this new 'inclusive masculinity' among boys attending three sixth forms (high school) there were no reports of bullying on the grounds of sexual orientation, or indeed for any other ostensible reason. Whereas homophobic bullying used to be a compulsory system for proving one's heterosexuality, the jock-ocratic social culture that supported this seems to be slipping at least among older school students. If this pattern is found in young age groups, it means that more boys will be able to sit at the top-of-the-hill, without fearing being pushed back down.

Afterword

In the Spring of 2012, I returned to my old high school to run with the team for two weeks. It had been 15 years since I left, and things had changed radically. Not only was there no homophobia on the team, but young men proudly discussed their other activities that none would have boasted about when I was in high school, or even when I was coaching. One boy talked about wanting to return to ballet lessons, another was establishing his career as a model, and most all of the boys were very soft in their gendered expression. Interesting, despite the time they took on their appearance, the love they outwardly express for each other on *Facebook* (and in person); or their feminised physical tactility (long hugs and massaging each other), they ran even faster than the boys did that I coached back in the macho 1980s. I guess I was right, masculinity had nothing to do with sexuality, and sexuality had little to do with athleticism. Boys can express a range of gendered behaviours on the team today, and homosexuality was not an issue, not even in the slightest.

References

Anderson, E. (2002) 'Openly gay athletes: contesting hegemonic masculinity in a homophobic environment', *Gender and Society*, 16: 860–877.

Anderson, E. (2005a) *In the Game: Gay Athletes and the Cult of Masculinity*, Albany, NY: State University of New York Press.

Anderson, E. (2005b) 'Orthodox and inclusive masculinity: competing masculinities among heterosexual men in a feminized terrain', *Sociological Perspectives*, 48: 337–355.

Anderson, E. (2008) '"Being masculine is not about who you sleep with…:" heterosexual athletes contesting masculinity and the one-time rule of homosexuality', *Sex Roles*, 58: 104–115.

Anderson, E. (2009) *Inclusive Masculinity: The Changing Nature of Masculinities*, New York, NY: Routledge.

Anderson, E. (2011a) 'The rise and fall of western homohysteria', *Journal of Feminist Studies*, 1: 80–94.

Anderson, E. (2011b) 'Inclusive masculinities of university soccer players in the American Midwest', *Gender and Education*, 23: 729–744.

Anderson, E. (2011c) 'Updating the outcome: gay athletes, straight teams, and coming out at the end of the decade', *Gender & Society*, 25: 250–268.

Anderson, E. (forthcoming) 'Inclusive masculinity in a physical education setting *Thymos: Journal of Boyhood Studies*.

Anderson, E., Adams, A. and Rivers, I. (2012) '"You wouldn't believe what straight men are doing with each other": kissing, cuddling and loving', *Archives of Sexual Behavior*, 41: 421–430.

Anderson, E. and McGuire, R. (2010) 'Inclusive masculinity theory and the politics of men's rugby', *Journal of Gender Studies*, 19: 249–262.

Bourdieu, P. (2001) *Masculine Domination,* trans R. Nice, Stanford, CA: Stanford University Press.

Connell, R.W. (1995) *Masculinities,* Berkeley: University of California Press.

Gill, D. L., Morrow, R. G., Collins, K. E., Lucey, A. B. and Schultz, A. M. (2006) 'Attitudes and sexual prejudice in sport and physical activity', *Journal of Sport Management*, 20: 554–564

Goffman, Erving (1963) *Stigma: Notes on the Management of Spoiled Identity*, Englewoord Cliffs: Prentice-Hall.

Griffin, P. (1998) *Strong Women, Deep Closets: Lesbians and Homophobia in Sport*, Champaign, IL: Human Kinetics.

Hekma, G (1998) '"As long as they don't make an issue of it...": Gay men and lesbians in organized sports in the Netherlands', *Journal of Homosexuality*, 35: 1–23

Kian, T. and Anderson, E. (2009) 'John Amaechi: changing the way sport reporters examine gay athletes', *Journal of Homosexuality*, 56:1–20.

Kimmel, M. S. (1994) 'Masculinity as homophobia', in H. Brod and M. Kaufman (eds), *Theorising Masculinities*, London: Sage.

McCormack, M. (2012) *The Declining Significance of Homophobia: How Teenage Boys are Redefining Masculinity and Heterosexuality*, New York: Oxford University Press.

McCormack, M. and Anderson, E. (2010) '"It's just not acceptable any more": the erosion of homophobia and the softening of masculinity at an English sixth form', *Sociology*, 44: 843–859.

McGuffey, C. S. and Rich, B. L. (1999) 'Playing in the gender transgression zone: Race, class, and hegemonic masculinity in middle childhood', *Gender & Society*, 13: 608–610.

Messner, M. (1992) *Power at Play: Sports and the Problem of Masculinity*, Boston, MA: Beacon Press.

Plummer, D. (1999) *One of the Boys: Masculinity, Homophobia and Modern Manhood*, New York: Harrington Park Press.

Pollack, W. (1998) *Real boys: Rescuing our Sons from the Myth of Boyhood*, New York: Henry Holt.

Pronger, B. (1990) *The Arena of Masculinity: Sports, Homosexuality, and the Meaning of Sex*, New York: St. Martin's Press.

Rivers, I. (2011) *Homophobic Bullying*: Research and Theoretical Perspectives, New York: Oxford University Press.

Southall, R., Anderson, E., Southall, C., Nagel, M. and Polite, F. (2011) 'An investigation of the relationship between college athletes' ethnicity and sexual-orientation attitudes', *Ethnic and Racial Studies*, 34: 293–313.

11 The role of Gay–Straight Alliances in addressing bullying in schools

Margaret Schneider, Robb Travers, Alex St. John,
Lauren Munro and Kate Klein

Introduction

In spite of a climate in Canada that is increasingly lesbian, gay, bisexual, trans and queer (LGBTQ) positive (Schneider and Dimito, 2008) homophobic bullying in schools is still endemic. There are many approaches to preventing bullying, but ultimately we believe that the most effective are those that change the school climate. We propose that Gay-Straight Alliances (GSAs) can be an effective way of addressing homophobic bullying. In this chapter we offer a description of how GSAs function in a large school system in Ontario, Canada and discuss how their unique context contributes to their effectiveness.

Canadian school system: brief overview

In Canada, education is the responsibility of the provinces. In Ontario, for historical reasons, there are two publicly funded school systems: the secular system, referred to as public school, and the Catholic school system. Both provide schooling from Kindergarten (4–6 years of age in Ontario, 5–6 years of age elsewhere) to grade 12 (17–18 years of age). The curriculum is determined by the provincial Ministry of Education and can be interpreted by local school districts. For example, while the mathematics curriculum is specific regarding what skill should be taught at what grade in school, sexuality education, which includes sexual orientation issues, and is taught in grades 1 (6–7 years of age) through to grade 8 (13–14 years of age) is comprehensive, but much less prescriptive. Thus, a particular school or school district can minimise discussion of sexual orientation or eliminate it altogether. The approach to sexual orientation in the Catholic school system, in terms of curriculum and the prohibition of GSAs, is doctrinaire and may contravene the Charter of Rights and Freedoms (Callaghan, 2011).

Homophobic bullying in Canadian schools

The documentation of homophobic bullying in school settings in North America is substantial, although most of the research to date has been conducted in the USA. However, Canadian-based studies do show that homophobic bullying is a significant problem, with a majority of sexual minority youth more likely to report bullying than their heterosexual counterparts (Williams *et al.*, 2005). In a study of teachers' experiences conducted by the first author and reported in detail elsewhere (Schneider and Dimito, 2008) a majority of participants had witnessed students being verbally harassed by other students because of their sexual orientation or because they were believed to be LGBTQ and half were aware of anti-LGBTQ graffiti on school property. In addition, nearly half were aware of teachers being harassed by students because they were LGBTQ or believed to be LGBTQ. One quarter were aware of students being assaulted by other students because they were LGBTQ or believed to be LGBTQ and nearly one quarter were aware of students who dropped out of school because of homophobic bullying.

Recently, *Egale*, a Canadian advocacy group for LGBTQ people, partnered with researchers from the University of Winnipeg and University of Manitoba to conduct a national study. Nearly 1,700 students (both LGBTQ and heterosexual) responded to an online survey. The results demonstrated that homophobic bullying in Canadian schools is, 'neither rare nor harmless but a major problem that schools need to address' (Taylor *et al.*, 2008: 2).

The major findings were as follows. A majority of students hear expressions and remarks such as, 'That's so gay', or 'faggot', 'queer', 'lesbo' and 'dyke' daily. A majority of the LGBTQ students reported being verbally harassed because of their sexual orientation/gender expression. One third of LGBTQ participants reported harassment involving text messaging or the Internet. Twenty-five per cent of LGBQ respondents had been physically harassed because of their sexual orientation and 40 per cent of the transgender students reported physical harassment due to their gender expression. A majority of respondents reported seeing homophobic graffiti at school. Most LGBTQ students reported feeling unsafe at school in comparison to only one fifth of straight students. Areas such as change rooms, washrooms and hallways were cited as particularly unsafe (a finding consistent with Chesir-Teran (2003) who recommends environmental audits of school-level heterosexism and homophobia). The results also indicated the failure of some school staff to address these issues.

As further evidence of the problem, Canadian teachers' groups have demonstrated concern by developing resources, for example, *Safe Schools: Breaking the Silence on Sexual Difference* (2002) published by the Saskatchewan Teachers' Federation, and *Seeing the Rainbow: Teachers Talk about Bisexual, Gay, Lesbian, Transgender and Two-Spirited Realities*, developed by the Canadian Teachers' Federation and the Elementary Teachers Federation of Ontario (2003) In addition, over the past decade there have been well-publicised individual instances of homophobic bullying and its consequences. In one case, Azmi Jubran (ironically, a heterosexual youth) launched a successful case against the North Vancouver School District before the British Columbian Human Rights Tribunal on the grounds that the education district personnel had done nothing to address homophobic bullying aimed at him (CBC News,

2005). In another case in British Columbia, Hamed Nastoh (also heterosexual) committed suicide as the result of abuse, including homophobic bullying, which ultimately resulted in the passage of the Safe Schools Act (British Columbia, Ministry of Education, 2006) prohibiting bullying and harassment in the schools on the basis of race, gender and sexual orientation (Mayencourt, 2006). The fact that many of these high-profile instances involved heterosexual youth speaks to the complex nature of homophobic bullying (Pascoe, 2011).

In 2006, a 13-year-old boy in the province of Ontario committed suicide as the result of bullying that started when he came out to a friend. The friend told everyone else, resulting in harassment face-to-face and online. A few days before his death some students stuffed him into a garbage can (Lakritz, 2008). Most recently, in October, 2011 an openly gay 15-year-old from Ottawa, Ontario ended his life after months of depression that his father attributes, in part, to homophobic bullying (Toronto Star, 2011). This particular case may represent the Canadian tipping point. Rick Mercer, a well-known political satirist and commentator expressed his outrage on his television series, *The Rick Mercer Report*, calling for action – the identification of the bullies in this particular instance – and challenging prominent gay Canadians to openly identify themselves and become role models. He was also interviewed on the popular CBC Radio current events program, *The Current*. This was followed by numerous phone-in talk shows on the topic as well as newspaper articles, containing numerous accounts of homophobic bullying (Woods, 2011; Zerbisias, 2011). By the end of 2011, two pieces of anti-bullying legislation had been proposed in Ontario's House of Commons.

Addressing school-based homophobia and the role of GSAs

Both Taylor *et al.* (2008) and Schneider and Dimito (2008) point to school policy as an important foundation for addressing homophobia. In Taylor *et al.* (2008), students who believed that their schools had anti-homophobia policies were much more likely than other LGBTQ students to feel that their school community was supportive; to feel comfortable talking to a counsellor or to classmates; to hear fewer homophobic comments and report that staff intervenes; and to report homophobic incidents to staff and their parents. They were less likely to feel unsafe at school and to have been verbally or physically harassed. Schneider and Dimito (2008) found that teachers working in school districts with an anti-homophobia policy felt more supported and protected and were more active in raising LGBTQ issues with colleagues and in the curriculum. As will be seen in the school system to be described below, policy played an important role as well.

Safe schools are places where students are not only free from verbal and physical harassment, but also places that give them a feeling of belonging, rather than being outsiders. There are many different approaches to making schools safe for LGBTQ students. These can include professional development for teachers, addressing LGBTQ issues in the curriculum and providing supportive counselling services. They can also be smaller projects such as ensuring that the library has relevant books and other resources available. Regardless of the strategies, there are some basic requirements for establishing a safe environment. Schneider's and Dimito's (2008) respondents were asked to indicate up to three things that they thought were needed for students to feel safe in their school. The responses fell into the following categories:

- *Policy and enforcement.* In order for any action to successfully take place there needs to be a clear foundation of policy supporting the safety and rights of all LGBTQ members of the school community. Furthermore, staff and administration must feel willing and empowered to implement the policy.
- *Social support.* Students need role models, both openly LGBTQ teachers as well as supportive heterosexual teachers. They need a safe contact person with whom they can talk, as well as a way of connecting with other LGBTQ students.
- *Resources.* These need to be available at a number of different levels. Teachers need staff training; LGBTQ students need material relevant to their lives; all students need exposure to the issues through curriculum.
- *Visibility.* Overall, LGBTQ issues need to be visible. The first three conditions are not sufficient, in and of themselves, if students are unaware of supportive staff, how to find resources, or whether or not their school district has any anti-LGBTQ discrimination policies. Visibility sends a message to LGBTQ students that they are a valued part of the school community and to heterosexual students that bullying is unacceptable.

GSAs can be an effective forum for addressing LGBTQ issues in general, and responding to homophobic bullying in the school setting. We will now describe the development of GSAs in one school district in Ontario, Canada and identify the key factors that allowed them to continue and succeed.

Research on GSAs

GSAs are school-based clubs that, at their best, are not just support groups. They are forums for both LGBTQ students and heterosexual allies to address homophobia and heterosexism in the school community. They provide support for LGBTQ students who are experiencing discrimination and provide a place for otherwise isolated students to enjoy a healthy social environment. But they also have a role as a hub for educational and political activities pertaining to homophobia and heterosexism (Doppler, 2000). This is an important theme and one to which we will return.

A handful of studies have shown that GSAs have a positive impact on LGBTQ students. In comparisons of schools with and without GSAs, LGBTQ students in schools with GSAs heard less homophobic language at school (Kosciw *et al.*, 2010; Szalacha, 2003), felt safer from harassment (Kosciw *et al.*, 2010;

Lee, 2002) and experienced less victimisation (Kosciw *et al.*, 2010; Heck *et al.*, 2011; Goodenow*et al.*, (2006). They were more likely to indicate that school personnel intervene when they hear homophobic language (Kosciw *et al.*, 2010); There were also positive mental health outcomes including improved academic performance (Lee, 2002), greater sense of connection with the school (Lee, 2002; Heck *et al.*, 2011; Kosciw *et al.*, 2010) and a general improved sense of well-being (Heck *et al.*, 2011) that extended into young adulthood (Toomey *et al.*, 2011). These are, of course, correlational studies and inferences regarding cause and effect must be made cautiously.

As with many interventions for LGBTQ youth, GSAs were historically based on a risk-reduction/mental health model, that focused on preventing the developmental problems associated with a stigmatised identity and associated risky correlates such as substance abuse, depression, suicide, etc. However, as schools became more concerned with diversity and equity, GSAs have increasingly incorporated a human rights perspective, often with a focus on critical pedagogy in which the social and power structures of the school and community, particularly heterosexism, are analysed and deconstructed (Mayberry, 2007; Macgillivray, 2005). This has resulted in an ecological understanding of GSAs, not just as isolated clubs supporting stigmatised youth, but as agents for social change within a larger community. Thus, their role in preventing homophobic bullying involves moving beyond being a 'hide out' by providing an impetus for changing the school environment. As one teacher, a participant in the study described below, observed:

> GSAs create a positive space. So when you walk into the GSA room you know that you're going to be accepted because the people in there accept you and are working as a community ... you work together with your GSA to create that bond of safe space and there are days where if you created it well enough it expands beyond those doors of that classroom ... it becomes a bigger picture.

Clearly, GSAs can have an important impact on the safety, mental health, school performance and experience of individual students. However, most researchers and practitioners agree that the ultimate value in GSAs lies in changing the social climate of the school. This means that GSAs must be visible, active and a significant part of the school community and must be sustainable from year to year, regardless of student or staff turnover. Key elements in sustaining GSAs include: equity and human rights policies that support the human rights of LGBTQ students; resources; key, committed staff members including administrators; community participation; and student leadership (Griffin and Oulette, 2002). The following pages will describe the role of all these elements as GSAs developed over several years to successfully address homophobic bullying in one school district.

The school district

The school district described here is in the Region of Waterloo, located in the south-west of the province of Ontario. The region is about one hour's drive from Toronto, the provincial capital. With a population of more than 500,000 it is one of the fastest growing areas in Ontario. Although a majority of the population is Caucasian, according to the 2006 census, 13 per cent of the population identified as being part of a visible minority including South Asian, Chinese, Filipino and Black. That figure had increased from the previous census by 40 per cent and no doubt it has continued to increase.

Although agriculture accounts for 65 per cent of the land use in the region, the economic base also includes business and industry (including car manufacturing, insurance companies as well as *Research In Motion*, maker of the *Blackberry*). It is home to two universities and one community college. The Region is a popular tourist destination, in part due to the heritage of the Mennonite and Amish settlers whose cultures continue to be evident. The Region also has a state-of-the-art concert hall, a symphony orchestra, a philharmonic choir and 13 public library branches. The average household income is above the national average (Region of Waterloo, 2011).

Although the region represents a mixture of rural and urban settings, it has become increasingly diverse and urbanised in the past decade. Yet, it remains politically conservative as indicated by the results of the recent provincial and federal elections, and is arguably socially conservative in many quarters. Thus, the success of GSAs in the school district cannot be simply attributed to the liberal perspective that is so often associated with urban areas.

The Waterloo Region District School Board (WRDSB) is one of the largest school boards in the province, serving approximately 60,000 students from kindergarten to grade 12. There are approximately 3,500 teachers and 2,000 support staff members. There are 17 high schools in total, some of which are distinctly urban and the rest residing in distinctly rural areas. There are GSAs in 16 high schools, including some in rural areas.

Development and sustainability of GSAs

The data reported here were collected as part of a larger, ongoing evaluation of GSAs being carried out by the second author. The present discussion is based on preliminary interviews with key informants: five teachers in the WRDSB; one community liaison person; one student and one former student. In addition, the second author had informal conversations with a vice principal, community leaders and several LGBTQ youth.

GSAs have existed in some schools in the WRDSB for about a decade, but it was a struggle to keep them viable. That changed about three years ago, when a community-based service, OK2BME (*'okay to be me'*), became involved with the WRDSB's GSAs. OK2BME is a group of services for LGBTQ youth in Waterloo Region. It operates under the umbrella of K-W Counselling

Services and in cooperation with Family and Children's Services of the Waterloo Region. The first step in this involvement took place about five years ago, when the Ontario Teachers' Federation had started a group for LGBTQ teachers who felt that they needed support. A staff person from OK2BME was invited to do a series of workshops for teachers at one of the schools identified as having a supportive atmosphere. After this, a link was established between teachers and a supportive community-based organisation.

The next step became possible in 2009, when Ontario's Ministry of Education and Training released the document entitled *Equity and Inclusive Education in Ontario's Schools: Guidelines for Policy Development and Implementation* (OntarioMinistry of Education and Training, 2009). This document set out a vision for an equitable and inclusive education system. It is largely concerned with racial discrimination, which is arguably the most conspicuous equity issue in the province. However, in several places it recognises all the prohibited grounds for discrimination as outlined in the Ontario Human Rights Code (Ontario Human Rights Commission, 2009), which include sexual orientation. The guidelines require schools to develop a supportive climate so that all students feel 'safe, welcomed and accepted' (Ontario Ministry of Education and Training, 2009: 27). Thus, the document opened the door to a much more vigorous effort to establish and maintain GSAs. It also required that each school district hire an equity officer. Its emphasis on community involvement was seen by staff at OK2BME as support for actively partnering with schools and it gave teachers a foothold in establishing and maintaining GSAs. The key informant from OK2BME noted,

> It's important for us to be active in community and community can be schools … Youth spend so much time in school … it all just made sense to have this partnership. We know the mental health issues, the amount of suicide, the stats related to that for LGBTQ youth who struggle and don't have supports. It makes sense to go into the schools and help the schools with their GSAs because that's a lot of what they talk about.

Since then OK2BME has been an important resource. There is one staff liaison person who dedicates much of her time to working with the schools. Having an expert in community development and LGBTQ issues has given structure and direction to the development of GSAs. The key informant noted:

> I think it's helped support the continuation of GSAs. Some of them were already started but were losing students, were losing interest. Teachers didn't really know what to do or how to facilitate or what their role was, so we've been able to go in and help them realign what they were doing or [suggest] ideas about how to keep and sustain a GSA. Lots of teachers … are eager to get one going but they don't know what it means and they don't know what to do. … We give them ideas of what they can do during that 50 minutes that they have instead of it just becoming a social club.

The liaison meets with teachers involved in GSAs as well as the WRDSB's equity officer four times a year. This GSA Leaders' Network is a chance for teachers to debrief. The liaison also provides psycho-educational resources for teachers and students. Thus, teachers and students have the needed support and knowledge base to develop their leadership skills. These meetings have been supplemented with two GSA annual conferences attended by both OK2BME and WRDSB staff, and students.

The liaison also helps students connect with age-appropriate LGBTQ activities in the larger community, such as counselling and recreational supports. In addition, OK2BME provides rainbow 'swag', such as lanyards, to distribute at school events. Teachers who display the swag are then easily identifiable as LGBTQ-positive. These increased resources provided impetus for organising various events. Individual schools have held Pink Days, Purple Days and Rainbow Days, to highlight the invisibility and inclusion of LGBTQ students and to raise awareness of homophobic bullying, and there are GSA dances and a Pride Prom at the end of the school year. The teachers who were interviewed agreed that the GSAs made LGBTQ issues more visible:

> Purple day was a ... big focus on anti-bullying around sexual orientation and gender issues ... We had a HUGE purple banner ... and we created hundreds of little purple ribbons, and then people could come down from homeroom to student activities to get them, and then we handed them out at lunch, but we'd also been asking people to dress in purple that day. And there was a really impressive response, more than I thought there would be. It brought about a lot of discussion ... We had parent-teacher interviews that night and I'm proud to say a lot of people left their purple on! ... We left our banner out in the evening for parents to come and sign, and at least be aware we were running it. I would say overall it was very successful and we seem to have a heightened awareness.

Another teacher noted:

> We're really focused on making sure [the kids get the connection between heterosexism and homophobia] and they really do. [We] sponsor things in the school that are working on heterosexism. So one of the amazing things they did this year was we sponsored the Valentine's Day dance, and I think at a grade 7/8 school that shows we've come far. And as the kids entered the dance we had "It Gets Better" stamps, and we had rainbow things, and all GSA stuff all into the dance ... so to me that was changing the traditional *very* heterosexist structure of the senior school.

These comments illustrate the necessary components for the development of effective GSAs. A foundation of policy mandated the appointment of key staff in the form of an equity officer and clearly delineated sexual orientation as an equity issue. This policy opened the door to community resources. The community resources helped train teachers and students to take leadership roles, which in terms seems to have sustained the GSAs.

Impact on school climate: did GSAs work?

Student: I got thrown in a locker when I went to the one school. I lasted 3 days there and I said, I'm transferring, I'm not staying here. [I'd like a school] where ... you can walk down the hall and [think], Oh look, they're not going to judge me, they're not going to say stuff. You're not going to hear people going, "whisper, whisper, whisper" beside you right? ... You don't hear those stupid slurs and that you could just be yourself and not worry, and not be made fun of for how you dress, or how you act, or who you like or anything like that.

Interviewer: What do you think schools can do to make that a reality?

Student: I think the biggest thing is awareness ... I think if more people ... start to feel more safe and come out, people will actually start to see the statistics ... I think it would be mind blowing for people to actually see, "Oh look in this classroom there's three gay students and you never would've thought." So I think if people were more aware of how many people there actually are but they're too scared to come out because of *them* and how they treat them I think it would be a big deal.

The same student also observed:

> The GSA [at our school] has a huge role. When you're walking around the school almost all of the teachers have the OK2BME lanyards, so you see a lot of the teachers are on the same page, that they wear the rainbow around saying , "Look this needs to be a safe school." It gives you hope [because] teachers are okay with it ... It makes an impact, right? You're walking down the hall [and think], "Oh look that teacher has an OK2BME lanyard, I feel safe like nothing's going to happen."

GSAs in the schools in WRDSB have made LGBTQ issues more visible. But what is the evidence that this made the school climate more positive for LGBTQ students? One teacher, talking about the impact on young people who have not come out, said:

> I think it's had [an impact]. This is my guess because you won't know until they come back in 5 years and say, "By the way I never came to your group but I saw your posters up." ... My guess is it's a huge difference just to know that it's a possibility at all. In my day it didn't even register as a maybe. It just wasn't on the radar. Now we've generated some GSA shirts [with the school name on them], so they've got our logo on it, a rainbow

logo, and a few staff members and some of their parents and brothers and people bought them. I made 30 this year and they were gone in no time.

Other teachers were not so sure:

> There probably are folks who know enough not to discuss it in a disparaging way or to be outwardly discriminatory. There are always those incidents and things you hear about that are said in the classroom and even more so the things that aren't addressed in the classroom so somebody yells, "Hey that's the gay kid," and you know ... the teacher doesn't do anything about it.

Some teachers make the distinction between the impact on overt homophobia in contrast to the impact on imbedded heterosexism, questioning whether there had been a significant impact on the latter:

> My question is [whether] it sometimes creates an illusion ... If we're going to deal with homophobia [we have to deal with] heterosexism ... [If not] it's like, "Oh, we have a multicultural club, and we *don't* deal with racism." And we deal with homophobia, but we don't deal with heterosexism.

Similarly, a pilot survey of 37 students involved in GSAs, conducted by the second author, provided mixed results. About half felt that their school's GSA increased the feeling of safety for LGBTQ students, and well over half felt that it made it easier for LGBTQ students to be out at school. Also more than half felt that it increased both staff and student acceptance of LGBTQ students. Everyone, except for one person, felt included, accepted and supported by their GSA. However, only about one third felt that the GSA activities decreased the use of derogatory words such as 'fag', etc. Approximately half felt that there had been backlash from other students and from staff.

There is also some inconsistency in interviews with students. When asked about bullying in general students often reported that they do not experience bullying. However, when asked about how their day went, or about specific behaviours it emerges that they have been verbally and sometimes physically harassed directly, or indirectly exposed to homophobic language. This speaks to the need for a longitudinal setting-level assessment as recommended by Chesir-Teran (2003) and described in Moos and Lemke (1983).

In summary, neither teachers nor students are unanimous when asked to quantify the impact of GSAs. However, they do agree that GSAs are potential agents of change and they all believe that the GSAs clearly fulfill a support role:

Teacher: We've talked about being an alternate family for ourselves and we really have each other and we need to support each other ... This year in particular was, at our school, difficult. One of their friends committed suicide recently here so we had a really tough, unusual year and that theme I would say ran throughout the year. So each meeting was really important ... A lot of them had their own struggles ... so we dealt a whole lot with everybody's struggles. We worked on self harm and keeping safe and looking after each other so it was a constant theme ... [The suicide] changed everything this year ... Whatever struggles they had it heightened their struggles. Whatever insecurities they had, it deepened them. It shook their foundation ... so I personally did a lot of suicidal intervention with this group in between the meetings ... and I'd be dealing with their counselor and other things all week and trying to help kids out with OK2BME just really trying to find support systems.

Conclusion

The GSAs in WRDSB are providing all the elements that teachers have said are necessary to eliminate homophobia in the schools. These are: social support, resources and visibility of LGBTQ issues, all founded on a clear policy. It would seem, then, that effective GSAs, that is GSAs supported by policy, resources, adequate leadership and community participation, can, over time, be an efficient way to address homophobic bullying in the schools because they have the potential to change the social context that tacitly supports bullying. Whether they can reach that potential has yet to be researched systematically.

Bullying takes place when individuals are devalued and therefore disempowered by virtue of their sex, race, physical appearance, sexual orientation, gender expression or other significant characteristics. However, anti-bullying strategies that simply address bullying behaviour do not address the social context that gives children and adolescents the idea that some individuals are more valuable than others. Furthermore, they do nothing to stop the 'whispering' that one student referred to – or other behaviours like whispering that don't precisely fall into the category of bullying. These behaviours can poison an environment and have similar severe consequences in the same way that more overt behaviours such as physical and verbal abuse do. Preventing bullying is about ensuring the safety of students. For a school to be truly safe, however, students must see themselves reflected in the school setting – in the curriculum, in the staffing, and in the activities. Even when bullying behaviour is under control in a school environment, an LGBTQ student cannot feel entirely safe if the underlying assumptions remain heterosexist, because as long as it is, that student remains an outsider in a stigmatising environment.

At their best, GSAs are not only safe havens for LGBTQ youth, but also serve as a forum for students to critically analyse and deconstruct their environment. In this way they can develop an understanding of heterosexism, how it is manifested and its impact upon them. That, in turn, gives them the tools to change their school environment, as is happening in the school system described here.

References

British Columbia, Ministry of Education (2006) *Safe Schools Act*. Available at: http:// www.leg.bc.ca/38th2nd/1st_read/m204-1.htm (accessed 22 February, 2012).

Callaghan, T. (2011) *Holy Homophobia: Doctrinal Discipling of Non-Heterosexuals in Canadian Catholic schools*, unpublished thesis, Ontario Institute for Studies in Education, University of Toronto.

Canadian Teachers' Federation and the Elementary Teachers' Federation of Ontario (2003) *Seeing the Rainbow: Teachers Talk About Bisexual, Gay, Lesbian, Transgender and Two-Spirited Realities*, Ottawa: Authors.

CBC News (2005) *Landmark win for bullying victim*. Available Http: http://www.cbc. ca/news/canada/british-columbia/story/2005/10/25/bc_jubran-bully20051025. html (accessed 25 October 2005).

Chesir-Teran, D. (2003) 'Conceptualizing and addressing heterosexism in high schools: a settings level approach', *American Journal of Community Psychology*, 31: 267–279.

Doppler, J. E. (2000) *A Description of Gay/Straight Alliances in the Public Schools of Massachusetts*, unpublished thesis, University of Massachusets-Amherst.

Goodenow, C., Szalacha, L. and Westheimer, K. (2006) 'School support groups, other school factors, and the safety of sexual minority adolescents', *Psychology in the Schools*, 43: 573–589.

Griffin, P. and Ouellett, M. L. (2002) 'Going beyond Gay-Straight Alliances to make schools safe for lesbian, gay, bisexual, and transgender students', *ANGLES: The Policy Journal of The Institute for Gay and Lesbian Strategic Studies*, 6: 1–8.

Heck, N. C., Flentje, A. and Cochran, B. N. (2011) 'Offsetting risks: high school Gay-Straight Alliances and lesbian, gay, bisexual, and transgender (LGBT) youth', *School Psychology Quarterly*, 26, 161–174.

Kosciw, J. G., Greytak, E. A., Diaz, E. M. and Bartkiewicz, M. J. (2010) *The 2009 National School Climate Survey: The Experiences of Lesbian, Gay, Bisexual and Transgender Youth in our Nation's Schools*, New York: GLSEN.

Lakritz, N. (2008) 'Homophobic bullying in schools can and does kill', *Calgary Herald* 30 January. Online. Available at: http://www.canada.com/calgaryherald/news/ story.html?id=cbc74181-3103-4366-bacf-bea306ede7ca (accessed 22 February 2012).

Lee, C. (2002) 'The impact of belonging to a high school gay/straight alliance', *The High School Journal*, 85: 13–26.

Macgillivray, I. K. (2005) 'Shaping democratic identities and building citizenship skills through student activism: Mexico's first Gay-Straight Alliance', *Equity and Excellence in Education*, 38: 320–330.

Mayberry, M. (2007) 'The story of a Salt Lake City Gay-Straight Alliance: identity work and LGBT youth', *Journal of Gay and Lesbian Issues in Education*, 4:13–31.

Mayencourt, L. (2006) *Mayencourt Meets with Hamed Nastoh Anti-Bullying Coalition*. Available at: http://www.lornemayencourtmla.bc.ca/EN/lorn's_local_news_2006/ mayencourt_meets_with_hamed_nastoh_anti-bullying_coalition/?andPH-PSES SID'9bcefa3feddfc5410267884bf3c04e (accessed 19 January 2006).

Moos, R. and Lemke, S. (1983) 'Assessing and improving social and ecological settings', in E. Seidman (ed.), *Handbook of Social Intervention*, Beverly Hills, CA: Sage.

Ontario Human Rights Commission (2009) *Ontario Human Rights Code*. Available at: http://www.ohrc.on.ca/en/resources/code (accessed 22 February 2012).

Ontario Ministry of Education and Training (2009) *Equity and Inclusive Education in Ontario's Schools: Guidelines for Policy Development and Implementation*, Toronto: Author.

Pascoe, C. J. (2011) *Dude, You're a Fag: Masculinity and Sexuality in High School,* Berkeley, CA: University of California Press.

Region of Waterloo (2011) *About Waterloo Region*. Available at: http://www. regionofwaterloo.ca/en/discoveringtheregion/aboutwaterlooregion.asp (accessed 22 February 2012).

Saskatchewan Teachers' Federation (2002) *Safe Schools: Breaking the Silence on Sexual Difference,* Saskatoon, SK: Author.

Schneider, M. and Dimito, A. (2008) 'Educators' beliefs about raising lesbian, gay, bisexual and transgender issues in the schools: the experience in Ontario, Canada,' *Journal of LGBT Youth*, 5: 49–71.

Szalacha, L. A. (2003) 'Safer sexual diversity climates: lessons learned from an evaluation of Massachusetts Safe Schools Program for gay and lesbian students', *American Journal of Education*, 110: 58–88.

Taylor, C., Peter, T., Schachter, K., Paquin, S., Beldom, S., Gross, Z. and McMinn, T. S. (2008) *Youth Speak Up about Homophobia and Transphobia: The First National Climate Survey on Homophobia in Canadian Schools. Phase One Report*, Toronto ON: Egale Canada Human Rights Trust.

Toomey, R. B., Ryan, C., Diaz, R. M. and Russell, S. T. (2011) 'High School gay-straight alliances (GSAs) and young adult well-being: an examination of GSA presence, participation, and perceived effectiveness', *Applied Developmental Science*, 15: 175–185.

Toronto Star (2011) 'Hundreds attend funeral for Jamie Hubley, bullied teen who committed suicide.' Available at: http://www.thestar.com/news/article/1073711 (accessed 21 October 2011).

Williams, T., Connolly, J., Pepler, D. and Craig, W. (2005) 'Peer victimization, social support and psychosocial adjustment of sexual minority adolescents', *Journal of Youth and Adolescence,* 34: 471–482.

Woods, M. (2011) 'Gay students bear "cycle of hate"', *Toronto Star*, 22 October. p. A6.

Zerbisias, A. (2011) 'Suicide and sexuality', *Toronto Star*, October 22, pp. IN1–3.

12 Planning and delivering interventions to promote gender and sexuality

Debbie Ollis

Introduction

> Starting secondary school was a big deal for Zoey. Pretty, smart and sporty, she was one of her small primary school's high achievers, so perhaps felt the transition to a large high school more than others. Keen to fit in, her new mobile phone came in handy as she made her first tentative forays into adolescent flirtation. Just 13, she began texting a boy she had met over summer who was a year older and regarded as one of the school's coolest kids. Then one night came an unexpected request: 'send me a photo.' Confused, Zoey sent back: 'what of?' He replied, "Take your clothes off." She didn't respond. But the boy did not let up and pestered her via text for several weeks – "everyone's doing it," "don't be frigid" – until one night, heart thumping, she took her phone into the family bathroom, took off her clothes, aimed the phone's camera at the mirror and took a picture of herself from the neck down. Seconds later she pressed "send" and the picture was his. She told no one but was sure the boy had shared the photo around because as she and her friends walked down to the school canteen at lunchtime they would pass the boy and his friends "and they would all sit there giving me these smirky looks." Zoey, by this stage halfway through year seven, started to receive texts from other boys asking for a photo. "So I went through the whole process again with two other guys," recalls Zoey, now 15. "I just wanted to make friends and be popular and I really thought if I did this they would become my friends."
>
> (Brady, 2011)

It is one thing to raise school and community awareness about the extent of gender and sexuality related bullying and violence, yet another to develop strategies and interventions that can deal with the complex and dynamic nature of how a situation such as Zoey's plays out in schools. This chapter is designed to assist those working with young people to translate the research and understandings on addressing gender, sexuality and bullying presented in this book into practice in schools. Drawing on current research on effective sexuality education, teacher practice, building respectful relationships and addressing gendered based violence, including homophobia, the chapter discusses and presents the key elements of planning and delivering successfully interventions for young people in schools.

Zoey's situation is a common story. However, dealing with it is a multifaceted issue for schools. Although the original texting (or 'sexting' as it is called) did not happen on the school grounds, it involved a number of the school's students. Zoey felt humiliated, became disengaged and refused to go to school. Zoey's parents were distressed and wanted the school to do something about it. Zoey's action was illegal, yet it could be argued that the boy's request for the photograph in the first place, and the subsequent fall-out it caused, is an instance of violence and bullying related to gender and sexuality. Would the situation be different if Zoey was a boy and the photograph had been distributed amongst a group of girls? If Zoey identified as lesbian, bisexual, trans, queer or questioning, would this change the situation and how to deal with it? These issues are complex and dynamic. The private nature of the situation and the blurred boundaries between school, home and responsibility makes such situations difficult for schools and those supporting young people.

Before exploring the key elements of a strategy to address the issues identified in Zoey's story and other examples of gender and sexuality related bullying and violence featured throughout this book, it is important to acknowledge that schools are but one part of a much larger picture (Home Office, 2011). Schools can and do make a difference. However, we need to be realistic about how much schools can do without broader structural change and departmental support. Change in schools is often instigated by the passion of a teacher or 'champion' wanting to make a difference (Adelman and Taylor 2007; Kroeger 2006). Just as the work of schools needs to be contextualised in this broader framework, so does the work of teachers and professionals implementing programmes in schools that aim to prevent violence and bullying and teach for positive gender and sexualities.

Gender and sexualities: a common framework

Teaching about gender, sexuality and violence has always presented challenges for schools. A lack of recognition, perceived and real opposition, teacher confidence and training, and competing curriculum priorities all present barriers to effective approaches in schools (Flood *et al.*, 2009; Meyer 2011; Ollis, 2010; Ollis and Tomaszewski, 1993; Smith *et al.*, 2011; United Nations Educational, Scientific and Cultural Organisation – UNESCO, 2009; US Agency for International Development – USAID, 2002). The recognition and funding of school based resources and a program is a cyclical process as governments respond to public incidents of violence and community concerns. The gendered nature of Zoey's story is a common feature of discussion, debate and resourcing in countries all over the Western world as parents and schools grapple with the impact of social media and access to technology.

In 2010 the Commonwealth Government of Australia allocated 2.5 million dollars to education schemes to prevent gender-based violence. Similar programmes have been seen in Canada and the UK (Home Office, 2011). UNESCO has also released international reports and resources to assist schools to address the issues (UNESCO, 2009). Many of these programmes have emerged under the agenda of respectful relationships. This has been done as a way of positioning violence in the context of relationships and in the hope that by building more respectful relationships, violence related to gender and sexuality will be reduced (Flood *et al.*, 2009; Lloyd and Nancarrow, 2009). It has also enabled a way of broadening the focus to include other forms of gender-based violence such as that experienced by young people who identify as LGBTQ (Hillier *et al.*, 2010). For example, one of the most recent interventions in Australia defined gender based violence to be inclusive of 'violence against gay, lesbian and transgender young people' (Department of Education and Early Childhood Development – DEECD, forthcoming: 5).

Over the past decade much of the work addressing gender, sexuality and bullying in Australia has been in the area of homophobia. National and longitudinal studies by Hillier *et al.* (1998; 2010) and Hillier and Harrison (2004) have shown an enormous impact on the visibility of sexual diversity in Australian schools, and on the development of resources and policies to support young people and schools to be affirming and proactive in combating homophobia. Like policies on sexual harassment and sexual abuse, some states in Australia have developed specific sexual diversity guidelines that require schools to be inclusive of all sexualities (Boston, 1997; DEECD, 2008a). National and state based resources have been developed with a clear focus on teaching about sexual diversity and gender in secondary schools in an inclusive and affirming way (Australian National Council for AIDS, Hepatitis C and Related Diseases – ANCAHRD, 2001; Department of Education and Training – DET, 2004; Shine, 2011). Teacher professional development has been implemented in most of the country. The most widely used resources by teachers of sexuality education are those that are inclusive of gender and sexual diversity and provide teachers with teaching sequences and ideas (Dyson, 2009; Smith *et al.*, 2011).

Consistent with the research presented in this book, schools in Australia remain the most likely place for abuse of LGBTQ young people to occur (Hillier *et al.*, 2010). In Australia the number of young people reporting abuse has actually increased to 80 per cent from 69 per cent in 1998 and 74 per cent in 2004. School based violence is also shown to increase young people's vulnerability to negative health outcomes, as the previous chapters have clearly illustrated. However, the latest research in Australia is suggesting that if schools have anti-homophobia education policies that are known to the students and deal specifically with homophobia as well as other bullying, LGBTQ are less likely to be abused or think about and engage in self-harm or suicidal behaviours (Hillier *et al.*, 2010).

As chapters elsewhere in this book have shown, gender and sexuality is likely to be the underlying theme evident in any violent incident in schools.

Much of it remains hidden because teachers and schools are reluctant to recognise, acknowledge and deal with it. School based sexuality education, sexual health, or sex and relationships education programmes also fail to teach about it because of a lack of teacher confidence, knowledge and concerns about parental and professional backlash (Carmody, 2009; Epstein and Johnson, 1998; Epstein *et al.*, 2003; Meyer, 2011; Ollis, 2009).

Even so, some schools defy these concerns and implement programmes and approaches that are inclusive and affirming of gender and sexuality, and challenge negative discourses. Drawing on Australian data from students and teachers involved in intervention studies, the remainder of this chapter will outline the elements of effective practice in planning and implementing programmes that have had some success in challenging negative discourses through teaching about gender, sexuality and violence.

Elements of effective practice

It always comes back to a 'whole-school' approach

There is not one policy document, programme or resource concerned with addressing gender and sexuality in a comprehensive way in schools that does not advocate the use of whole school approach (Health Canada, 2003; ANCAHRD, 1999; International Planned Parenthood Federation – IPPF, 2006; UNESCO, 2009; USAID, 2002). Strategies are most effective as part of a whole school approach that acknowledges both the agency of individuals (Kehler and Martino, 2007; Renold, 2006) and the influence of broader social structures such as gender, class, ethnicity/culture and power in the construction of sexualities and gender (Flood *et al.*, 2009; Meyer, 2011).

Zoey was targeted because she was a girl. Crabbe and Corlett (2010) argue that although 'sexting' may be consensual, it can also serve to reinforce and amplify gender inequality in line with cultural attitudes that position men and women differently, and strengthen the double standard. This happens in the context of an online world in which sexual images, most often sexualised images of women and girls are readily available, including pornography (Mitchell *et al.*, 2007). Zoey was in transition from primary to high school, a documented stress period, in which issues of violence and bullying have been shown to occur (Langenkamp, 2009).

Whether an incident is about gender and power in heterosexual relationships, violence and bullying between girls over sexuality issues or related to homophobia, an effective whole-school approach needs to start from the assumption that sexuality and gender are positive foundations of young people. It links information and critical thinking with agency, choice and support of diversity (Population Council, 2010; Ferguson *et al.*, 2008; Formby *et al.*, 2010; Ollis, 2002; Sieg, 2003; Sinkinson, 2009). It further conceptualises issues such as violence and bullying as intimately connected to the concept of improving sexual health as outlined by the World Health Organisation (WHO):

> Sexual health is a state of physical, emotional, mental and social well-being in relation to sexuality; it is not merely the absence of disease, dysfunction or infirmity. Sexual health requires a positive and respectful approach to sexuality and sexual relationships, as well as the possibility of having pleasurable and safe sexual experiences, free of coercion, discrimination and violence.
>
> (WHO, 2011)

A whole-school approach to improving the sexual health of young people and challenging negative discourses around gender and sexuality involves the whole school community (school leadership, teachers, parents, caregivers, elders, school authorities, students and community agencies who work with schools) working towards a comprehensive approach to adolescent health (Clift and Jensen, 2005; DEECD, 2008b; Department for Education and Employment – DfEE, 1999; Ferguson *et al.*, 2008; Healy, 1998; Ollis, 2003), enhanced by strong leadership that is participatory and democratic (Blackmore, 2004; Hargreaves, 2004; Hargreaves and Goodson, 2006; Walker, 2004). It involves developing a common understanding and code of practice (ANCAHRD, 2001; Flood *et al.*, 2009).

This means the development of policies and procedures that all school staff will understand and know how to implement consistently if a situation such as Zoey's arises. As simple as it sounds, research shows a clear link between the visibility of policies, teacher intervention and students feeling safe (Glover *et al.*, 1998; Hillier *et al.*, 2010; Education and Skills Committee, 2007; Kosciw *et al.*, 2008). It also means providing professional learning/ continuing professional development for staff and parents to increase visibility, recognition and understanding of the gendered nature of this type of incident as well as the legal ramifications (Ollis, 2009). Zoey's actions were illegal. Sending a sexually explicit image of a minor on the Internet or phone is classed as distributing pornography in Australia and many other developed nations. Physical and verbal abuse of a gay student is assault in Australia and elsewhere. It would also mean that students are engaged in education about sexual health and relationships that increases the awareness, recognition and understanding of the nature and impact of gender based violence, including the legal, moral, ethical and human rights implications. Education would enable students to critically explore the social constructions of gender, sexuality, power and homophobia. Parents and teachers would be aware of their own responsibility in promoting respectful relationships and in keeping young people safe (Health Canada, 2003; ANCAHRD, 1999).

However, a whole-school approach is often difficult to achieve because of teacher resistance and discomfort (Buston *et al.*, 2002), or discomfort from the school administration (Ollis, 2010). Differing moral and ethical paradigms and cultural contexts also mean that some schools have different legal and ethical considerations in relation to some issues, such as homophobia, making a consistent approach impossible to achieve (Carmody, 2009). Even so, many schools manage their approach to these whole school issues with interventions that show real improvements in teacher practice and student engagement.

What interventions work?

The answer to this question is contextual. Schools differ in their cultures and their approaches. One school may be proactive in implementing preventative work in sexual harassment, but is reluctant to address homophobia. Others may have policies but no consistent implementation strategies. Some schools may have comprehensive teaching and learning programmes but are unwilling to deal with incidents of gender and sexuality related violence in the school ground or sports fields. Others may be reluctant to be proactive at a whole school level for fear of school reputation. Regardless of how the schools are positioning gender and sexuality issues, or what the catalyst for action has been, there are some key considerations that have been shown to assist in planning and implementing programmes that can help to bring about some positive change.

The most consistent element is the crucial role that teachers can play in bringing about change and in challenging homophobia and sexism. Incentives and coercion are not effective with teachers. Teachers and those working with young people need to develop at the very least, a recognition of the importance of a safe and supportive school environment that is inclusive of gender and sexuality. Then it may be possible to develop teachers' willingness, commitment and the confidence to engage in interventions that are health promoting and sex and gender positive (Epstein and Johnson, 1998; Meyer, 2011; Ollis, 2010, 2011).

Teachers make the difference

Over the past twenty years I have worked with teachers and students in schools and universities to develop effective strategies for teaching about gender, sexuality and violence. This work has led me to believe that professional learning/continuing professional development is essential to assist teachers. Professional learning/continuing professional development enables teachers to develop knowledge, comfort, confidence, commitment and an inclusive and affirming framework to understand and position these issues. To do this teachers have to reflect upon and examine their own attitudes, school attitudes, community attitudes and examine the implications of not addressing these issues for the young people they teach. I have often used the notion of safety as a starting point because it provides a common and evidence based approach that all teachers can relate to. As earlier chapters illustrate, the research shows that many students experience discrimination, violence and bullying on the basis of their gender and sexuality. Every teacher is responsible for the safety of their students regardless of their own values and attitudes to sexuality. Teachers have statutory 'duty of care', or are in loco parentis, as it is referred to in Australia. Starting with safety also enables a move from a moral and ethical standpoints to one of ensuring schools are safe and supportive learning environments.

The importance of sexuality education

Although providing a safe and supportive environment is the responsibility of the whole school community, a whole school approach also requires a targeted teaching intervention (Flood *et al.*, 2009). Potentially, any discipline area can provide a framework for exploring issues of gender, sexuality and violence but traditionally this is most likely to be in the arts and social sciences. In itself this is a rationale for why all teachers require some professional learning/ continuing professional development to ensure they are not reinforcing traditional and discriminatory notions of gender and sexuality and are equipped to effectively address homophobia, sexism and other forms of gender based violence. It also indicates the need to provide a separate, sustainable context for teaching about these issues. Sex and relationships education (SRE), where it exists, is the most common context in which curriculum guidelines and resources are found (Formby *et al.*, 2010; UNESCO, 2009; WHO, 2011).

In a recent study of respectful relationships education in Australia (Ollis, 2011), interviews with teachers highlighted the difficulty of teaching about gender, sexuality and violence in contexts other than health and sexuality education. Although all teachers maintained that professional learning/continuing professional development had increased their understanding and preparedness to teach about gender and violence this was not the case in practice. Consistent with the findings of other research, the subject context was an important factor in teachers' willingness to cover sensitive sexuality issues (Ollis, 2009). As the following example demonstrates the teachers who implemented the programme in the context of SRE were confident and had a positive experience in comparison to those who had implemented it as part of an English unit:

> The kids loved it overall ... Yeah and I enjoyed taking it ... being we are health teachers, then they expect it ... we are accustomed to using group work, and role play and those sorts of strategies (SRE teacher).
> ... I found the programme challenging. I found the kids hard work ... the topics, scenarios and transgender case study did not engage the Yr. 8 students ... All struggled with the term 'partner' (English teacher).

There are a number of reasons why the teachers who had been directed to use the materials in their English classes struggled. The content and activities were radically different to the approaches with which they were comfortable. Although they had articulated an understanding of the importance of teaching about gender and sexuality following a two-day professional learning/continuing professional development workshop, they found it difficult to run the activities with the students. They reported that the material was confronting, and they found it hard to work with the students – resulting in one teacher recruiting community workers to conduct the lessons (Ollis, 2011).

It is important to prepare teachers and other professionals to address these issues in schools. Several studies have explored the enabling factors that are necessary to shift teachers from a position of hostility or indifference to one of commitment to the principles of inclusiveness and affirmation and prepare them to teach the issues in the classroom (Epstein and Johnson 1998, Ollis, 2010; Sinkinson, 2009).

Key factors in implementing and planning programmes in schools

Relevant and up-to-date teaching approaches

Teachers need effective teaching tools and resources that can assist them to address sensitive issues with students. In two recent studies of school-based interventions (Ollis, 2011; Ollis and Meldrum, 2009) students were clear about the approaches they found effective and relevant. Studies show that an activity-based approach to learning about gender, sexuality and violence engages the students (Carmody, 2009; Martino *et al.*, 2005; Ollis, 2009, 2011; Ollis and Harrison, 2010; Ollis and Meldrum, 2009). Students referred to the connection between doing and remembering: 'informative and even a little fun. I enjoyed how the activities get you involved and up and around in the classroom … you learn more' (Ollis, 2011), 'it was a completely different way to learn cause you can put it into practice, it was more of a reality' (Ollis and Meldrum, 2009).

Being able to talk about issues such as sexuality, gender, violence against women and homophobia also features as important, as it increases understanding and confidence and reduces fear (Ollis, 2011):

> Yeah, 'cause it's the sort of thing if you don't know about it, it's sort of scary. Whereas, people who get called gays and stuff like that, it's all blown out of proportion way too easily because we don't have a greater understanding of it … I think we need to do a course or something just to get people's confidence up to be able to talk about that sort of thing (Grade 9 boy, 14–15 years of age).

Teaching and learning experiences that build empathy, develop understanding, raise awareness and provide the opportunity for reflection appear to be highly valued by students and are seen as effective strategies to include in interventions designed to teach about and explore issues of gender, sexuality and violence (Ollis, 2011):

I think this was better than normal curriculum, because I think people understood more of what people actually feel ... especially cause you get to see what other people think ... It's very important that students are aware of what can happen in relationships ... getting students to see what gender based violence can do ... It raised awareness over some of the sensitive topics we otherwise wouldn't discuss. It was fun and I enjoyed it as well as learnt heaps ... reflections were a hassle, though they made you think about what you have done (Grade 9 girl, 14–15 years of age).

The combination of relevant content and engaging teaching approaches is clearly an important intervention strategy. If students can engage with the material then there is a greater chance of learning taking place. Research consistently shows that the opportunity to talk and make sense of their social worlds is an important aspect of effective approaches for students (Keddie and Mills, 2007; Martino *et al.*, 2005). Nevertheless, unless teachers can develop the knowledge and confidence to work with students around sensitive sexuality issues such as homophobia and other gender and sexuality issues, resources and teaching approaches become irrelevant. Teachers need professional learning/continuing professional development and training to use available interventions effectively.

The importance of professional learning/continuing professional development

We've been sent all this wonderful, huge, expensive resource ... must have cost them a squillion to produce. A great big box with all these packages and videos from the government, no instructions, I have no clue what it's about or what's in it. It's been sitting there now for three months and I haven't had a chance to even look inside it and I just think, they've obviously spent lots of money and lots of time producing this, getting it out to schools, getting it copied to every school and I'm not using it ... You'd be better off spending less money producing it and more money in-servicing people on how to use it.

(Ollis, 2009: 202)

Although a well-developed resource can assist teachers to address issues such as sexuality, homophobia and other gender-based violence including family violence, pornography, sexual assault and sexual harassment (Imbesi, 2008; Ollis, 2011; Smith *et al.*, 2011), good teaching and learning strategies alone are not sufficient to ensure that this is carried out in a positive and effective manner. Rather, research indicates that professional learning/continuing professional development that provides relevant discipline knowledge, skills and personal exploration of values and attitudes is extremely important. Further, and possibly more important, is the additional components of ongoing support and follow-up. It is often through pilot programmes that additional support becomes available to teachers to develop the sense of safety, comfort and confidence needed to use resources that address gender-based violence (Imbesi, 2008; Meiers, 2004; Ollis, 2011).

Basic elements for effective practice

Confidence and professionalism

The opportunity to engage in targeted PL/CPD has been shown to be crucial in building teachers' personal and professional confidence to cover sensitive sexuality issues such as gender, sexuality, violence and homophobia (Bowen *et al.*, 2004; Buston *et al.*, 2002; Freeman *et al.*, 2003; Ollis, 2011; Sinkinson, 2009; Tutty *et al.*, 2002). One European study cited in Flood *et al.* (2009), maintained that a lack of teacher training was the key impediment to an effective violence prevention programme. Moreover, programmes also need to be long enough in duration to enable a developmental and sequential approach (Flood *et al.*, 2009). In one study this sequential and developmental approach appeared to give teachers a sense that they were 'the experts ... having done the latest training'. Unlike most available professional learning, 'it was two days, not just a couple of hours after school' (Ollis, 2009: 202).

Having a solid framework

Implementing programmes via professional learning/continuing professional development needs to be more than providing teachers with a set of teaching and learning strategies. Teachers need to develop a sound understanding of the evidence base that can help provide a rationale for why they should have a role in addressing gender- and sexuality-related bullying and violence in their schools based programmes. For many teachers professional learning/ continuing professional development might be the first time they have the opportunity to consider research on young people, sexuality, bullying and the implications for their practice (Harrison and Ollis, 2011; Ollis, 2009, 2011). In addition, the exploration of current frameworks for working with young people around sexuality, such as health promotion, inclusion, positive sexualities and harm minimisation, has been shown to increase a sense of professionalism and theoretical understanding (Queensland Education, 2004; Evans *et al.*, 2009; Harrison and Ollis, 2011; Mugford and Nelson, 1996; Ollis, 2009):

> Given me a sort of theoretical basis. I think that's always a strong thing to work from, for me anyway. I mean they can give me any activity you like, bit unless it's got some connection. Unless it's hanging pegged on something, I find it really hard, I need to know why I'm doing what I'm doing.
>
> (Ollis, 2009: 175)

The importance of practice

Being able to test out and develop some clear parameters for their pedagogical practice is an important element in preparing teachers to teach about gender and sexuality related bullying and violence (Flood *et al.*, 2009; Ollis, 2009, 2011):

> It's really hard to put down on paper sometimes how something's meant to be run, the spirit of the activity, you know, and the best thing, the best workshops I've been to are the ones where you actually do the activities that you're going to do with kids. Because then you can see, this is where I need to make very clear that the kids know this, or this is where I have to give them this instruction, or this is the arrangement of the room, or this is the materials I need to have ready.
>
> (Ollis, 2009: 202)

Professional learning/continuing professional development that is conducted in a manner that mirrors the classroom processes has an enabling impact. Change in practice arises when teachers are able to see and experience the activities first-hand. This enables them to develop a sense of what to expect and an understanding of how students may feel. It provides the opportunity to anticipate possible questions and backlash from addressing sexual diversity and positive sexualities. It also enables teachers to see how to run the activities, including setting necessary boundaries and questioning techniques (Harrison and Ollis, 2011; Leahy *et al.*, 2004; Ollis, 2010, 2011).

Exploration of values and attitudes

Education about gender and sexuality is risky business for teachers because it is concerned with issues that can invoke a moral or ethical response and, if not conducted appropriately, can set up blame and shame. Research has demonstrated that the opportunity to explore and challenge personal attitudes and positions is not only highly valued by the teachers, but is instrumental in bringing about a change in practice for many teachers (Harrison and Ollis, 2011; Ollis, 2009, 2011). The power of activities that require teachers to explore personal positioning to sexual diversity and gender on shifting negative attitudes and exclusive approaches to teaching sexuality has been shown in a number of studies in Australia (Harrison and Ollis, 2011; Leahy *et al.*, 2004; Ollis, 2010, 2011). Teachers commonly refer to this as being the most valuable part of professional learning/continuing professional development. It provides the opportunity for teachers to explore how they feel about sexuality related issues in a supported learning environment prior to working with students, other staff and parents. It can also impact positively on teachers' ability to set up supportive learning environments (Ollis, 2010, 2011). One study showed that attitudinal change was greatest for teachers who struggled personally with issues of sexuality:

I surprised others and also myself in the workshop that knows me. I hope that this has flittered down into my teaching. Sometimes I need to check myself and find myself questioning some statement that particular the boys make that I previously may let slide or thought that I agree, so why would I question the kids.

(Ollis, 2010: 225).

Taking the extra step – 'supported risk taking'

This book has aimed to illustrate the complex and sensitive nature of addressing issues of gender- and sexuality-related bullying and violence in schools. Teacher anxiety about personal safety, students' ability to cope with the topics and potential student and teacher sexism and homophobia can result in teachers being reluctant to teach about these issues even after they have done extensive professional learning/continuing professional development (Flood *et al.*, 2009; Ollis, 2010, 2011). If teachers are not provided with what I call 'supported risk taking' to try using activities with students and testing out strategies, they will avoid them and continue with their old comfortable routines. In one study, I asked teachers to use activities that looked at transgender, gender and power and sexual diversity (ANCAHRD, 2001). Many teachers commented on how surprised they were that they had been able to carry out the activities without any negative consequences, revealing they would not have selected these to use with students had they not been requested to:

It's forced me to actually get into it. I can't pussyfoot around it, I had to do some certain activities today and it's actually turned out a really good learning experience for me because I think it's too easy to get given a resource and then just pick out the ones that are nice and easy to do...

(Ollis, 2009: 206).

Teachers need to be supported whilst they trial difficult and potentially sensitive activities. This means providing a structure that enables alternatives to the isolated teacher approach characteristic of most classrooms. Alternatives like team teaching with experienced teachers or with the trainers may provide some solutions. One model developed by a sexual assault centre in Australia (Imbesi, 2008) utilises the slow withdrawal of support. However, this programme is resource intensive and very difficult to sustain (Flood *et al.*, 2009). Common amongst successful programmes is the opportunity for teachers to be provided with follow-up and reflection as part of this supported risk taking. They need to have the opportunity to reflect on their practice. This can be difficult for schools and school systems, and means that if teachers are to be supported to do this work we need to rethink how we provide training, feedback and follow-up.

Feedback and follow-up

Providing support and follow-up after an initial training programme can be difficult and expensive, yet several studies indicate that they are crucial if change in practice is to be sustainable (Harrison and Ollis, 2011; Imbesi, 2009; Ollis, 2009, 2011). Commonly such follow-up tends to emerge through research projects that require teachers to reflect on their practice rather than being built into programmes. Such projects have shown the importance of being able to reflect on practice for developing confidence:

> I've really achieved a lot and I've come out feeling a lot better about it and more confident myself ... The confidence is growing in that I don't profess to be the guru but I'm on a learning curve that's steep, and I'm quite enjoying it.
>
> (Ollis, 2009: 207).

It also serves as a catalyst and reminder for the teachers to revisit and review resources. One teacher, in a study that explored the use of a resource to teach about gender and sexual diversity, 'kept going back and forth to the material, re-reading, getting on the Internet, hunting' (Ollis, 2009: 207)

Conclusion

To return to Zoey's situation, it is important to summarise the key elements of what is needed to effectively plan and implement programmes in schools that effectively address this illustration of gender- and sexuality-related bullying and violence or any other identified in this book. A school will need a whole-school approach, in which the issues are everybody's responsibility. Policy should be visible, and enacted by all staff. Support and affirmation would be visible for LGBTQ students, and students would know that issues would be dealt with if they arose. Teachers should have access to professional learning/continuing professional development that enabled them to develop a strong sense of the importance of schools and teachers in addressing sexuality, gender and bullying issues. SRE teachers and other relevant teachers will clearly need to have access to professional learning/continuing professional development which will enhance or further ground their knowledge, skills and personal understandings of gender and sexuality. It is important that those teachers feel that they have the confidence to teach these issues in an affirming way. Furthermore, by ensuring that teachers are prepared to deal with the issues outlined in this chapter and in previous chapters, we can ensure that students access educational experiences that address sexuality, gender and bullying that is affirming of diversity, and enables the development of those skills that build respectful relationships in a safe environment.

References

Adelman, H.S. and Taylor, L. (2007) 'Systemic change for school improvement', *Journal of Educational and Psychological Consultation*, 17: 55–77.

Australian National Council for AIDS, Hepatitis C and Related Diseases (1999) *Talking Sexual Health: National Framework for Education About STIs, HIV/AIDS and Blood-Borne Viruses in Secondary Schools*, Canberra: Author.

Australian National Council for AIDS, Hepatitis C and Related Diseases (2001) *Talking Sexual Health: A Learning and Teaching Resource for Secondary Schools*, Canberra: Author.

Blackmore, J, (2004) 'Restructuring educational leadership in changing contexts: a local/global account of restructuring in Australia', *Journal of Educational Change*, 5: 267–288.

Boston, K. (1997), *Homophobia in Schools*, Sydney, NSW: Department of Education and Training.

Bowen, L. K., Gwiasda, V. and Brown, M. M. (2004) 'Engaging community residents to prevent violence', *Journal of Interpersonal Violence*, 19: 356.

Brady, N. (2011) 'Scourge of the school yard: how one rash moment can ruin a young life', *The Age*, 10 July. Available at: http://www.theage.com.au/technology/technology-news/scourge-of-the-school-yard-how-one-rash-moment-can-ruin-a-young-life-20110709-1h84z.html (accessed 22 February 2012).

Buston, K., White, D., Hart, G. and Scott, S. (2002) 'Implementation of a teacher-delivered sex education programme', *Journal of Health Education Research*, 17: 59–72.

Carmody, M. (2009) *Sex and Ethics: The Sexual Ethics Education Program for Young People*, Melbourne: Macmillan.

Clift, S. and Jensen, B. B. (eds) (2005) *The Health Promoting School: International Advances in Theory, Evaluation and Practice*, Copenhagen: Danish University of Education Press.

Crabbe, M. and Corlett, D. (2010) 'Eroticising inequality: technology, pornography and young people', *Domestic Violence Resource Centre Victoria Quarterly*, 3: 1–6.

Department of Education and Early Childhood Development (2008a) *Catching On Everywhere – Part 1 Program Planning: Concepts and Policy*, Melbourne: Author (Sexuality Education Program Development for Victorian Schools).

Department of Education and Early Childhood Development (2008b) *Catching On Everywhere – Part 2 School Practice in Sexuality Education*, Melbourne: Author (Learning Programs Division Office for Government School Education).

Department of Education and Early Childhood Development (forthcoming) *Stepping Out Against Gender-Based Violence: A Teaching and Learning Resource to Build Respectful Relationships in Secondary School*, Melbourne: Author.

Department of Education and Training (2004) *Catching On*, Melbourne: Author (STD/HIV Prevention Education Project).

Department for Education and Employment (1999) *National Healthy School Standard: Guidelines*, Nottingham: Author.

Dyson, S. (2009) 'Girls and well-being: why educators ahould promote respectful relationships in school programs', *Redress: Journal of the Association of Women Educators*, 18: 8–13.

Education and Skills Committee (2007) *Bullying: Third Report of Session*, London: The Stationary Office.

Epstein, D. and Johnson, R. (1998) *Schooling Sexualities*, Buckingham: Open University Press.

Epstein, D., O'Flynn, S. and Telford, D. (2003) *Silenced Sexualities in Schools and Universities*, Stoke-on-Trent: Trentham Books.

Evans, S., Krogh, C. and Carmody, M. (2009) *Time to Get Cracking: The Challenge of Developing Best Practice in Australian Sexual Assault Prevention*, Melbourne: Australian Institute of Family Studies.

Ferguson, R. M., Vanwesenbeeck, I. and Knijn, T. (2008) 'A matter of facts ... and more: an exploratory analysis of the content of sexuality education in the Netherlands', *Sex Education*, 8: 14.

Flood, M., Fergus, L. and Heenan, M. (2009) *Respectful Relationships Education: Violence Prevention and Respectful Relationships Education in Victorian Secondary Schools*, Melbourne: Department of Education and Early Childhood Development.

Formby, E., Hirst, J., Owen, J., Hayter, M. and Stapleton, H. (2010) 'Selling it as a holistic health provision and not just about condoms ...: sexual health services in school settings: current models and their relationship with sex and relationships education policy and provision', *Sex Education*, 10: 423–35.

Freeman, E., Strong, D., Cahill, H., Wyn, J. and Shaw, G. (2003) 'Enhancing professional practice: an innovative professional development strategy to support teachers in school-based mental health promotion', *Journal of In-service Education*, 29: 277–294.

Glover, S., Burns, J., Butler, H. and Patton, G. (1998) 'Social environments and the emotional wellbeing of young people', *Family Matters*, 49: 11–16.

Hargreaves, A. (2004) 'Inclusive and exclusive educational change: emotional responses of teachers and implications for leadership', *School Leadership and Management*, 24: 287–309.

Hargreaves, A. and Goodson, I. (2006) 'Educational change over time? The sustainability and nonsustainability of three decades of secondary school change and continuity', *Educational Administration Quarterly*, 42: 3.

Harrison, L. and Ollis, D. (2011) 'Preparing pre-service teachers to teach sexuality education in the middle years: barriers and enablers ', paper presented to *Australian Teacher Education Assocaition Conference*, Melbourne, July 2011.

Healy, C. (1998) 'Health promoting schools: learning from the European project', *Health Education*, 98: 21–26.

Health Canada (2003) *Canadian Guidelines for Sexual Health Education*, Ottawa: Author (Population and Public Health Branch).

Home Office (2011) *Together We Can End Violence Against Women and Girls: A Strategy*, London: Author (National Mental Health Development Unit).

Hillier, L., Dempsey, D., Harrison, L., Beale, L., Matthews, L. and Rosenthal, D. (1998) *Writing Themselves In: A National Report on the Sexuality, Health and Well-Being of Same-Sex Attracted Young People*, Melbourne: La Trobe University: Australian Research Centre in Sex, Health and Society.

Hillier, L. and Harrison, L. (2004) 'Homophobia and the production of shame: young people and same sex attraction', *Culture, Health and Sexuality*, 61, 79–94.

Hillier, L., Jones, T., Monagle, M., Overton, N., Gahan, L., Blackman, J. and Mitchell, A. (2010) *Writing Themselves in 3 (WTi3): The Third National Study on the Sexual Health and Well-being of Same-Sex Attracted and Gender Questioning Young People*, Melbourne: La Trobe University: Australian Research Centre in Sex, Health and Society.

160   *Debbie Ollis*

Imbesi, R. (2008) *Sexual Assault Prevention Program for Secondary Schools (SAPPSS) Report*, Melbourne: CASA House.

Imbesi, R. (2009) 'Issues of masculinity and violence and the current boys' debate in Australia', *Redress: Journal of the Association of Women Educators*, 18: 9.

International Planned Parenthood Federation (2006) *IPPF Framework for Comprehensive Sexuality Education CSE*, London: The International Planned Parenthood Federation.

Keddie, A. and Mills, M. (2007) *Teaching Boys*, Crows Nest, NSW: Allen and Unwin.

Kehler, M. and Martino, W. (2007) 'Questioning masculinities: interrogating boys' capacities for self-problematization in schools', *Canadian Journal of Education/ Revue Canadienne de l'Education*, 30: 90–112.

Kosciw, J. G., Diaz, E. M. and Greytak, E. A. (2008) *National School Climate Survey 2007: The Experiences of Lesbian, Gay, Bisexual and Transgender Youth in our Nation's Schools*, New York: GLSEN.

Kroeger, J. (2006) 'Stretching performances in education: the impact of gay parenting and activism on identity and school change', *Journal of Educational Change*, 7: 319–337.

Langenkamp, A. G. (2009) 'Following different pathways: social integration, achievement, and transition to high school', *American Journal of Education*, 116: 69–97.

Leahy, D., Horne, R. and Harrison, L. (2004) *Bass Coast Sexuality Education Project: Needs Analysis and Professional Development Evaluation Report*, Geelong: Deakin University (Consultancy and Development Unit, Faculty of Education).

Lloyd, L. and Nancarrow, H. (2009) *Time for Action: The National Council's Plan for Australia to Reduce Violence Against Women and their Children, 2009–2021*, Canberra: National Council to Reduce Violence Against Women and Their Children.

Martino, W., Mills, M. and Lingard, B. (2005) 'Interrogating single-sex classes as a strategy for addressing boys' educational and social needs', *Oxford Review of Education*, 31: 237–254.

Meiers, M. (2004) 'Asking the right questions: probing teachers' experience of the impact of professional development on classroom practice and student learning', paper presented to *Australian Association for Research in Education Conference*, University of Melbourne, November, 2004.

Meyer, E. (2011) *Gender and Sexual Diversity in Schools*, New York: Springer.

Mugford, J. and Nelson, D. (1996) *Violence Prevention in Practice: Australian Award Winning Programmes*, Canberra: Australian Institute of Criminology.

Mitchell, K., Wolak, J. and Finkelhor, D. (2007) 'Trends in youth reports of sexual solicitations, harassment and unwanted exposure to pornography on the internet', *Journal of Adolescent Health*, 40: 116–126.

Ollis, D. (2002) 'The time is right: addressing sexual diversity in health education', *Health Education Australia*, 2: 5.

Ollis, D. (2003) 'Talking sexual health: promoting partnerships to create a whole school approach', *Journal of Health Education Association*, 3: 4.

Ollis, D. (2009) *Sexualities and Gender in the Classroom: Changing Teacher Practice*, Cologne: Lambert Academic Publishing.

Ollis, D. (2010) 'I haven't changed bigots but …: reflections on the impact of teacher professional learning in sexuality education', *Sex Education*, 10: 217–230.

Ollis, D. (2011) 'A "respectful relationships" approach: could it be the answer to preventing gender-based violence?', *Redress: Journal of the Association of Women Educators*, 20: 19–26

Ollis, D. and Harrison, L. (2010) 'Getting over the embarrassment', presented at the *Australian Association of Research in Education Conference*, Melbourne, November 2010.

Ollis, D. and Meldrum, K. (2009) 'Girls talking about girls' issues: the importance of girls-only health and physical education in promoting well-being', *Redress*, 18: 21–30.

Ollis, D. and Tomaszewski, I. (1993) *Gender and Violence Project: Position Paper*, Canberra: Department of Employment Education and Training.

Population Council (2010) *All One Curriculum,* New York: Author.

Queensland Education (2004) *Promoting Positive Gender Relationships: A Report of a Study into the Feasibility of Developing and delivering Curriculum Through Queensland State Schools to Promote Positive Gender Relationships*, Queensland: Author (Office for Women and Curriculum Strategy Branch).

Renold, E. (2006) '"They won't let us play ... unless you're going out with one of them": girls, boys and Butler's "heterosexual matrix" in the primary years', *British Journal of Sociology of Education*, 27: 489–509.

Shine, S.A. (2011) *Teach it Like it Is: A Relationships and Sexual Health Curriculum Resourse for Teachers of Middle Schools*, Kensington, SA: Sexual Health Information Networking and Education Inc.

Sieg, E. (2003) 'Sex education and the young–some remaining dilemmas', *Health Education*, 103: 34–40.

Sinkinson, M. (2009) '"Sexuality isn't just about sex": pre-service teachers' shifting constructs of sexuality education', *Sex Education*, 9: 421–436.

Smith, A., Schlichthorst, M., Mitchell, A., Walsh, J., Lyons, A., Blackman, P. and Pitts, M. (2011) *Results of the 1st National Survey of Australian Secondary Teachers of Sexuality Education 2010*, Melbourne: Latrobe University: Australian Research Centre in Sex Health and Society.

Tutty, L. *et al.* (2002) *School-Based Violence Prevention Programs: A Resource Manual to Prevent Violence Against Girls and Young Women*, Calgary: University of Calgary (National Strategy on Community Safety and Crime Prevention).

United Nations Educational Scientific Cultural Organization (2009) *International Technical Guidance on Sexuality Education*, Paris: Author

US Agency for International Development (2002) *Unsafe Schools: A Literature Review of School-Related Gender-Based Violence in Developing Countries*, Washington, DC: Author.

Walker, J. (2004) 'Parents and sex education – looking beyond the birds and the bees', *Sex Education*, 4: 239–254.

World Health Organisation (2011) *Violence Against Women: Intimate Partner and Sexual Violence Against Women* (Fact sheet No. 239). Available at: http://www.who.int/ mediacentre/factsheets/fs239/en/ (accesed 20 October 2011).

13 Discourses of sexuality and gender considered

Ian Rivers and Neil Duncan

Introduction

The aim of this book was to bring together a series of authors from different countries and different disciplines to consider bullying using sexuality and gender as a framework. Such a perspective has provided an opportunity for scholars, activists and trainers to discuss their own experiences of research, their own perspectives on research they and others have conducted, past and present, and their understandings of how sexuality and gender are considered, informed by and acted upon within educational contexts.

This edited collection bears witness to the fact that different discourses about bullying exist in different countries and according to the different disciplines from which scholars derive their theoretical and methodological standpoints. No one discourse takes precedence over the other, however, it is important that we understand how these different discourses have emerged and how they can be understood in order to better the lives and educational experiences of young people in schools today. There also remain significant gaps in our knowledge of the interplay between sexuality and gender within the context of education. Do we, for example, still presume that what works for lesbian and gay young people will also work for bisexual, transgender or 'queer' young people? How many resources and role models currently exist that allow us to provide positive reinforcement to bisexual young people, those who politically and socially identify as queer, and indeed those who are transgender? Do we continue to construct stories of gender that offer biologically rather than socially determined explanations of why men and women differ? Are critical discourses included in curricula that open the minds of young people to alternative, socially constructed explanations of the world in which they live and the roles they have accepted or been given?

Arguments that proffer a more liberal, constructed or critical approach to understanding sexuality and gender also challenge political and religious dogmas that perhaps educators and policy makers will find difficult to defend to traditionalists or conservatives. But we must also remember that 'tradition' is no more than recognition of longevity, and conservativism an adherence to tradition. Traditions fall away and are forgotten when they no longer serve a useful social purpose, and perhaps this is where some of the more traditional views of sexuality and gender need to go. Indeed, in the UK, after decades of discrimination, the primarily Conservative coalition government has pushed ahead with its commitment to equal marriage. Even those cabinet ministers who once voted in favour of Section 28 of the Local Government Act (1988) which sought to prohibit 'the promotion of homosexuality as a pretended family relationship' are now supporting equal marriage. Traditions change and so too do conservatives – both politically and socially.

A more critical eye

How then do we bring a more critical eye to the education of young people on issues of sexuality and gender? In the penultimate chapter, Debbie Ollis points to the fact that one key lies in the training of teachers and a commitment to professional learning and continuing professional development throughout a teaching career. Perhaps one starting point for this is this book. Here educationalists, psychologists and sociologists provide a rich seam of information and data upon which to construct training events for teachers, administrators, local government officers and, of course, parents and guardians. However, we do not provide a single message for readers; this book offers multiple perspectives, including some that challenge accepted understandings of the plight of LGBTQ young people in schools.

For example, Mark McCormack's chapter (Chapter 8) illustrates that fact that there are new ways of looking at the very nature of the language used by young people in schools. 'That's so gay' may no longer be a term that is used and understood by young people to relate specifically to one or another's sexuality. Rather it has been adopted by young people today to signify something that is unfashionable or just not very good. Of course, the fact that 'gay' remains a word with a negative connotation is, without question, to be bemoaned, but should a teacher or parent necessarily identify this as homophobic bullying? It may instead be part of the 'fag discourse' (Pascoe, 2007) or 'gay discourse' (McCormack, 2012) that now pervades our schoolyards and classrooms globally.

Additionally, Eric Anderson's work, born from his own experiences as an 'out' gay high school coach (see Chapter 10), shows us that the nature of broader understandings of masculinity has indeed changed. This is something that we saw gradually emerge in the popular press in the early 1990s when journalist Mark Simpson first coined the phrase 'metrosexual' to illustrate the new wave of men who took care of their appearance and were less inhibited in their expression of emotion (Simpson, 1994). Anderson's work, signified by his theory of inclusive masculinity, demonstrates that heterosexual young men are now engaging in behaviours that once would have led to suspicions of homosexuality. He argues that the licence granted to these young men extends to so-called 'homoerotic horseplay' without any public challenge to their heterosexual identity. Yet, Anderson *et al.*, (2012) have also shown that while, young men, particularly college and university students, can 'kiss' as a mark of friendship, such behaviour is regulated through the presence of alcohol, or through the public acknowledgement by peers of a longstanding friendship between individuals. Thus while a jock-ocratic culture may be diminishing, the nature of masculinity remains regulated to a degree by limitations on acceptable behaviour between two heterosexual men. We have yet to fully understand how prevalent they are, and how these new forms of masculinity impact upon gay male intimacy or, indeed friendships between heterosexual young men and gay or bisexual young men.

Dorothy Espelage, in her chapter (Chapter 4), has demonstrated that, despite changes in the construction of masculinity by young heterosexual men towards other young heterosexual men, there is little to celebrate in terms of the way in which young men develop understandings of their relationships with young women. She argues that there is an inherent link between traditional forms of masculinity, homophobia and sexual violence perpetrated against women. Based upon cross-sectional and longitudinal studies, she has argued that there is now sufficient evidence to suggest that homophobic teasing established by middle school (11–14 years of age) is likely to predict more extremes of behaviour in later years, including the perpetration of sexual violence.

The victimisation of girls is a theme further explored by Dawn Jennifer (Chapter 5) and Siân Williams (Chapter 6) who both continue to exlore the impact of traditional gender norms upon school behaviour. In these chapters we have not only seen the reinforcement of traditional notions of what it means to be male or female played out among school-aged children, we have also seen the ways in which sexual aggression is expressed. While Siân's chapter focuses particularly on the gender conflicts that arise at school, Dawn's chapter draws our attention to the fact that traditional gender norms are reinforced by both sexes and not simply by boys seeking dominance over girls. Girls themselves engage in sexual aggression against one another, and use whispering, rumour mongering and social isolation to reinforce hierarchies and denigrate the status of other girls through the use of labels such as 'slapper', 'tart', 'tramp' and 'slag'.

The link between bullying behaviour and sexual violence is one which, perhaps, we have been reticent to address in schools because it places much more emphasis on the need for early intervention when bullying is detected. If as Dorothy Espelage suggests there is a link between homophobic bullying and sexual or intimate partner violence in later years, then it becomes even more important that we employ interventions that address issues of sexuality early on and, significantly, view education more broadly as an apprenticeship for life and not one solely focused upon academic attainment. Hence a school environment that is accepting of diversity and that encourages young people to discuss issues of sexuality is one that is healthy and serves a social as well as educational purpose.

Gay–Straight Alliances (GSAs) in schools aim to offer such environments. They not only ensure that LGBTQ young people are supported by their heterosexual peers, they also demonstrate to all members of the school community that homophobia will not be tolerated and that there must be respect for all regardless of their sexual orientation or transgender status. As Margaret Schneider and her colleagues have shown (Chapter 11), GSAs provide most of the elements teachers feel are necessary to eliminate homophobic bullying. They offer social support, act as a resource and, most important of all, offer visibility for LGBTQ issues. Where they are supported by proactive policies, material resources, effective leadership and community participation, Schneider *et al.* have suggested that, over time, they can be an efficient way to address homophobia (and now potentially aspects of sexual violence) because they change an environment that perhaps ignored or tacitly condoned bullying behaviour.

Cyberspace, bullying and sexuality

Changing the school environment from one that ignores or tacitly condones bullying to one that challenges it and supports all students regardless of their sexual orientation or transgender status is but the first step. As both Siân Williams (Chapter 6) and Ian Rivers (Chapter 3) have shown, bullying today extends beyond the school environment and now invades the recreational spaces and homes of victims. In years gone by, bullying was something that tended to happen only within a restricted few hours (the school day). Home provided a respite for the weary victim, but not any more. The advent of the internet and young people's access to mobile/cell phone technology means that bullying is now a 24-7 activity. Messages can be sent at any point during the day or night, images can be uploaded, pictures distributed and websites set up in seconds from any home computer or smart phone. Both Siân and Ian have shown that much of the cyberaggression young people are exposed to is sexual in nature. Ian has demonstrated how girls are more likely to be exposed to aggressive sexual solicitation than boys – often by members of the opposite sex. However, as Dawn Jennifer noted in her chapter (Chapter 5), it is not always the case that sexual aggression is perpetrated by members of the opposite sex, and sometimes girls may entrap targets by posing as boys or by exploiting their knowledge of their target's romantic or sexual interests when freindships end (see Rivers and Noret, 2010).

Many of the concerns associated with young people's vulnerability online also apply to young people with disabilities or special education needs. A recent study conducted at the University of Cambridge on behalf of the Anti-Bullying Alliance (McLaughlin *et al.*, 2011) has shown that children with special educational needs may be particularly targetted by bullies online. McLaughlin and her colleagues have suggested that, in the absence of successful social relationships offline, some young people with special educational needs (particularly those on the autistic spectrum) find friendship online in more structured and focused interactions. Such vulnerability can also extend to sexual exploitation online and, at the moment there is very little research exploring this issue among children and young people with special educational needs.

Notwithstanding this, Neil Duncan's chapter (Chapter 9) does provide an opportunity for us to reflect upon the ways in which we view children and young people with special educational needs and/or disabilities. Quite often we forget that they too have emerging sexualities that will not only seek expression but may also be LGBTQ. Young people with learning difficulties may be at risk of greater exploitation by those who seek out young people to exploit sexually. They may, in some cases, be the victims of more sexually aggressive bullying, ridiculed for their unpopularity and by extension inability to develop romantic relationships. Online they may become the targets of those bullies who may encourage them to take, send or post 'selfies' (pictures of their bodies unclothed) which are then distributed.

In his chapter, Neil also focuses on the imagery that surrounds young people as they grow up. How does a young person with a physical impairment react to the images in magazine and on the internet that constantly surround him or her? Where are the images that show young people with disabilities that they are attractive and desirable human beings too? As Neil argues all too often we infantalise or ignore the sexuality of disabled young people and this too can alienate them from their able-bodied peers: in effect it forces us to segregate able-bodied from disabled young people according to our own and society's prejudices surrounding disability and sexuality. Such infantalisation can not only result in further bullying as sex becomes very much a part of the discourse of teenagers, it too has the potential to drive young people to seek information and perhaps even sexual experiences via the internet.

Next steps

Anyone who works in an educational context will know that there is a growing number of resources available ostensibly to address general bullying, sexual bullying, homophobic bullying, bullying on the grounds of special educational needs and/or disability, cyberbullying and that promote better sex education. However, there are few resources that bring all of the components together. It is important that we acknowledge the complexity of young people's lives and not shy away from taking bold steps to develop policies and resources that address the issues raised in this book. Such policies and resources need to be sensitive to the changing nature of young peoples' discourse, and also make sense of the seemingly conflicting stories that emerge from research. As we have noted, while there is evidence to suggest that the nature of heterosexual masculinity is changing, we do not as yet know if this is mirrored among gay and bisexual men, or if there has been a concomitant shift in the way in which young people view women and their role within society.

We must better understand how sexuality and gender are understood with the context and school and also provide educators with greater clarity around these issues through professional learning/continuing professional development. There is such diversity in the ways in which these issues are raised in teacher training that we cannot be sure, even within a national context, that all newly qualified teachers have an appreciation of the ways in which bullying manifests itself and the ways in which it intersects with issues of gender or gender-expression and sexuality. There is a need for programmes of development in professional practice that ensure that either at state level or national level, teachers are well-versed both in the literature and methods used to counter bullying, particularly where it is sexual in nature. Of course, there will be resistance but that resistance is often born of a belief that discussions relating sexuality and particularly homosexuality have no place in the classroom. Yet, without these discussions young people are left with little effective guidance and will seek information from other sources, usually the internet, which is perhaps more stark and more likely to expose them to risk than if they were provided with opportunities to develop and understanding these issues within a structured learning environment.

Concluding comments

Bullying does not just affect young people at school, it affects families and teachers too. It makes growing up and the process of learning a constant source of stress and anxiety. It also has the potential to impact upon people's lives long after they have left school. We should not ignore the legacy that bullying leaves those who have suffered it. It is incumbent upon educators to ensure that young people leave their charge confident, able and fully equipped to take their place in the world. No young person who faces bullying daily because of his or her sexual orientation should ever be told by a headteacher or school principal that the best solution is to, 'leave the school as soon as possible … you're not considering going to the sixth form here are you?' (Rivers, 2012). Similarly no adult should ever live a life haunted in the following way by the memories of their schoolyard bullies:

> For a long time, I had been calling it shame, but I realised recently that I think it might be flashbacks. It doesn't just contain shame, but also fear, pressure to be different than I am, the feeling of being scary to other people, a feeling like I'm on a slippery slope and can do nothing right, a black alone feeling, sadness, a strong self-consciousness, feeling diminished, and other things. It's more complex than just one feeling. I can go from knowing that someone is fine with me and my gayness, to all at once, because of a look on their face or maybe even my own word choice, feeling extremely unsure of myself, feeling like I'm a big ugly sickening monster to that person, not knowing how they feel about me. It's like a sudden realisation of who I am in the world, but it isn't who I am now, but who I was in the world back then. It feels like I'm back there.
>
> (Rivers, 2012)

References

Anderson, E., Adams, A. and Rivers, I. (2012) '"You wouldn't believe what straight men are doing with each other": kissing, cuddling and loving', *Archives of Sexual Behavior*, 41: 421–430.

McCormack, M. (2012) *The Declining Significance of Homophobia: How Teenage Boys are Redefining Masculinity and Heterosexuality*, New York: Oxford University Press.

McLaughlin, C., Byers, R. and Oliver, C. (2011) *Responding to Bullying among Children with Special Educational Needs and/or Disabilities*. Available at: http://www.anti-bullyingalliance.org.uk/media/13561/SEND_bullying_validating%20local%20 practice.pdf (accessed 24 June 2012).

Pascoe, C. J. (2007) *Dude, You're a Fag*, London: University of California Press.

Rivers, I. (2012) 'Bias-based bullying: its impact and intersections with new media', keynote address to the *National Centre Against Bullying Biennial Conference*, Melbourne Convention and Exhibition Centre, June, 2012.

Rivers, I and Noret N. (2010) '"I h 8 u": findings from a five-year study of text and email bullying', *British Educational Research Journal*, 36: 643–671.

Simpson, M. (1994) 'Here come the mirror men', *The Independent*, November 15, p. 3.

Index